WELFARE STATE CHANGE

Welfare State Change

Towards a Third Way?

edited by
JANE LEWIS
and
REBECCA SURENDER

OXFORD
UNIVERSITY PRESS

OXFORD

UNIVERSITY PRESS

Great Clarendon Street, Oxford OX2 6DP

Oxford University Press is a department of the University of Oxford.
It furthers the University's objective of excellence in research, scholarship,
and education by publishing worldwide in

Oxford New York

Auckland Bangkok Buenos Aires Cape Town Chennai
Dar es Salaam Delhi Hong Kong Istanbul Karachi Kolkata
Kuala Lumpur Madrid Melbourne Mexico City Mumbai Nairobi
São Paulo Shanghai Taipei Tokyo Toronto

Oxford is a registered trade mark of Oxford University Press
in the UK and in certain other countries

Published in the United States
by Oxford University Press Inc., New York

British Library Cataloguing in Publication Data
Data available

Library of Congress Cataloging in Publication Data
Data available
ISBN 0-19-926672-7 (hbk.)
ISBN 0-19-9266735 (pbk.)

1 3 5 7 9 10 8 6 4 2

Typeset by Newgen Imaging Systems (P) Ltd., Chennai, India
Printed in Great Britain
on acid-free paper by
Biddles Ltd., King's Lynn

CONTENTS

LIST OF CONTRIBUTORS

Professor Helmut Anheier – London School of Economics, UK.

Dr Giuliano Bonoli – Department of Social Work and Social Policy, University of Fribourg, Switzerland.

Professor Jochen Clasen – Department of Applied Social Sciences, University of Stirling, UK.

Mr Daniel Clegg – Department of Social Policy and Social Work, University of Oxford, UK.

Professor Mary Daly – School of Sociology and Social Policy, Queen's University, Belfast, Northern Ireland.

Dr Hartley Dean – London School of Economics, UK.

Professor Jane Lewis (Editor) – Department of Social Policy and Social Work, University of Oxford, UK.

Professor Ruth Lister – Department of Social Sciences, Loughborough University.

Professor Janet Newman – Open University, UK.

Dr Martin Powell – University of Bath, UK.

Dr Rebecca Surender (Editor) – Department of Social Policy and Social Work, University of Oxford, UK.

Dr Stuart White – Jesus College, University of Oxford, UK.

I

Policy Contexts and Concepts

1

Modern Challenges to the Welfare State and the Antecedents of the Third Way

REBECCA SURENDER

During the past decade a new politics of the welfare state has been identified in a new wave of literature on welfare state change. Subjected to strong pressures during the 1980s and 1990s, welfare systems underwent a period of 'intense renovation' (Bonoli and Palier 2001), and the search for solutions heralded, according to some, a new emerging welfare orthodoxy. However, opinions vary considerably as to whether to characterize these changes in terms of retrenchment, restructuring, or resilience, or indeed whether the changes are heading in a similar direction in different national contexts (Deacon 2002; Leibfried 2002; Pierson 2001; White 2001). This book sets out to examine recent welfare state change in relation to the Third Way—an equally contested topic. Defining the content and consequences of a so-called Third Way in social policy has become an increasingly important part of the debate about the future of the welfare state and social democratic politics.

According to early proponents, largely those in think tanks and the political arena, the Third Way reflects an attempt by contemporary social democracies to forge a new political settlement which is fitted to the conditions of a modern society and new global economy, but which retains the goals of social cohesion and egalitarianism (Halpern and Mikosz 1998). It seeks to differentiate itself as distinct from the political ideologies of the New Right and Old Left. Though commonly linked to the US Democratic Party in the Clinton era, it can also be traced to the political debates and discourses in European social democratic parties during the mid-1990s, most notably in the United Kingdom, Germany, and the Netherlands. In social policy terms the model attempts to transcend the fixed alternatives of the state and the market. Instead, civil society, government, and the economy are viewed as interdependent and equal partners in the provision of welfare; and the challenge for government is to create equilibrium between these three pillars. The individual is to be 'pushed' towards self-help and independent, active citizenship, while business and government must contribute to economic and social cohesion (Blair 1998; Blair and Schröder 1999).

Others, however, remain sceptical, arguing that the model does not comprise a political philosophy or set of strategies that are coherent or distinctive. Described variously as 'vaguely mystical' (Wheeler 1998), 'a slippery concept' (Bashevkin 2001), and a form of 'political product differentiation' (Wood 1998), much of the early debate focused on classification and definition. For many, the Third Way was no more than a compromise between competing systems of economic organization (capitalism and socialism), principles of resource allocation (market and state), or ideologies (Left and Right). For Giddens, however, an early proponent of a Third Way paradigm, the Third Way precisely does not lie between Left and Right but is *beyond* Left and Right (Giddens 1998). For Giddens, the Third Way represents the renewal of social democracy in a changed, 'globalized' environment where the solutions of the Old Left have become redundant while those of the Right are reactionary. Similarly, for Gamble and Kelly (1998), the Third Way signals the creation of a new and heterodox alignment of ideas that recognizes that there has been a sharp break in political continuity, rendering many former political certainties obsolete. Driver and Martell (2003) differ only in the terms of expression, arguing that, while Left and Right remain 'important markers' for contemporary politics, the Third Way does combine them in significant new ways, with policy implications that break with established debates and alternatives. However, while Giddens asserts that this new social democratic agenda is integrated and distinctive, Driver and Martell conclude that there is not space just for one Third Way but for many, with varying values and policy positions. White (1998) uses similar language, defining the Third Way as a large and contested conceptual space. While White suggests that there is no (single) 'big idea' but rather an accumulation of 'small to medium-sized' ideas which together add up to something 'big', he is one of the earliest to begin to identify key characteristics of Third Way thinking (White 1998). As he argues in Chapter 2 of this volume, ideas about mutualism, employment-centred social policy, and asset-based egalitarianism signal receptivity to new ways of achieving traditional Left goals. Greater egalitarianism is to be achieved not through income redistribution but by action to affect the initial distribution of skills, capacities, and productive endowments. Equally important, the state should be seen as the guarantor but not necessarily as the direct provider of 'opportunity' goods.

As the chapters in this volume illustrate, all Western industrialized countries have undergone a process of social democratic modernization and substantial welfare state restructuring, with policies—whether labelled Third Way or not—that arguably are at one with many of the ideas of the

Third Way. Many European social democrats were well ahead of the British Labour Party, despite its professed position as the standard-bearer of this new welfare. Dutch social democrats were adopting a pragmatic approach to the market before 1997, promoting deregulation, tax reductions, and the work ethic, 'flexicurity' and training in the labour markets, and reallocation of resources from social security to other areas such as education. The Swedes at an even earlier juncture were at the forefront of developing active labour market policies based on education and training, with Denmark also pursuing a conscious strategy of labour market flexibility and activation (Kuhnle 2001). A new and aggressive emphasis on cost containment has pervaded much welfare reform in Europe and has resulted in cuts across the board in replacement rates or basic amounts in most sickness or family benefits, and an erosion of universal benefits more generally (Ferrera, Hemerijck, and Rhodes 2001). New ways of fighting poverty and social exclusion have resulted in more targeted means-tested benefits and in-work benefits and wage subsidies. Equally across Europe the idea that welfare policy needs to be more responsive to changes in family formation and gender roles and more attuned to balancing work and family life seems to be taking hold (Lewis 2002). Finally, in almost all states there has been a growing attention to the welfare role played by the market, family, and voluntary organizations, and a growing acceptance of the view that 'state monopoly' of welfare may not necessarily be a good thing (Kuhnle 2001).

It is of course not only European countries that have pursued new strategies. The administrations of Hawke and Keating in Australia, Clarke in New Zealand, and Chrétien in Canada also undertook bold policy reforms—many of which, it has been argued, provided blueprints for the New Labour programme (Johnson and Tonkiss 2002; Pierson and Castles 2001). As in European states, welfare reforms under Australian and New Zealand Labour administrations and the Canadian Liberal Party combined neo-liberal measures with traditional progressive objectives to rationalize provision and to regulate the activities of welfare recipients. A 'work-based' emphasis on welfare reforms geared towards shifting people from benefits into work resulted in opening up access to employment, a move to in-work benefits, and enhanced access to childcare. Social justice was now concerned to direct benefits to those in greatest need and to address the problems of low pay and child poverty through changes in the tax and benefit system.

Interpretations of what is happening, however, depend in large measure on the level of change that is being discussed. For example, in virtually all Western welfare states it is possible to identify a greater emphasis on linking an individuals entitlement to cash benefits with his (and increasingly also her) responsibility to undertake training or to work. However, the nature of what are commonly referred to as welfare-to-work programmes differs hugely from country to country, reflecting the importance of national traditions in respect of both policies and political ideas (Pierson 2001). Furthermore, while in the case of this specific example it may be possible to argue that there is convergence in terms of principles and policy goals alongside considerable cross-national variation in policy mechanisms, it is far from easy to reach agreement on a list of broad, overarching principles informing all recent social policy changes in Western welfare states. Other difficult issues also remain. First, not all current centre-left governments pursuing similar policy goals choose to identify with the Third Way and, second, some of the policies that are often identified with a Third Way approach are not confined to political parties of the centre-left. For example, both Bush and Blair have expressed enthusiasm for a greater role for the voluntary or 'third' sector, and in particular social provision by 'faith-based' organizations. It is clear that, in order not to be misled by single examples or case studies, it is important to look across a range of policy fields, goals, and instruments.

This volume seeks to provide a critical understanding of the origins, content, and consequences of recent social policy reform in relation to the notion of a Third Way in industrialized economies systems of welfare. In particular, it examines substantive areas of public policy since it is indeed the case that it is in their 'detailed practical effects, rather than in their general philosophy' that Third Way policies ultimately will have to be judged (Kaletsky 1998). By presenting a detailed examination of the main developments that have arisen in the four primary spheres of welfare provision—the state, the labour market, the third sector, and the family—the text considers how far the complex mixture of continuity and change signals a significant shift towards a new mode of welfare. While it is more difficult to tie down a 'Third Way vision' of social policy than perhaps it was to do for 'Thatcherism' or the neo-liberal agenda of the1980s, as the chapters in this volume will show, there is increasing evidence that centre-left parties have changed their approach to social policy-making. There is some convergence in the broad tenor of their approaches, even if substantial diversity remains in terms of political rhetoric and policy mechanisms.

However, a further question needs to be posed. If we accept that some distinctive Third Way agenda in social policy has emerged in advanced welfare state societies, how do we explain why a full-blown and explicit Third Way discourse was prominent in a relatively small number of countries, most notably the US and UK, but relatively absent in most others? Why did Democrat and Labour politicians in these two countries become conspicuous standard-bearers for this controversial and potentially risky political path while other European and Antipodean centre-left administrations instituted similar reforms with less fanfare and announcement? Early accounts of the rise of a Third Way influence on social policy have tended to emphasize macro-level economic and sociological factors as the key drivers of change; globalization, fiscal crisis, and post-material affluence, to name a few (Giddens 1998). However, while these broad trends provide a general framework with which to analyse current reforms, the indicators are not fine-grained enough to explain differences between states. Why, for instance, if politicians in different countries have perceived the same broad trends, have they responded with such different political discourses?

This chapter will argue that, in order to understand why a Third Way agenda has been embraced unequivocally and visibly in some contexts but introduced more stealthily in others, the political nature and context of policy formation needs to be integrated into the analysis. That is, to understand the emergence of either Third Way policies or rhetoric, an analysis of the interaction between macro-socio-economic factors and political dynamics is required. It is undoubtedly the case that the broad internal and external pressures for reform currently being experienced by all advanced welfare economies have helped to push current patterns of welfare arrangements in a similar direction. However, an analysis of the political context surrounding the trajectory of social policy reform in the US and UK suggests that electoral and political considerations rather than ideological factors explain why the promotion of Third Way reform assumed an evangelical tone in these countries but not others. Conversely, an examination of the Australian case indicates that political traditions and institutional arrangements are equally salient factors in explaining the rejection of an aggressive new labelling of the policy agenda in many countries, and to this extent classic 'new institutionalist' and 'path dependence' theories of change (Pierson 2001; Swank 2002) continue to be relevant.

However before examining the factors underpinning the new welfare arrangements in these particular cases, it is necessary first to consider the general antecedents of welfare state restructuring experienced by most welfare states. What are the factors that have driven so many traditional pro-welfare social democrats, within a relatively short period of time, to introduce more radical, and arguably more restrictive, measures than their conservative or liberal predecessors (Clasen 2002)? What are the changing social political and economic circumstances that require traditional forms of social democratic welfare to be revised? Understanding these factors is essential not only for determining the extent to which new welfare arrangements represent a distinctive and cohesive programme of restructuring and modernization—a new politics of welfare—but also for assessing its likely robustness and durability. It is to these questions that this chapter will first turn.

1. Current Pressures on the Welfare State

During the past three decades, governments in advanced industrialized societies have found it increasingly difficult to meet both the traditional welfare needs and the new welfare risks of their populations. The nature of the challenges confronting welfare states during the 1970s and 1980s are well understood (Pierson 1994; Taylor-Gooby, 1991; Castles 1998) and include the 'usual suspects' of economic, social and demographic change. The reform strategies adopted by Western governments during this period have been documented, and theories of welfare state retrenchment, demise, convergence, and change debated (Pierson 2001; Leibfried 2001).

Prominent in any discussion of the determinants of current welfare state restructuring is of course globalization and the changing international economy. Put simply, this thesis states that contemporary processes of market liberalization, 'transnationalization', and cross-border economic activity have diminished the powers of nation-states. In particular, the demise of the fixed exchange system and the increase in the quantity and availability of liquid capital has heightened international capital mobility and shifted power from the state to the market (Scharpf 2001), forcing a reordering of the objectives and priorities of policy-making.

Dependent on capital for wealth generation and economic stability, the state becomes reliant on its ability to secure the conditions that will prevent any 'haemorrhaging' of investment finance or 'social dumping' (the scenario that firms operating where social wages are low are able to undercut the prices of competitors, forcing higher-cost firms to go out of business or to relocate to low social-wage economies). These conditions include low taxation, fiscal austerity, labour market flexibility, and deregulation. Traditional commitments of social democratic administrations to higher levels of taxation, public expenditure, and full employment have, so it is argued (Baker 2002), been severely constrained. In place of a traditional welfare state has now come a 'competition or Schumpeterian state' that focuses on making economic activities more competitive internationally rather than on promoting social welfare (Jessop 1994).

A different though related set of arguments concerns technological developments that affect patterns of work and employment, reducing opportunities for less-skilled workers and subjecting substantial parts of the labour force to new risks and uncertainties (Taylor-Gooby 2003). Although these changes have been more extensive in some industrialized economies than others, the consequences of a more unequal and complex labour market are increasingly being felt everywhere (Scharpf and Schmidt 2002). Rapid technological change has widened the gap between low and high skilled workers, while regulations, particularly in continental welfare systems, designed to protect low-skilled labour when it had a more prominent place in the market now serves as a major obstacle for low-skilled 'outsiders' seeking employment (Leibfried and Obinger 2001). The increase in part-time work and more interrupted and diverse career patterns add to the complexity and require major adjustments to the education and social security systems. The redesign of incentive structures together with social investment aimed at human capital formation, quintessential Third Way strategies, are thus visible in several countries.

A further aspect of globalization is what Giddens (1998) refers to as a 'sideways squeeze' on national government by trans-national agencies which take over various of its administrative or regulatory functions. The impact of the European Union (EU) is one such example. Analysis of European social policy increasingly points to the growing impact of European integration on convergence towards one (broad) model. One compelling account comes from Leibfried and Pierson (2001) who argue that the process of European integration has eroded both the legal authority and the regulatory capacity of member states to determine national policy. The EU intervenes both actively—by enacting social policy initiatives of its own through the European Commission, the Council of Ministers, and the European Court of Justice—and more indirectly by the imposition of market compatibility requirements that restrict and redefine the social policies of member states. Regulations and 'benchmarking' governing health and safety in the workplace, retirement and pension schemes, education, labour mobility, and freedom to provide services and benefits all impinge on the design and reform of national policy.

However, what is most significant for the purposes of this discussion is that the direction of EU reform has been consistently away from a Polanyian 'protective reaction against market relations' and towards policies directly connected to labour market participation. While acknowledging that social policies in mixed economies have always interacted in a variety of complex ways with markets, the authors nevertheless conclude that *'never before has the construction of markets so visibly and intensively shaped the development of social policy initiatives'* (Leibfried and Pierson 2001).

It is in this sense then, many would argue that the forces of globalization are transforming the welfare systems of industrialized societies and shaping both the goals and methods of centre-left governments. Not only do the economic processes of liberalization of international trade and economic exchange constrain centre-left administrations, the growth of new trans-national structures broadens the activities of government to a more multi-tiered role of governance. Both forces push government in the direction of retrenchment and adaptation, towards developing new social and generational contracts, and towards utilizing more market-based instruments and solutions.

A second category of determinants of the new welfare arrangements, though partially stemming from these economic changes, is nevertheless more sociological in nature. There is evidence to support the view that a key element behind the modernization agenda of many social democratic parties at the close of the twentieth century was a sociological analysis of the changing size and character of the working class, and the implications of these changes for long-term electoral prospects (Heath, Jowell, and Curtice 2001). In all advanced industrialized societies, the post-war period has seen a decline in the size of the working class, making it clear to traditional centre-left parties that it will be increasingly difficult for them to win electoral majorities. However, not only has the working class shrunk in size, the remains of it has changed significantly in character. Class boundaries have blurred and the more affluent members of the working class have converged with the lower-middle classes in their aspirations and lifestyles. In particular they have become more individualistic and materialistic (Cerny and Evans 2000) and are becoming increasingly detached from the collectivist politics of traditional Left parties.

The social aspect of this systemic change was captured early on in Inglehart's (1971, 1977) notion of 'postmaterialism': that growing affluence had shifted the value priorities of Western citizens from substantive material needs to post-material concerns such as quality of the environment and minority rights. Additionally, the rise of a more educated, media-savvy public, together with the erosion of the traditional family model (with a severing of the link that saw young people rely on family for education and employment), all contributed to increasing individualism.

In the 1990s a serious attempt to connect a theory of these macro-sociological changes to current welfare policy strategies was made by, among others, Anthony Giddens (1998). Compression of time and space, the questioning of authority and knowledge, increasingly media-led experience, and awareness of diversity all combined to undermine traditional ideologies and force citizens to make their own guidelines, that is, the reflexive individual in an era of 'reflexive modernisation' (Giddens 1994). The era of reflexive modernization meant a new basis for politics. Though he titles his book *Beyond Left and Right*, Giddens actually suggests a modification of these categories. He argues that the aim of the Left should be to reconsider equality as a means, not an end—a means towards the goal of emancipation per se, whether that is poverty elimination, social cohesion, or economic growth. Welfare too should become redefined to meet 'life politics' concerns, become indeed part of a 'generative politics' that empowers people, not through direct financial redistribution but through 'positive welfare'.

There is a case to be made, it would seem, that sociological processes are affecting the welfare systems of industrialized societies and shaping the policies of centre-left governments. If the argument is correct that modern society is becoming more individualistic and that there has been a weakening of social class, then modern centre or Third Way parties may be the inevitable outcome. Equally, if an empowerment principle galvanizes individuals—individuals with increasing levels of education, networks, skills, and range of experiences—to confront traditional leaders and 'get things done themselves', a delegitimization of welfare 'dependency', and a Third Way notion of 'asset-based egalitarianism' may also follow.

This review of some of the factors that have driven Third Way policy has for reasons of space omitted other possible precursors. Accounts of fiscal pressures resulting from population ageing (OECD 1998), the independent role of ideology and the intellectual climate (Harris 2002), and the collapse of communism in Soviet Russia and Eastern Europe (Giddens 2002) have all featured in recent literature. Competing for intellectual influence within the Third Way debate are exponents of communitarianism. For these writers, most notably Etzioni (1995, 1997), the retreat from traditional welfare and collectivist solutions is driven not by fiscal or efficiency concerns but rather moral ones. Modern society, according to these writers, displays a decline in both moral and civic spheres, reflected in the rise in crime and disorder, disrespect and apathy towards political participation, a rejection of family values, poor educational achievement, and low aspirations. The solution to this social degeneration lies in the move from 'society' to 'community', that is, from statutory provision to private and voluntary effort. The regeneration of the community as the locus for moral interaction is essential, since it is through communities that individuals and groups encourage one another to 'reasoned judgment and virtuous action' (Etzioni 1995). While communitarianism is thus concerned with a moral agenda set within a social rather than an economic or political context, it has nevertheless contributed to the discourse surrounding a 'new welfare'. Key among the objectives of communitarians is to place the burden of responsibility on recipients rather than government and to substitute 'obligation' for an 'entitlement' form of provision (Harris 2002). The thesis thus supports a move from a centralized welfare state to a more developmental, associational form of welfare, equally favoured by other Third Way advocates.

It is also important to note that the changes identified here, and as theorized by Giddens and others, are not of course without their contradictions and critics. Mouzelis (2001), for example, challenges the assumption that social changes constitute structural forces to be adapted to, without fully recognizing an often overt *political* strategy by agents with interests, and that some individuals hold more power vis-à-vis these structures than others. Leggett (2002), Rhodes (2000), and others have also argued that Giddens and other advocates of a globalization thesis fall into a sociological reductionism as they take globalization for granted, as something to respond to rather than as a contingent political project by those governments, business, and media institutions adhering to an economically conservative ideology.

These criticisms are important and will continue to play a role in the shaping of the Third Way debate. Nevertheless, it would be obtuse to deny that the profound social and economic changes discussed so far have, to more or less the same degree, been experienced by all advanced industrialized societies over roughly the same time period, and therefore do indeed explain much of the similarity in the direction of welfare reform currently under way in these countries—whether explicitly labelled 'Third Way' or not. Deindustrialization, economic competition, supranational structures of governance, changing class relationships, and greater cultural diversity have undoubtedly provoked a shift in the architecture of welfare systems. It is true that the precise mix and force of the structural challenges facing individual economies vary, and that there exist different national trajectories of welfare state 'adjustment' leading to what some have termed 'divergent convergence' in policy responses (Hinrichs 2002; Seeleib-Kaiser 2000). The importance of different domestic economic challenges also needs to be recognized (Castles and Timomen 2003). Nevertheless, some clear patterns are discernible. Welfare reforms geared towards shifting people from benefits to work, a reduced role for state delivery of services, a shift from insurance-based provision to means-tested assistance, a greater emphasis on education, training, and unemployment schemes— all revolving around reinvigorated notions of 'reciprocal obligation'—are prominent among Nordic, Continental, and English-speaking welfare states.

Again, however, the question needs to be posed: if we accept that the emergence of the Third Way has occurred within the context of globalization and the transformation of the class society into the market society, why were the welfare reforms that resulted from these changed circumstances highlighted as a decisive and ideological change in some countries, but depicted more routinely as programmatic modification in others?

2. The Third Way: A Political Response to Electoral Pressures?

While we must be cautious about drawing conclusions from the experience of a small number of cases, an examination of the US and UK suggests strong similarities in the factors that drove the aggressive rebranding of the centre-left in both countries. 'New institutionalist' theories have tended to focus on historical factors such as path dependency or organizational arrangements of government when explaining welfare state change—for example, the extent to which unitary versus more fragmented forms of government provide veto points, or the role of coalitions. As an examination of the Australian case shows, while these variables are undoubtedly significant and intermediary in nature because they mediate the impact of structural developments on policy-making, it is clear that other political factors, such as electoral considerations, and sometimes more idiosyncratic factors such as intra-party conflicts and the role of party leaders, also need to be included in any analysis.

Stephen Skowroneck (1997) and others have argued that the strategies pursued by Clinton should be understood as the ideological expression of 'pre-emptive presidential leadership'. That is, pre-emptive leaders build political support by adopting some of the more popular ideas of their rivals and combining them with their own parties' more traditional appeal. The crucial point is that these leaders are operating in the general context of an inhospitable ideological environment and are thus limited in their capacity to shape the political world. For the US Democrats, we see that the series of humiliating defeats throughout the 1980s and the crisis of confidence and legitimacy that ensued required radical and bold new measures. Thus, the development of the Third Way as a visionary call to arms was fundamentally pragmatic and electorally driven.

The Shaping of the Third Way in the US

The rise of the Third Way in the US must be located within a major political dynamic that can be traced to the collapse of the liberal consensus underpinning the expansion of New Deal and Great Society programmes. Party political division stemmed from perceived policy failures and, between 1968 and 1972, the Democratic Party split into two factions: New Left versus southern and moderate/conservative Democrats. Some have argued that the split was in part based on diverging values: New Left and post-materialist values such as minority rights, the environment, and pacifism, versus southern and moderate Democratic values concerned with the traditional 'bread and butter' issues of the white working class (Hale 1995). However, for the purpose of this analysis the crucial issue is that, from McGovern's landslide defeat in the 1972 presidential election to the Dukakis loss in 1988, New Left Democrat candidates failed to capture a majority.

It was thus during the period 1982–92, amid the political and intellectual machinations that preceded the Clinton presidency, that a new strategy was formulated. Conservative Democrats, feeling estranged from their party by the New Left, began to formulate a position that later became recognizable as the Third Way. However, it is clear that, not only did the former disagree with the latter on principle, but the question of *power* motivated this emerging strategy (Wier 1998). Arguing that their party was unelectable because its values were out of line with the majority of American voters, the first expression of a Third Way reformulation came from the House Democrat Caucus's Committee of Party Effectiveness (CPE) in 1982, formed by Rep. Gillis Long and Al From (Baer 2000). Feeling the party's policy documents put abortion, gay rights, and gun control ahead of crime and other issues more salient to the public, the CPE began advocating a message of 'national interest, not special interest'. Its 1982 publication *Rebuilding the Road to Opportunity* proposed a return to pre-1968 issues such as economic growth and opportunity, not entitlement, though controlled investment and education. New Deal liberalism was placed within the context of globalization and an economically individualist electorate wanting smaller government. This was the embryonic Third Way.

Although this strategy gained the support of some elected Democrats that election year, it was ultimately the Reagan landslide, in which Walter Mondale lost all states but his own—Minnesota—and Washington, DC, which boosted the credibility of From and Long's basic mathematical complaint that the party was appealing to only a third of voters and repelling swing voters concerned with federal beneficence to the 'undeserving poor'. However, it required another electoral defeat, for Dukakis in 1988, to bring fresh impetus to the cause of modernization. The DLC adopted new aggressive tactics, formed a think tank, the Progressive Policy Institute (PPI), and took advice from the Heritage Foundation about the conflation of fundraising, marketing, and policy. The substance of policy emerging from PPI was confidently divergent from Democrat policy; for instance, PPI's first proposal was to expand the Earned Income Tax Credit instead of raising the minimum wage, so placing work ahead of redistribution. By the time of Clinton's first victory in 1992, then, the Third Way had been defined, elucidated through a range of policies, and gained institutional support. The 1996 election, however, proved the zenith for the Third Way in the US. Clinton's 1995 budget called for spending cuts and a balanced budget, welfare reform structurally changed the relationship between government and citizen, and traditional policies were redefined along Third Way lines. The DLC sought to add gravitas to the Third Way as an ideology by locating it within a Western centre-left political revival, reflected in the 1998 public dialogue between Clinton, Blair, and Prodi, then between Clinton, Blair, Schröeder, D'Alema, and Wim Kok in 1999. A broader ideological vision was generated which located specific Third Way policies in 'a new historical stage' in which globalization created a need to apply 'basic American principles to changing circumstances'.

What is resoundingly clear is that the role of institutions and electoral politics, namely, the rejection of New Left principles by moderate Democrats as a means to power, were instrumental to the Third Way's 'rise' in the US.

The Shaping of the Third Way in the UK

Others have argued similarly that the move to an explicit Third Way discourse in the UK was provoked in great measure by the Labour Party's loss of credibility in the 1980s and 1990s and need to re-establish an image of being able to govern (Clasen 2002; Heath, Jowell, and Curtice 2001; Bonoli and Powell 2002). The process of so-called modernization that culminated in New Labour's victory in 1997 after eighteen years out of office, like the New Democrats' rise to power, should be viewed as a gradual process though with a number of distinct phases (Heffernan 1998). Its origins should perhaps be traced to the decade of Neil Kinnock's leadership of the party between 1983 and 1992, since it was he who first vigorously argued that 'harsh electoral reality' dictated that the party could not rely 'merely on a combination of the dispossessed, the traditional, and the increasingly fragmentary working class and minority groups for the winning of power'. Changing patterns of employment (away from manual work in unionized manufacturing industry), the fragmentation of traditional working class communities, and the ageing of the population (with older people tending to vote Conservative) led many at the time to predict that the 'forward march of Labour had been halted' (Hobsbawm and Jaques 1981).

Despite the doubts of many that Labour could ever again be a major political force, the party began the gradual process of broadening its appeal by returning towards the centre of the political spectrum and discarding its extremist and 'loony left' image. Concentrating on internal reforms, the leadership expelled left-wing members, weakened the influence of the trade unions, and strengthened its own power relative to that of the activists (Driver and Martell 2002). With fewer public displays of disunity, the party became a more centralized and effective campaigning organization, with techniques drawn from the media, marketing, and advertising. However, despite strenuous attempts at party reform and continued 'modernization' (including discarding its commitments to nationalize the banks, renationalize the utilities, and adopt unilateral nuclear disarmament), the electoral pay-off at both the 1987 and 1992 general elections was relatively modest.

It was not until Tony Blair, Gordon Brown, and fellow modernizers assumed power within the party in 1994 that a different pace and style of modernization was forced through. A number of radical and far-reaching institutional, ideological, and image changes were instituted. Clause IV of the Labour party's constitution was abandoned as were plans to renationalize industries that the Conservatives had privatized; Keynesian interventionist strategies designed to secure full employment were replaced with a broad acceptance of market forces and a neo-liberal commitment to low inflation. Most crucially, previous commitments to high levels of taxation and public expenditure, which the modernizers believed had seriously damaged past electoral chances, were discarded (Savage and Atkinson 2001). Like its New Democrat soul mates across the Atlantic, Labour worked aggressively to distance itself from special interest groups—in this case the trade unions—asserting that the unions would receive 'fairness not favours'. To symbolize and crystallize these changes, the modernizers rebranded their party 'New Labour'. By the time it was elected to power in May 1997, it had a new constitution, new policies, new internal structures, and a new image, causing one commentator to claim that 'a revolution had occurred in British party politics' (Seyd 1998).

Some have asserted that Labour's eventual victory in May 1997 was a triumph of style over substance (Hewitt and Gould 1993). Spin doctors, computerized marketing techniques, and voter 'profiling' were certainly all employed in the New Labour armoury. Many of the strategies were borrowed from the New Democrats in the US, and some of the Blair team had been on the campaign trail in the 1992 US presidential elections. Like Clinton, Blair proved a magnetic and compelling leader, able to communicate with the electorate in a reassuring and convincing manner. Others, however, have argued that it was less this 'popular touch' or organizational slickness that finally secured victory for Labour than the substance of policy—Third Way policy (Driver and Martell 2002). What is more certain, however, is that electoral ambitions and political expediency appear to be the main underlying drivers of the hard-line redefining of policy in both the US and the UK.

It is clear however that several other factors were also needed in order for the qualitative change in the policy agenda to occur. Kitschelts (2001) argues that 'unpopular policies' can be pursued by centre-left governments if the right 'strategic configurations of party systems' are in place. Among the key variables are electoral trade-offs, office-seeking leadership, and intra-party conflicts, which give modernizers the upper hand. We see these conditions present in the US and UK cases. Another key variable that is beginning to be identified is the decisive role of the party leader, and this too has some resonance for the US and UK cases. While the role of collective actors—for example, the trade unions or social partners—has been linked to welfare state adaptation, the role of individuals such as party leaders has received less attention. However, Ross (2000) highlights the pivotal role of Blair himself in the success of the Blairite project and it seems that the motives, interests, and capabilities of the New Labour and Democrat leaderships may be important ingredients in explaining why their respective parties were willing to embark on 'path-breaking' change. What we witness in these case studies is that political argumentation and justification can play an independent and vital role in political processes and welfare state change. Once in power, both Clinton and Blair became powerful and articulate figureheads for their movements, and each managed to create a public understanding of the need for reform.

Equally, an examination of events in Australia suggests that 'political system factors' also affect parties' and governments' strategic choices. Facing many of the same economic vulnerabilities of globalization and deindustrialization as its Anglophile counterparts, and responding with similar measures, the Australian Labor Party nevertheless characterized its reform package as 'The Australian Way' rather than a new 'Third Way'. Any understanding of this difference must acknowledge the institutional constraints faced by the central government from coalition or corporate arrangements which made it extremely difficult for it to pursue an openly radical or path-breaking strategy.

The Shaping of the Third Way in Australia

For much of the post-war period, the ALP, at the federal level, found itself out of government. In 1983, however, under the leadership of Bob Hawke, it won its first federal election since 1974, and then went on (under Hawke and later Paul Keating) to win a staggering five further federal elections before finally being defeated in 1996.

Nevertheless, unlike its UK counterpart, when the ALP first came to power in 1983 it did not frame itself as pursuing a Third Way or even an innovative political agenda, but rather as restoring peace and stability after the intense industrial struggles under the Fraser administration. Yet from its very first year in office the Hawke government did embark on a series of radical economic and social reforms, which can be interpreted as a first iteration of the Third Way in Australia (Pierson and Castles 2001). An aggressive programme of privatization, deregulation, and public sector cuts ensued. Reforms to the welfare state emphasized raising living standards by improving wages and labour market conditions rather than through extensive welfare provision. Policies were geared to shifting people from benefits to work and individuals were encouraged to be 'active' recipients of welfare by participating in education, training, and unemployment schemes (Johnson and Tonkiss 2002). Many of the Hawke–Keating reforms also altered the relationship between state and citizen and exemplified a Third Way approach. Pension reform was explicitly designed to reallocate the costs of pension provision to the private sector and to individuals themselves, leaving the state to guarantee provision only for those on low incomes. The use of income-contingent loans as a funding device for higher education was instituted as were new (non-government) forms of delivery mechanisms for a range of benefits and welfare services.

If most of the social policies of the Hawke–Keating governments bore the hallmarks of Third Way reform, and arguably were the blueprints for subsequent US and UK programmes (Johnson and Tonkiss 2002), why were they not portrayed more aggressively as a radical and paradigmatically new approach to welfare—as in the United States and Britain? If both Hawke and Keating described themselves as 'breaking new ground' and in reality did so, why did neither invoke the logic of a Third Way?

Indeed, in direct contrast to the American and British experience, in which 'newness' was politically of the essence, both Hawke and Keating were keen to present themselves as lying within the mainstream of the Australian labour tradition (Pierson and Castles 2001). Any explanation of the unwillingness of the ALP to rebrand itself must be rooted in an understanding of the neo-corporatist context in which it operated. An important difference between Australian and British (and American) governments lies in their respective relationships with the trade unions. The Australian neo-corporatist 'Accord' provided for a wages policy and social contract based on an agreement between the government and the Australian Council of Trade Unions (ACTU). As there had been no equivalent of Thatcher's attacks and dismantling of militant unions, the ALP was forced to work closely with the ACTU. The emphasis was thus on achieving consensus between government, unions, and key employer groups, particularly through the establishment of tripartite advisory bodies. The need to take a powerful union movement with them meant that the entire programme of the ALP between 1983 and 1996 was carried through in a series of Accords with the ACTU. It was this political pragmatism that led to the ALP's strategic decision not to reposition itself ideologically.

It appears, then, that, whether referred to as 'Third Way' or not, many similarities in the welfare reforms adopted by the US, the UK, and Australia can be identified, and this also holds true for other industrialized welfare states, as some contributions to this volume will show. However, in order to understand why an explicit discourse of policy reconfiguration and reform was actively embraced in some countries but avoided in others, an analysis of the impact of both the political history and constraints of institutional structures is necessary. In a context such as the Australian one, where much depends on negotiation and compromise with other 'power centres and veto players', it may be perfectly rational not to commit too clearly to policy positions which may antagonize important partners (Busch 1999). The same analysis holds true for European corporatist or federal states, in particular Germany, and, as other authors later argue, in part explains why the initial enthusiasm for the Third Way project quickly faded from political discourse in that country.

We begin, then, with a set of welfare state changes that are by no means easy to characterize, and a set of political ideas and approach to social policy that are much debated by commentators. It is important to note that we also began this project agnostic about the nature of the relationship between welfare state change and an identifiable set of political ideas. Explanations may be sought in political pragmatism (as argued in this chapter), rapid structural change, or an identifiable and coherent set of principles. There is certainly no consensus among the contributors to this volume. However, the contributions do emphasize the importance of identifying and discussing the role of political ideas, rhetoric, and strategy; policy goals and mechanisms; and ideas and practices in respect of the governance of social policy. There has been considerable rethinking on the part of governments when it comes to social policy, in particular about the central set of relationships between the labour market, the family, and the state, and about the role of the state and the nature of governance. Very little of the post-war welfare settlement remains unquestioned, whether the nature of the risk to be addressed; the nature of entitlements and the form of conditionality to be applied; or the best means of making provision—whether via cash payments or services. If the former, whether via insurance, social assistance, or more individual asset-based mechanisms, and if the latter, how much should be financed and provided by the

state, the market, and the third sector. Furthermore, left-of-centre political
parties have had to rethink their approaches to social provision in relation
to earlier, and usually strongly held, ideas of 'the proper thing to do' in
respect of 'welfare', as well as in response to socio-economic change and
specific political conjunctures.

The following chapters further probe and develop these issues, and in
doing so assess the success of current social democratic administrations in
developing a distinctive new agenda in social policy. The theoretical
debates and empirical research presented in all three sections evaluate the
tensions and dilemmas involved in the process of creating welfare change,
as well as its impact on the traditional concerns of social policy, namely,
social solidarity and citizenship.

3. Scope and Organization of the Book

Part I traces the political and historical developments surrounding a Third
Way agenda in social policy and develops a conceptual framework by
which it can be appraised. White explores two issues central to the debate
over the welfare philosophy of the Third Way: first, how egalitarian it is,
and second, whether its emphasis on contractualism constitutes a break
with social democratic tradition. White's analysis suggests that, while less
egalitarian than most other social democratic philosophies, a Third Way
stress on welfare contractualism is not unique or incongruent with other
notions of social justice. He identifies key ideas that underpin the Third
Way approach in the UK, and suggests that these may be shared cross-
nationally, although different countries will be starting from different
places. However, on the basis of a comparative analysis, Bonoli and
Powell argue that there is more similarity between European governments
in terms of their policies than in respect of ideas at the level of political
rhetoric, although there is evidence of agreement on values at an overarching level. Nevertheless, there is, they think, more similarity between
what governments are doing than what they are saying.

Part II focuses on those areas that are central to the restructuring of welfare states and to the new thinking about welfare: the role of the state, the
labour market, the family, and the third sector. As Newman and Anheier
show, new approaches to governance, filtered through ideas about modernization, enabling, and partnership, are an essential part of the new welfare arrangements. Both contributors grapple with one of the major issues
raised in this chapter: the extent to which Third Way ideas, as opposed to
structural forces, are drivers of change. Clasen and Clegg concur with
Bonoli and Powell's argument regarding the similarity of policy in

European states. Looking at labour market reforms in the UK, France, and Germany, they conclude that actual policy has been more similar than might be suggested by the political rhetoric in each case. The authors further illustrate the arguments presented in this chapter, namely, that while a Third Way discourse has had programmatic utility for the Blair government, the opposite may have been the case in the other countries. Daly is of the view that there is new thinking about the relationship between the state, the family, and the market, but joins those who are sceptical about how far this is attributable to an identifiable Third Way approach. Nevertheless, these chapters show the renegotiation of relationships and boundaries between the state and civil society; between welfare provision, the labour market, and the family; and between citizens and the state, which taken together amount to a major reconceptualizing of welfare states and social policies.

Part III returns to the task of understanding what constitutes a Third Way approach to social policy-making. Both Lister and Dean do this through an exploration of basic concepts. Lister takes up the idea of 'the social investment state', a concept used by political proponents of the Third Way and in academic analysis in both the UK and Canada. Dean focuses on concepts that are well-established in the study of social policy and have historically been key goals of left-of-centre political parties: equality, citizenship, and social cohesion. Dean examines in particular the impact of social policies under New Labour on these goals. Taken together, these chapters further clarify the extent to which recent approaches to social policy-making can be characterized as 'new'. Both authors express doubts about the direction that policy has taken. Finally, Lewis seeks to bring together the new ideas about policies and governance explored in Part II, and to illustrate the complexity of their interaction in relation to one policy field in the UK— namely, childcare—which because of the central rethinking of labour market and family policies has become a focus of attention in many Western European welfare states and at the EU level.

The most difficult issue of all is whether the new thinking about social policy, whether explicitly labeled Third Way' or not, can actually deliver the goods. We cannot yet know, but the chapters in this book do give a sense of the extent to which the approach to social policy-making is being reworked in many countries, as well as drawing attention yet again to the old adages that politics and context matter. There may not be a strongly identifiable vision of a Third Way, but common strands can be identified in recent approaches to policy-making across welfare states, and they bring with them new tensions and contradictions. The situation is finely balanced for those who wish to promote social solidarity alongside markets.

References

Baer, K. (2000). *Reinventing Democrats: The Politics of Liberalism From Reagan To Clinton*. Lawrence: University of Kansas Press.

Baker, A. (2000). 'Globalisation and the British Residual State', in R. Stubbs and G. Underhill (eds.), *Political Economy and the Changing Global Order*. Toronto, Canada: Oxford University Press.

Bashevkin, S. (2001). *Road-Testing the Third Way: Welfare Reform in Canada, Britain and the United States* (Working Paper No. 4). School of Public Policy and Research, UCLA.

Blair, T. (1998). *The Third Way*. London: Fabian Society.

—— and Schroeder, G. (1999). *Europe: The Third Way/Die Neue Mitte*. London: Labour Party.

Bonoli, G. and Palier, B. (2001). 'How Do Welfare States Change? Institutions and their Impact on the Politics of Welfare State Reform in Western Europe', in S. Leibfried (ed.), *Welfare State Futures*. Cambridge: Cambridge University Press.

—— and Powell, M. (2002). 'Third Ways in Europe?', *Social Policy and Society*, 1/1: 59–66.

Braun, D. and Busch, A. (eds.) (1999). *Public Policy and Political Ideas*. Cheltenham: Edward Elgar.

Busch, A. and Manow, P. (2001). 'The SPD and the Neue Mitte in Germany', in S. White (ed.), *New Labour: The Progressive Future?* Basingstoke: Macmillan.

Cerny, P. and Evans, M. (2000). *New Labour, Globalisation and the Competition State*. Cambridge, MA: Harvard University Press.

Clasen, J. (2002). 'Modern Social Democracy and European Welfare State Reform', *Social Policy and Society*, 1/1: 67–76.

Driver, S. and Martell, L. (2000). 'Left, Right and the Third Way', *Policy and Politics*, 28/2: 147–61.

—— —— (2002). *Blair's Britain*. Cambridge: Polity Press.

Etzioni, A. (1993). *The Spirit of Community: The Reinvention of American Society*. New York: Touchstone.

—— (2000). *The Third Way to a Good Society*. London: Demos.

Ferrera, M., Hemerijck, A., and Rhodes, M. (2001). 'Recasting European Welfare States for the 21st Century', in S. Leibfried (ed.), *Welfare State Futures*. Cambridge: Cambridge University Press.

Giddens, A. (1994). *Beyond Left and Right*. Cambridge: Polity Press.

—— (1998). *The Third Way. The Renewal of Social Democracy*. Cambridge: Polity Press.

—— (2002). *Where Now for New Labour?* Cambridge: Polity Press.

Green Pedersen, C., van Kersbergen, K., and Hemerijck, A. (2001). 'Neo-Liberalism, The "Third Way", or What? Recent Social Democratic Welfare Policies in Denmark and the Netherlands', *Journal of European Public Policy*, 8: 307–25.

Hale, J. (1995). 'The Making of the new Democrats', *Political Science Quarterly*, 110: 207–32.

Halpern, D. and Mikosz, D. (1998). *The Third Way*. London: Nexus.

Harris, P. (2002). 'Welfare Rewritten: Change and Interlay in Social and Economic Accounts', *Journal of Social Policy*, 31: 377–98.

Heath, A., Jowell, R., and Curtice, J. (2001). *The Rise of New Labour*. Oxford: Oxford University Press.

Heffernan, R. (1998). 'Labour's Transformation: A Staged process with no Single Point of Origin', *Politics*, 18: 101–6.

—— (2001). *New Labour and Thatcherism: Political Change in Britain*. Basingstoke: Macmillan.

Hewitt, P. and Gould, P. (1993). 'Lessons from America: Learning from Success— Labour and Clinton's New Democrats', *Renewal*, 1: 45–51.

Jessop, B. (1994). 'The Transition to Post-Fordism and the Schumpeterian Workfare State', in R. Burrows and B. Loader (eds.), *Towards a Post-Fordist Welfare State?* London: Routledge.

Johnson, C. and Tonkiss, F. (2002). 'The Third Influence: The Blair Government and Australian Labor', *Policy and Politics*, 30/1: 1, 5–18.

Kitschelt, H. (2001). 'Partisan Competition and Welfare State Retrenchment: When Do Politicians Choose Unpopular Policies?', in P. Pierson (ed.), *The New Politics of the Welfare State*. Oxford: Oxford University Press.

Kuhnle, S. (2001). 'The Nordic Welfare State in a European Context: Dealing With New Economic and Ideological Challenges in the 1990s', in S. Leibfried (ed.), *Welfare State Futures*. Cambridge: Cambridge University Press.

Le Grand, J. (1998). 'The Third Way begins with Cora', *New Statesman*, 6 March: 26–7.

Leibfried, S. (ed.) (2001). *Welfare State Futures*. Cambridge: Cambridge University Press.

—— and Obinger, H. (2001). 'Welfare State Futures', in S. Leibfried (ed.), *Welfare State Futures*. Cambridge: Cambridge University Press.

—— and Pierson, P. (2000). 'Social Policy', in H. Wallace and W. Wallace (eds.), *Policy-making in the European Union*. Oxford: Oxford University Press.

Lewis, J. (2002). 'Gender and Welfare State Change', *European Societies*, 4: 331–57.

OECD (1996). *Ageing in OECD Countries: A Critical Policy Challenge* (Social Policy Studies No. 20). Paris: OECD.

—— (1998). *Maintaining Prosperity in an Ageing Society*. Paris: OECD.

Pierson, C. (2001). *Hard Choices: Social Democracy in the Twenty First Century*. Cambridge: Polity Press.

—— and Castles, F. (2001). *Australian Antecedents of the Third Way*. Grenoble: ECPR.

Putnam, R. (1995). 'Bowling Alone: America's Declining Social Capital', *Journal of Democracy*, 6: 65–78.

Rhodes, M. (2000). 'Desperately Seeking a Solution: Social Democracy, Thatcherism and The Third Way in British Welfare', *West European Politics*, 23/2: 161–86.

Ross, F. (2000). 'Framing Welfare Reform in Affluent Societies: Rendering Restructuring More Palatable?', *Journal of Public Policy*, 20/3: 169–93.

Savage, S. and Atkinson, R. (eds.) (2001). *Public Policy Under Blair*. Basingstoke: Palgrave.

Scharpf, F. (2001). 'The Viability of Advanced Welfare States in the International Economy: Vulnerabilities and Options', in S. Leibfried (ed.), *Welfare State Futures*. Cambridge: Cambridge University Press.

—— and V. Schmidt (eds.) (2000*a*). *Welfare and Work in the Open Economy. Volume 1: From Vulnerability to Competitiveness*. Oxford: Oxford University Press.

—— —— (eds.) (2000*b*). *Welfare and Work in the Open Economy. Volume 2: Diverse Responses to Common Challenges*. Oxford: Oxford University Press.

Seeleib-Kaiser, M. (1999). 'Welfare Systems and the Conditions of Globalisation: Divergence, Convergence and Divergent Convergence', *Zeitschrift für Sozialreform*, 45/1: 3–23.

Seyd, P. (1998). *New Labour Triumphs: Britain at the Polls*. Chatham, NJ: Chatham House.

Skowronek, S. (1997). *The Politics Presidents Make: Leadership from John Adams to George Bush* (2nd edn.). Cambridge, MA: Harvard University Press.

Swank, D. (2002). *Global Capital, Political Institutions and Policy Change in Developed Welfare States*. Cambridge: Cambridge University Press.

Vandenbroucke, F. (2001). 'European Social Democracy and the Third Way: Convergence, Divisions, and Shared Questions', in S. White (ed.), *New Labour: The Progressive Future?* Basingstoke: Palgrave.

White, S. (1998). 'Interpreting the Third Way: Not One Road But Many', *Renewal*, 6/2: 17–30.

—— (2001). 'The Ambiguities of the Third Way', in S. White (ed.), *New Labour: The Progressive Future?* Basingstoke: Palgrave.

2

Welfare Philosophy and the Third Way

STUART WHITE

> We want to draw a line below which we will not allow persons to live and
> labour, yet above which they may compete with all the strength of their
> manhood. We want to have free competition upwards; we decline to allow
> free competition to run downwards.
>
> (Winston Churchill, *Liberalism and the Social Problem*)

Since the late 1990s, parties and governments of the centre-left have
frequently described themselves as offering a 'Third Way'. Even where
the term itself is displaced by some other phrase, such as 'progressive
governance', the sense of a new, distinctive political project remains.
Moreover, the reform of existing welfare arrangements is clearly central
to this project. How should we characterize this project philosophically?
In what ways is its thinking about welfare continuous with the mainstream
social democratic tradition? In what ways does it break with (perhaps even
threaten) this normative tradition?

In debating these questions, two issues seem to be particularly important. The first issue concerns how far and in what sense the Third Way is
egalitarian. Social democrats have historically seen the welfare state as
part of a 'strategy of equality' (Tawney 1964). Some sense that the Third
Way lacks the same underlying egalitarian ambition. The second issue
concerns the emphasis in Third Way rhetoric and policy on welfare contractualism. Welfare provision is seen in the Third Way as one side of a
contract between state and citizen. The other side of the contract is that the
citizen should meet certain behavioural standards, for example in relation
to job search or training. Benefits, in the Third Way view, can and sometimes should be conditional on satisfying these standards (both cash benefits and some public services). Critics argue that this represents a clear

I would like to thank Alan Deacon for many helpful discussions of contractualism; Selina Chen,
Ben Jackson, Michael Jacobs, Neal Lawson, Marc Stears, and Adam Swift for various discussions about the Third Way and egalitarianism; and Jane Lewis and Rebecca Surender for their
comments on an earlier version of the chapter.

break with the principle of 'social citizenship' that T. H. Marshall saw as embodied in developed welfare states (Marshall 1950), a principle which is thought by the critics to entail a policy of unconditional entitlement to benefits. Contractualism is presented as an idea foreign to social democracy, an alien import from other ideologies (typically of dubious North American origin) such as the 'communitarianism' of Amitai Etzioni or the 'New Paternalism' of conservatives like Lawrence Mead. In short, the claim is that the Third Way is *not egalitarian enough* and is *too contractualist* to be regarded as embodying a social democratic philosophy of welfare. It is, at worst, a moderately humanized version of neo-liberalism, and at best a kind of hybrid that plucks and combines ideas from other philosophies, socialist, liberal, and conservative (a view presented by Freeden 1999).

This chapter explores these two issues at the heart of the debate over the welfare philosophy of the Third Way. How egalitarian is the Third Way? Does its emphasis on contractualism constitute a break with a social demo-cratic welfare philosophy? Focusing on the Anglo-American Third Way, and particularly on the British case, I argue that there are discontinuities with the historic social democratic mainstream, but that the picture is more complicated than the critics suggest.

To what extent do my conclusions about the welfare philosophy of the Third Way generalize to other nations that have experienced governments of a supposedly Third Way orientation? Cross-national generalizations about welfare philosophy and Third Ways are difficult. One reason is that Third Way politics, perhaps especially in the area of welfare, is strongly path-dependent: political imperatives, mediated by national systems of economic and welfare governance, typically constrain political actors to reform in a way that does not break too radically with policy inheritances. When proponents of the Third Way, or 'progressive governance', meet at international conferences,[1] they may share a rhetoric and a set of policy concerns (such as welfare-to-work and reform of public services): they may all sign up, in a broad-brush way, to the value concepts and policy themes outlined in section 1 below. But a US New Democrat and a Swedish 'modernizing' social democrat nevertheless start from very different places in terms of their institutional and policy inheritances; they espouse different concrete policy programmes (see Clift 2003 on the sub-stantial policy differences between New Labour in Britain and continental European social democratic parties); and these differences in policy inheri-tance and advocacy are also likely to correlate with real, underlying

---

[1] An example would be the Progressive Governance conference organized under the auspices of Policy Network in London in July 2003. For details of participants and related papers, see www.progressive-governance.net.

philosophical differences. There is, to be sure, no logical reason why the two cannot inhabit the same philosophical space in spite of their different policy inheritances and programmes. But in so far as the philosophy of political actors is to some extent adaptive to perceptions of what is feasible, and policy inheritances and current programmes influence actors' perceptions of the feasible, different policy inheritances and programmes will translate into (and will in turn be consolidated by) different implicit philosophies. A second factor that should caution against cross-national generalization about the philosophy underpinning Third Ways in welfare is that the ideas of the left or centre-left in a given nation will of course be shaped in part by ideological traditions particular to that nation. Think, for example, of the distinctive influence on the French centre-left of a self-conscious republican tradition. Thus, what goes for the British or US cases cannot be assumed to apply straightforwardly to other national Third Ways (and, indeed, one should be wary of assuming too much similarity between the British and US Third Ways). In the case of Third Ways outside of 'Anglo-America' (Gamble 2003), the utility of this chapter may lie less in any specific conclusion I draw about the welfare philosophy of the Third Way than in the framework I use to explore this question, a framework that can be readily applied to other national cases.

1. The Third Way: The Core Value and Policy Framework

Let us begin by charting some of the basic ideas that define the Third Way. In an earlier study, I argued that the Third Way can be seen, as Steven Lukes puts it, as a 'rhetorically-defined space' marked out by commitment to certain core values and a preference for certain sorts of public policy (see White 2001; Lukes 2003).

On the face of it, the core value concepts of the Third Way are not hard to discern. Consider the following passage from the Arnold Goodman Charity Lecture given by Tony Blair in 1993:

A modern notion of citizenship gives rights but demands obligations, shows respect but wants it back, grants *opportunity* but insists on *responsibility* ... Binding all this together is the notion of rebuilding a modern view of *community*, where interdependence and independence are both recognised, where the existence of a strong and cohesive society is considered essential to the fulfilment of individual aspiration and progress. (Blair 1996: 218, 220, emphasis added)

The value concepts highlighted here are the same as those that Bill Clinton used to kick off his run for the presidency in October 1991: '... [we seek] a New Covenant, a solemn agreement between the people and their government, to provide opportunity for everybody, inspire responsibility throughout our society and restore a sense of community to our great nation' (Greenberg 1995: 214; see also Klein 2002: 38–9).

'Opportunity, responsibility, community': this is the central rhetorical trinity of Third Way politics. Of course, these terms can be unpacked in different ways according to one's underlying political philosophy. Over time, as more literature advocating the Third Way has accumulated along with actual policies that are said to embody Third Way values, it has become possible to discern a dominant, quasi-authoritative interpretation of these concepts. However, even when the Third Way was in its infancy, there were some clear constraints on how these value concepts could plausibly be construed, some indications of what was intended by this rhetoric. So, for example, 'opportunity' certainly seems to mean more than the formal opportunity to earn and pursue happiness that one would have in a simple free-market society. Often linked with the idea of 'social inclusion', it signifies at least a baseline of effective opportunity for self-development and material advance. On the other hand, it is emphatically not shorthand for 'equality of outcome', an idea that is routinely rubbished by proponents of the Third Way (for more detail, see the discussion in section 2 below).

For its part, 'responsibility' is not equivalent to the classical liberal notion of self-reliance, the idea that the individual should stand on his or her own feet without any assistance from government. If that were what Third Way advocates meant by responsibility, then the commitment to responsibility would contradict their commitment to opportunity, given that the latter does imply some right to assistance. Relatedly, such a classical liberal understanding of responsibility is in flat contradiction to some flagship Third Way policy ideas such as more generous in-work benefits for the low-paid. On the other hand, the theme of 'responsibility' does seem to mark a difference between the Third Way and *some* earlier currents of social democratic thought. A major current of post-war social democratic thought in Britain is characterized by what one might call a flight from moralism, by a growing unwillingness to define and enforce certain behavioural standards of citizenship, at least as a condition for the receipt of welfare. David Piachaud (1993) refers to this mind-set as 'mid-century Fabianism', while Alan Deacon (2002) refers to it as the 'quasi-Titmuss paradigm'. Richard Titmuss was a firm believer in universalism as against means-testing and, for the most part, he also tended in his later, published work to downplay, or simply ignore, questions about the possible negative behavioural effects of welfare (Deacon 2002: 17–22).[2] Many later social policy scholars from the 1960s to the 1980s

---

[2] Titmuss's views in this area were not fixed, however. John Welshman has shown that, even in his later years, Titmuss held to a complicated, nuanced, and ultimately somewhat confused

followed his lead in this respect, regarding such behavioural concerns as symptomatic of a discredited voluntarist explanation of deprivation, and as likely in practice to lead to policies that would unfairly stigmatize and punish the disadvantaged (Deacon 2002: 22–6). The receipt of welfare came to be seen, in this paradigm, simply as an unconditional entitlement. Gareth Davies has charted the rise of a similar current of 'entitlement liberalism' in the USA in the 1960s (Davies 1996). The Third Way emphasis on 'responsibility' is clearly meant to mark a break with this approach to welfare. As Tony Giddens puts it, in the closest thing we have to an official Third Way manifesto:

One might suggest as a prime motto for the new politics, *no rights without responsibilities* . . . Old-style social democracy . . . was inclined to treat rights as unconditional claims. With expanding individualism should come an extension of obligations. Unemployment benefits, for example, should carry the obligation to look actively for work . . . (Giddens 1998: 65)

As discussed further below, Giddens is here echoing a slogan of the US communitarian movement which emerged in the 1980s, though this is not to say that the underlying idea does not have roots also in British social democratic thought.[3]

The term 'community' is so vague that it is readily appropriated by ideologists across the political spectrum from anarchists to fascists. One way of understanding its import in a Third Way context is as a derivative of the first two value concepts. If there is sufficient 'opportunity', then nobody suffers 'social exclusion', which seems necessary for 'community'. If people meet their responsibilities, then nobody will be free-riding unfairly on the efforts of others, and this, too, seems necessary for 'community'. Thus, 'community' refers to the quality of social life made possible by securing 'opportunity' and general respect for 'responsibility'. But 'community' is also something that helps to produce these goods, not just a product of them. As 'social capital', it is an asset that can help to secure opportunity and to nurture a stronger sense of civic responsibility.

---

view about the relative importance of structure and agency in causing social problems, though this picture is more evident from private correspondence and unpublished writings than from his published work. Welshman also emphasizes that Titmuss and his students were inclined to stress structural factors over behavioural factors in explaining social problems because they were reacting against a narrowly behavioural approach adopted by psychiatrists in the 1950s. See Welshman (2001).

[3] Nor should one assume that the turn from unconditional entitlement to contractualist notions of welfare is confined to Anglo-America. It is reflected also, for example, in the recent work of the French social theorist and commentator Pierre Rosanvallon, an influential figure in the 'social liberal' wing of the French centre-left (Rosanvallon 2000; Bouvet and Michel 2001).

30 *Stuart White*

'Community' is both an end that is realized through 'opportunity' and 'responsibility', and a crucial means to their realization.

If these are the values of the Third Way, how do its proponents envisage advancing these values? If we focus specifically on welfare policy, there seem to be at least four key, organizing policy themes (the reader should imagine me slipping into the character of a Third Way enthusiast as I describe them).[4]

1. *Asset-based egalitarianism.* State welfare provision should seek not merely to alleviate disadvantage but to build assets so that people are more able to avoid disadvantage. This enables us to expand opportunity, and so increase fairness, while at the same time improving competitiveness and efficiency (see Commission on Social Justice 1994; Brown 1995, 1999; Giddens 1998, especially 99–128 on the 'social investment state'). One major focus of concern must be human capital: a better-educated work-force is essential to improving the perceived trade-off between employ-ment and earnings equality in post-industrial economies. This brings educational policy to centre stage and, if we take a longer view, under-scores the importance of early-years intervention to foster child develop-ment in pre-school years. Fighting 'social exclusion' also requires attention to financial asset-building amongst the worst-off. To this end, government should encourage financial institutions geared to the needs of low-income groups, such as credit unions, and should provide generous subsidies to low-income savers combined with financial literacy pro-grammes (HM Treasury 2001). Even more radically, the government can provide all citizens on maturity or birth with a basic capital grant (Ackerman and Alstott 1999; Nissan and Le Grand 2000; Kelly and Lissauer 2000), an idea that finds expression in New Labour's Child Trust Fund policy (see HM Treasury 2001, 2003).

2. *Welfare contractualism.* 'Opportunity' must be combined with 'responsibility'. Thus, benefits for the out of work should be made condi-tional on active job search and retraining (Giddens 1998: 65, 116–17). In post-industrial labour markets, it is essential to redistribute to boost the incomes of the low-paid (since low pay for some is the price of high employment). But the form of redistribution should be seen to reward work rather than laziness, pointing towards programmes such as the Earned Income Tax Credit (Clinton) and Working Families Tax Credit

---

[4] This list of policy instruments is similar to that presented in my earlier essay (White 2001), but I have amended it slightly in light of policy developments since the late 1990s. A fuller list would also have to include an account of the conception of macroeconomic policy associated with the Third Way, which is in fact more complicated than the standard 'end of Keynesianism' inter-pretation suggests. For a helpful discussion of this issue, see Annesley and Gamble (2003: 146–9).

(New Labour). In the past, the Left has tended to explain social problems such as poverty, unemployment, and crime in terms of structural barriers, the Right in terms of individual agency (see, for example, Mead 1986, 1992). This is a false and disabling dichotomy. To get to grips with entrenched social problems of these kinds, government must address itself to both structural barriers and individual agency. Contractualism, in a context of supportive, asset-building policies, expresses this post-structuralist conception of social problems and of how to tackle them (see Deacon and Mann 1999).

3. *Re-engineering public services: state as guarantor, not necessarily provider*. To meet the objective of 'opportunity', the state must play an active role in securing the provision of certain basic services to all, such as health care and education. However, we should not remain uncritically wedded to the idea that the state should directly provide such services. In some cases, it may be appropriate for the state to finance the service while contracting out immediate provision to private, for-profit companies or to the voluntary sector. Where the state retains a provider role, moreover, it may be appropriate to reorganize the system of service delivery, employing devices such as quasi-markets and making greater use of performance indicators backed up by inspection regimes and perhaps new non-profit 'public interest companies' as service providers (on which see Lea and Mayo 2003: 17–26). If the conservative median voter is to get better value for his/her tax monies, and if provision is to match the expectations of a more individualist society, it is vital to re-engineer public service provision in (at least some of) these ways so that they are more efficient and responsive (Policy Network 2003). No specific approach is to be privileged; the key is open-minded experimentation with a view to finding what works.

4. *Mutualism and the re-engagement of civil society*. The theme of re-engineering public services is linked to a fourth policy theme: 'mutualism' and the effort to build and engage associations within civil society to help address social problems and deliver public services. Credit unions have a vital role in combating financial exclusion (Brown, Conaty, and Mayo 2003). 'Public interest companies', with mandates to involve the communities they serve in managing service provision, may have a role in running hospitals or schools (Lea and Mayo 2003). Time banks can be used to help encourage volunteering (New Economics Foundation 2001). More generally, policy objectives will not be met if the government simply does things to or for individuals. The government needs intermediaries close to the ground to work with it, and so must design policy interventions and services in ways that build and engage communities of relevant 'stakeholders' with whom it can work in 'partnership'.

These policy themes are seen not only as individually desirable but as mutually supportive. A quintessential Third Way policy idea would combine elements of all four policy themes: it would be, perhaps, an intervention to build assets (human or financial) which offers new opportunities in return for the assumption of certain personal responsibilities, which draws in part on the private and/or voluntary sectors for programme delivery, and which seeks to build and engage with civil society in the process of delivery. In combining these policy themes, the policy would neatly express the interconnectedness of 'opportunity', 'responsibility', and 'community'.

2. Is the Third Way Egalitarian?

With this account of the core Third Way value and policy framework in place, let us now explore the welfare philosophy it embodies in more detail. As noted above, two key issues here concern how egalitarian the Third Way is, and the consistency of welfare contractualism with a philosophy of social citizenship. I shall consider the egalitarianism issue first, turning to the relationship between contractualism and social citizenship in the next section.

The Third Way is committed to 'opportunity'. But how egalitarian is its understanding of this value? In considering this question, it will help to step back momentarily and consider what sorts of things cause inequalities. Simplifying a little, we can discern at least four important sources of inequality (derived from Nagel 1991: 102–9):

E1 *Discrimination*: inequality in access to education and employment attributable to admissions, hiring, and related decisions made on the basis of personal characteristics that are not relevant to the candidate's merit.

E2 *Social background inequality*: inequality in opportunity due to differences in social background encompassing inequalities in access to and quality of education (not explained by E1), inequalities due to differences in family environment and parenting capacity, and inequalities in resources in early adulthood.

E3 *Natural endowment inequality*: inequality in natural abilities affecting the earnings capacity of the individual and/or imposing disabilities that imply special resource needs.

E4 *Differences in effort and lifestyle choice*: differences between people in effort and lifestyle choice that impact upon their final levels of incomes and welfare.

Third Way rhetoric often refers us to 'equality of worth' as a core value (for example, Blair 1998: 4). However, by itself this notion doesn't tell us very much about the egalitarianism of the Third Way. For the pertinent question is this: if you believe that people have equal worth, which of the four sources of inequality listed above will you (*ought* you to) regard as objectionable and, thus, as a possible target for corrective state action? Merely emphasizing 'equality of worth' risks obscuring this basic issue.

One can distinguish four basic positions on this issue. First, there is what we may call the *weak meritocrat* position, which objects only to the inequality grounded in E1. On this view, it is unfair if a better-qualified person is rejected for a job on the grounds of personal characteristics that are unrelated to job performance, such as race, gender, or sexual orientation. The state should prohibit this. But it is inappropriate for the state to try to tackle the other listed sources of inequality, either because the resultant inequalities are essentially legitimate or because any concerted effort to tackle them would come at an objectionably high price in terms of other values (such as liberty).

Second, there is a *strong meritocrat* position. The strong meritocrat objects not only to inequalities grounded in E1 but also to those grounded in E2. Qualified support for this strong form of meritocracy can be found in Miller (2000). On this view, the inequalities due to E2 are illegitimate and the state ought to do a lot to tackle them, though most strong meritocrats would concede that it is unfeasible fully to eliminate such inequalities without unacceptable limitations on family life. Inequalities due to E3 and E4 are accepted as legitimate. The strong meritocrat will argue that at least some of these inequalities are just because they are connected with more skilled and harder-working people getting what they 'deserve' (see Miller 2000: chs. 7–9).

Third, there is a *supermeritocrat* position which objects to inequalities grounded in E1 through E3. Proponents of this view argue that the strong meritocrat position is, as Ronald Dworkin puts it, 'fraudulent' (Dworkin 1985: 207). The strong meritocrat objects to the weak meritocrat because there cannot be genuine 'equality of opportunity' if we do not tackle inequalities grounded in E2 as well as E1. The supermeritocrat similarly objects to the strong meritocrat that there is no genuine equality of opportunity if we ignore the inequalities grounded in E3. The classic statement of this argument is found in John Rawls's *A Theory of Justice* (though one also sees a clear anticipation of it in Émile Durkheim's lectures on civic morals; see Durkheim 1992: 219–20). Rawls argues that, if it is unjust for people to be disadvantaged by the bad luck of being born into one social class rather than another, it is equally unjust for them to be disadvantaged by bad luck in the genetic lottery: 'There is no more reason

to permit the distribution of income and wealth to be settled by the distribution of natural assets than by historical and social fortune' (Rawls 1999:
63–4). Thus, supermeritocrats like Rawls argue that earnings inequalities
that have their roots in unequal natural endowments are not deserved.
In principle, these inequalities should be taxed away. They are justifiable
only to the extent that they improve the material position of the 'worst-
off group' (roughly speaking, the class of low-skilled manual workers),
for example by providing the more gifted with extra incentives to work
(see Rawls 1999: 65–70). Rawls says conflicting things about E4-type
inequalities, but Dworkin is emphatic that they are essentially legitimate
(see Dworkin 1985: 205–8, 2000: 65–119).[5] In his view, we fail to show
citizens equal respect if we require some of them to subsidize the costly
or imprudent lifestyle choices of others: provided that we have properly
tackled the inequalities grounded in E1–E3, the hard-working and the
entrepreneurial should not have to subsidize the lazy and the risk-averse.

Finally, there is the *equality of outcome* position which objects to all of
the listed sources of inequality. The ideal here is of strict income equality
or, more typically, of strict income equality modified to account for disabilities and other special needs. Some proponents of this view might
allow for moderation of the ideal on incentive grounds (as, for example,
Karl Marx does in his account of the first stage of communist society;
see Marx 1976), though they may also envisage a transformation in the
character of productive motivation that diminishes the need for special
incentive payments.

Now, where does the Third Way stand in relation to these four types of
egalitarianism? As suggested above, proponents of the Third Way clearly
reject the equality-of-outcome position. This position provides them with
a convenient rhetorical punching-bag against which they can assert their
claim to be different from earlier currents of the Left. This is the 'abstract
equality' that, according to Blair, has in the past 'stifled opportunity'
(Blair 1998: 3).

What about the supermeritocratic position advanced by Rawls and
Dworkin? This, too, seems to be a position that supporters of the Third
Way reject. A key claim of Rawls and Dworkin is that the naturally gifted

---

[5] In *A Theory of Justice*, Rawls suggests that 'willingness to make an effort' is bound up with
social background and natural ability in a way that makes it inappropriate to try to differentiate
distributive shares between individuals on the basis of effort (see Rawls 1999: 64, 274).
However, in *Justice as Fairness* he denies that those who choose to do no work are entitled to
the basic income share guaranteed to the worst-off, implying that some differentiation according to effort is appropriate (see Rawls 2001: 179). One should also note that, at the policy level,
Dworkin accepts that it will be difficult to make a fully accurate distinction between disadvantage due to brute luck and that due to choice, and is willing to tolerate some subsidy of the lazy
and risk-averse as a feature of any real-world transfer scheme (see Dworkin 1985: 208).

arc not inherently deserving of higher reward for the development and employment of their talents than the less gifted. This idea runs counter to the clear meritocratic spirit of Blair's description of what he means by 'opportunity for all': 'The Left . . . has in the past too readily downplayed its duty to promote a wide range of opportunities for individuals to *advance themselves and their families*' (Blair 1998: 3, emphasis added). Or consider: '*Talent and efforts should be encouraged to flourish* in all quarters, and governments must act decisively to end discrimination and prejudice' (Blair 1998: 3, emphasis added). One could, at a stretch, square these words with a Rawlsian understanding of justice by arguing that Blair intends only that the talented should 'flourish' and 'advance themselves' to the extent that this maximizes the prospects of the worst-off. But there is no qualification to this effect in Blair's text. Moreover, Blair's comments should be seen in the context of the work of the Commission on Social Justice. The Commission explicitly eschewed Rawls's theory of justice, affirming that the more talented are to some (completely unspecified) extent inherently 'deserving' of or 'entitled' to higher reward (see Commission on Social Justice 1993: 12–14). This is not to say that there is not some ambivalence in the Third Way literature about the ideal of meritocracy (weak or strong). In his first effort to tell us what the Third Way is, Giddens goes out of his way to emphasize that the Third Way does not see equality in meritocratic terms: meritocracy is presented as harsh, socially disruptive, and self-contradictory (Giddens 1998: 101–2). But in a more recent work he tells us that 'a meritocratic approach to equality is inevitable'; that 'We should want a society that is more egalitarian than it is today, but which is meritocratic and pluralistic . . .' (Giddens 2001: 38).

It seems reasonable, then, to regard meritocracy as central to Third Way thinking about equality, though this is not to say that the Third Way reduces straightforwardly to either of the two meritocratic positions identified above. On the one hand, the Third Way conception of 'opportunity for all' certainly goes beyond what is consistent with the weak meritocrat position. Whereas the weak meritocrat is concerned only with the barriers posed by discrimination, Blair's 'opportunity for all' clearly does embrace a concern for barriers rooted in class and family background as well as discrimination. In Blair's words: 'Gross inequalities continue to be handed down from generation to generation, and the progressive Left must robustly tackle the obstacles to true equality of opportunity' (Blair 1998: 3). In the case of New Labour, there is a large array of policy proposals and initiatives that reflect this concern: Sure Start, Education Action Zones, the New Deal for Communities, and so on.

However, if the Third Way is not equivalent to the weak meritocracy position, nor does it conform to that of strong meritocracy. There are two important differences. First, there is a difference between wanting equality of opportunity in the strong meritocrat's sense, and the Third Way goal, as articulated by Blair, of 'opportunity for all'. The latter concept does not necessarily point towards people being *equal* in terms of their opportunity, but to their all having a *decent floor* of opportunity. Securing this may require interventions that go well beyond what the weak meritocrat would accept, but it need not take us as far in tackling social background disadvantage as the strong meritocrat demands. Certainly—with the important exception of anti-discrimination policy—the practice of Third Way governments, such as the New Labour government, reflects a concern with ensuring a basic floor of opportunity for all rather than with equality of opportunity (though one must be wary about inferring values from policies in a direct manner as policies may reflect a compromise of values in the light of constraints). A strong meritocrat, for example, would typically wish to strike at inequalities in inherited wealth by taxing wealth transfers heavily and redistributing the proceeds, perhaps as some kind of universal capital grant (Ackerman and Alstott 1999). As noted above, New Labour has introduced a modest capital grant scheme, the Child Trust Fund. But it was striking that in government discussion of the policy no linkage with reform of inheritance tax was made, despite the prominence of this linkage in some of the background, academically rooted literature (Ackerman and Alstott 1999; Nissan and Le Grand 2000). 'Inclusion' is, again, a threshold concept, not one that necessarily intimates *equality* in opportunity. In this respect, then, the Third Way stands to the 'right' of the strong meritocrat position.

In another respect, however, it also stands to the 'left' of this position. Third Way advocates do not seem committed to the strict meritocratic view that it is inappropriate for the state to take any action to correct or compensate for disadvantage due to poor natural endowments (the E3-type inequalities). To be sure, Third Wayers stand with meritocrats in rejecting the Rawlsian view that all earnings inequality attributable to differences in natural endowments is morally arbitrary, and is just only if it somehow works to the advantage of the 'worst-off'. But this does not mean that they are indifferent to the position of those born with severe disabilities or who, even with a decent education, will be unable to command much of a wage. In Blair's words: 'Social justice must be founded on the equal worth of each individual, whatever their background, *capability*, creed or race' (Blair 1998: 3, emphasis added). In the case of severe disability, the operative slogan is: 'Work for those who can, security for those who cannot.' In the case of low earnings capacity, there is indeed an optimism about the possibility of education and retraining boosting people's earnings potential, but this is surely tempered by a realism about the long-term need for redistribution to support the low-paid; in-work benefits are not seen as a temporary expedient that can be dispensed with at some point in the future. Once again, the position seems to be captured by some kind of sufficiency or threshold principle: proponents of the Third Way do not want to see people pushed below some basic standard of living as a result of poor natural endowments. This represents an important qualification to a strictly meritocratic perspective (one shared by Miller 2000).

Third Way reservations about unqualified meritocracy (weak or strong) are perhaps also related to another important strand of egalitarian thinking, one that we have not yet mentioned. Some philosophers have recently criticized the egalitarianism of thinkers such as Dworkin for being, as they allege, too much concerned with the distribution of resources as opposed to the quality of social relations. They argue that, for a society to be egalitarian, it is necessary and sufficient that its social relations embody an ethos of equal respect, an absence of domination and oppression, and that all are able to participate in political life. Distributional issues are important, on this view, but the idea is that we should derive our view about the correct distribution of income and wealth by considering what distribution is necessary to create a culture of equal respect, prevent domination, and enable political participation. I shall refer to this type of egalitarianism as *relational egalitarianism*. It is forcefully defended in Anderson (1999).

It is not difficult to see how a relational egalitarianism of this kind might excite anxieties about meritocracy. First, there is the threat from meritocracy to a culture of equal respect. Here we return to the argument of Michael Young in his classic *The Rise of the Meritocracy* (Young 1958). Young's book asks us to consider how the successful and unsuccessful would view one another in a society that is meritocratic in the strong sense identified above. He argues that the successful, assured that they really are on top because they deserve to be, will become filled with a sense of innate superiority, while those at the bottom will seethe with resentment because they are unable to blame anyone but themselves for their lot. This is hardly the basis for a culture of equal respect. Second, wealth inequalities between the successful and unsuccessful in a meritocracy, weak or strong, could quite conceivably be such as to render the unsuccessful vulnerable to personal domination by the successful and to undermine political equality in all but a formal sense. Similar concerns about the quality of social life underlie Giddens's initial wariness about meritocracy. Echoing Young, he writes that '. . . a radically meritocratic society would create deep inequalities of outcome, which would threaten social cohesion' (Giddens 1998: 101).

However, there seems to be one important difference between relational egalitarianism and the Third Way approach to equality. Both can agree that the concerns described above imply the need for a floor constraint to meritocracy. But what about a ceiling constraint, an upper limit on levels of income and wealth? The relational egalitarian must be prepared to keep this open as a possibility. It is interesting that, in his first effort to articulate the Third Way, Giddens employs the idea of 'social exclusion' in a double-edged way, to refer both to 'exclusion at the bottom' and to exclusion at the top: '. . . a withdrawal from public institutions on the part of more affluent groups, who choose to live separately from the rest of society. Privileged groups start to live in fortress communities . . .' (Giddens 1998: 103). However, while acknowledging that the problem is an effect of widening income and wealth inequalities, Giddens does not suggest taxes on the rich to tackle it. No ceiling constraint on income and wealth is envisaged.

3. Contractualism and Social Citizenship

Let us now turn to the controversy over welfare contractualism. According to some critics, welfare contractualism marks a break with a philosophy of 'social citizenship' identified as the foundation of the modern welfare state in T. H. Marshall's influential essay, 'Citizenship and Social Class' (see, for example, King 1999; King and Wickham-Jones 1999). Relatedly, as noted above, it is claimed that contractualism reflects the influence of philosophical currents outside the social democratic tradition such as Etzioni's 'communitarianism' (Etzioni 1994, 1996).

Communitarianism emerged as a public intellectual movement in the US in the early 1990s, associated with academics such as Amitai Etzioni, William Galston, and Mary Ann Glendon. Communitarians argue that they come to rescue liberal society, not to bury it. The stability of a liberal society depends on citizens shouldering certain responsibilities and possessing related virtues. After a long and in some ways desirable period of expanding individual rights and weakening traditional norms of sexuality and family life, it is time, they say, to switch the emphasis to the definition of civic responsibilities and the cultivation of civic virtue. This perspective obviously fits neatly with a call for greater 'reciprocity' in welfare (Deacon 2002: 75–6), though it is fair to say that welfare reform as such does not feature very highly in major statements of the communitarian agenda such as the 'Responsive Communitarian Platform' (see Etzioni 1994: 251–67). Communitarian ideas have certainly helped shape the Third Way. They influenced the early rhetoric and policy themes of the Clinton Democrats and, in turn, New Labour. The language of balancing rights and responsibilities is already evident, for example, in the 1994 report of the Commission on Social Justice. It is important, however, to appreciate the basic amorphousness of 'communitarianism'. The core ideas of responsibility and virtue (not to mention community) can be unpacked in many different ways, depending on one's background political philosophy. One can readily imagine conservative communitarianisms, civic republican communitarianisms, and liberal communitarianisms, and Etzioni has edited volumes in which these distinct, potentially conflicting perspectives all find a voice (see Etzioni 1995, 1998). Similarly, it can be argued that there is a communitarianism already existing within the social democratic tradition, a point I shall now try to explain.

In Britain, ideas of social citizenship or of 'social rights' emerged in tandem with efforts to articulate theories of social justice. A particularly influential theory in this respect is the functionalist theory of social justice (see White 1999 and, for a particularly acute analysis, Jackson 2003). Finding maturity in the work of more radical 'New Liberals' such as John Hobson and Leonard Hobhouse (Hobson 1996; Hobhouse 1912, 1994), this theory explicitly informs the work of R. H. Tawney and Harold Laski (especially Tawney 1948, 1964), and key elements of the theory are still discernible in Tony Crosland's *The Future of Socialism* (1956). At the base of the theory are two ideas:

1. *Fair pay for productive function.* Every person performing a valuable productive function should receive, as of right, 'such remuneration as serves to stimulate and maintain its effective performance', that is, at least sufficient to cover basic needs.
2. *Fair opportunity for productive function.* Everyone 'capable of performing some useful social function . . . should have the opportunity of doing so . . .' (Hobhouse 1994: 100).

Implicit in these two ideas is a conception of social rights: a right to a decent minimum social wage and, relatedly, to the productive opportunity needed to earn such a wage. Left to itself, a free-market capitalist economy will not respect these rights. Concerted state action and expenditure will be needed to secure them:

It is for the State to take care that the economic conditions are such that the normal man [sic] who is not defective in mind or body can by useful labour feed, house, and clothe himself and his family. The 'right to work' and the 'right to a living wage'. . . . are integral conditions of a good social order. (Hobhouse 1994: 76)

Note that Hobhouse does not say here that the state should simply *give* people food, housing, and clothing, regardless of their work effort. To do this would disconnect income from productive effort, which is contrary to the fundamental functionalist premise of, as Hobhouse puts it, equating 'social service and reward' (Hobhouse 1994: 100). Rather, the state should ensure that people have *reasonable access to* a civilized standard of living, that is, that they can achieve this standard of living given a willingness to make a reasonable productive effort. It is this reasonable access to a decent social wage that people have a right to. (It is perhaps worth noting here how the Edwardian Labour Party repeatedly proposed a Right to Work Bill that would guarantee relief work for the unemployed rather than provide welfare as an alternative to work; see Freeden 1978: 212–15.) Now, there is no violation of this right if the state conditions the receipt of certain basic goods on willingness to make a reasonable productive effort. Hobhouse points clearly in this direction:

... given the opportunity of adequately remunerated work, a man has the power to earn his living. It his right and his duty to make the best use of this opportunity, and if he fails he may fairly be treated as a pauper ... (Hobhouse 1994: 79)

The implication of this should be clear. Here we have a conception of social rights, grounded in a theory of social justice that is indisputably central to the mainstream social democratic tradition in Britain, which is perfectly compatible with welfare contractualism. As I have explained elsewhere, there is no basis in Marshall's text for ascribing to him a view of social rights that differs fundamentally from the functionalist view described here (White 2000: 511–12; see also Powell 2002).[6] Thus, the claim that the Third Way breaks with the social democratic tradition because of its welfare contractualism per se does not stand up. Proponents of the Third Way might, indeed, turn the tables on the critics and argue that, by endorsing contractualism, the Third Way is returning to a long-standing social democratic conception of welfare and citizenship that was unfortunately eclipsed by the rise of the quasi-Titmuss paradigm in the 1960s and 1970s. In connection with this, it is interesting to note how Blair does appeal back to social democratic thinkers of the pre-war era—Hobhouse, Hobson, Tawney, G. D. H. Cole—in trying to support his claim that 'Duty is a Labour Value' (see Blair 1996: 4–21, 236–42).

When one takes a closer look at the social democratic functionalists, however, the attempt by Third Way proponents to appropriate them seems

[6] The idea that contractualism and social democracy are incompatible also seems odd when one looks at the issue in a broader comparative perspective. The active labour market policy of Swedish social democracy, for example, has always embodied strong contractualist assumptions, reflecting a philosophy of welfare and citizenship similar to that of the British functionalists (Tilton 1990). Commentators on the British case often argue that policies such as the New Deal reflect the influence of welfare-to-work ideas from the USA (King and Wickham-Jones 1999). But while there is doubtless some truth in this, Scandinavian practice also seems to have been influential (Annesley and Gamble 2003).

very problematic. First, when the functionalists criticized people for living off society without working, their target was not primarily people on welfare but people living off various kinds of 'functionless property', forms of private property that entitle their owners to income flows not matched by any personal productive service. Targets for criticism included landlords enjoying urban ground rents inflated by the industry of others, and those living off inherited wealth (see Hobhouse 1994: 90–6; Tawney 1948: ch. 5). The functionalists proposed a range of fiscal measures to eliminate this kind of private property, and were very critical of those who complained about the supposedly idle poor while ignoring the scandal, as they saw it, of the idle rich. Hobhouse writes:

The moralist is . . . concerned lest we should insist too much on rights and too little on duties . . . The only doubt is whether the stern disciplinarians . . . fully realize the revolutionary nature of their doctrine. If a system is wrong which maintains an idle man in bare necessaries, a system is much more wrong which maintains an idle man in great superfluity, and any system which allows the inheritance of wealth on the great scale is open to criticism on this score . . . (Hobhouse 1912: 16–17)

Second, while the functionalists were concerned foremost with ensuring that all workers received at least a decent minimum social wage, they were also concerned with the degree of inequality in reward above the minimum. The basic formula they employed was that inequality in reward between skilled and unskilled workers is permissible if it promotes the common good: 'Inequality in circumstance is reasonable, in so far as it is the necessary condition of securing the services which the community requires . . .' (Tawney 1964: 112). Depending on how one construes 'common good', this view is strikingly close to the Rawlsian view that inequalities are justifiable only if they work to the benefit of all, skilled and unskilled alike (see Jackson 2003: 99–104). Of course, on the face of it, the Rawlsian view has the implication that, if skilled workers are very selfish, policy-makers may have to permit very large special incentive payments to such workers or see a sharp drop in production from which everyone will suffer. This has lead some egalitarians to argue that attention must be given not only to the formal rules within which economic cooperation takes place but to the ethos that governs how people work within these rules (see Cohen 2000). Interestingly, the social democratic functionalists shared this concern, calling for the gradual cultivation of a more community-minded, public-spirited work ethic. Hobhouse again:

There are in truth other motives to action than those of direct and proportionate pecuniary reward. There is the hope of advancement, of social esteem, there is the pure love of work, and the desire to serve society . . . [Such motives] are indeed diminished by a social system which makes material success the main object of respect, and tends to regard devotion to the public service as either humbug or simplicity. But they can never be extinct, and we have but to curtail the field of the other impulses which compete with them in human nature, and they will of themselves expand to all their original vigour. (Hobhouse 1912: 116)

These aspects of social democratic functionalism are basically absent from the Third Way. While there are occasional references to inheritance tax in Third Way literature (for example, Mandelson and Liddle 1996: 128), and occasional screeds directed at 'fat cat' corporate executives (see Giddens 2002: 41), the Third Way simply does not interrogate the morality of property incomes in the systematic way that the functionalists did. It takes the essential legitimacy of these incomes as a given. And, as we saw in the previous section, the emphasis in Third Way thinking is with making sure that nobody falls below a minimally decent standard of living and labour-market opportunity. There is not much concern about inequality above the minimum, and certainly no notion that we might try to promote a communitarian service ethic in society so as to help compress earnings inequality: Third Way 'communitarianism' does not go so far.

4. Conclusion

To conclude, how does the Third Way stand in relation to the social democratic tradition? Many critics tend too readily to assimilate social democracy with what Deacon calls the quasi-Titmuss paradigm. They neglect the current within social democratic thought that draws on the functionalist theory of social justice, and this leads them to overstate how innovative the Third Way is in its acceptance of welfare contractualism. Relatedly, their neglect of the functionalist tradition means that they fail to see the contestability of the notions of 'social rights' and 'social citizenship' that they appeal to in their normative criticism of Third Way contractualism. We have seen, in our discussion of the functionalists, that it is perfectly intelligible to speak of contractualist social rights. Merely appealing to the bare notions of 'social rights' and 'citizenship' in criticism of contractualism will not do, for the content we give to these terms depends on what one takes to be the correct theory of social justice.

Defenders of the Third Way are aware of their affinities with the social democratic functionalists. They are happy to appeal back to their language of duty and responsibility. Nevertheless, the critics have a point when they claim that the Third Way is not egalitarian. The Third Way is not egalitarian if by 'egalitarian' one is referring to something like the supermeritocratic position defended by Rawls. Nor is it full-bloodedly meritocratic, in either the weak or the strong sense distinguished above. Its philosophy is better described as 'sufficientarian': what matters is that everyone have a decent level of lifetime labour-market opportunity and, relatedly, access to a decent standard of living. This, and the fact that the Third Way contains no systematic moral evaluation of property incomes, marks an important difference with the social democratic functionalists. They too were suffi-cientarians for the short run; but they embedded their short-term reform agenda in an account of the deeper, longer-term goals of social democracy that was more ambitiously egalitarian. For the Third Way, by contrast, constraining capitalism to deliver a decent minimum of opportunity and living standards *is* the long-term vision.

Of course, it could be that, in present economic and electoral circumstances, the Third Way represents pretty much the upper limit of what can be done as an alternative to neo-liberalism. I am not sure that this is so, but I do not have the expertise to say that it is not. Even if this were true, however, we should not fall into the trap of thinking that, if the Third Way *is* the upper limit of what can feasibly be done, it therefore makes for a just society (Cohen 1995). We should keep firmly in mind the distinction between the questions 'What is to be done?' and 'What is just?' If there is an indisputable fault in Third Way thinking and rhetoric, typified in the writings of Blair and Giddens, it lies in a tendency to lose sight of the difference between these questions. By doing this, Third Way proponents arguably seek to effect too deep a reconciliation of social democrats to perceived economic and electoral constraints; they seek not merely a realism or pragmatism about the pursuit of egalitarian ambition but an unwarranted repudiation of egalitarianism as an ambition.

References

Ackerman, B. and Alstott, A. (1999). *The Stakeholder Society*. New Haven, CT: Yale University Press.

Anderson, E. (1999). 'What is the Point of Equality?', *Ethics*, 109: 287–337.

Annesley, C. and Gamble, A. (2003). 'Economic and Welfare Policy', in S. Ludlam and M. Smith (eds.), *Governing as New Labour: Policy and Politics under Blair*. Basingstoke: Palgrave.

Blair, T. (1996). *New Britain: My Vision for a Young Country*. London: Fourth Estate.

—— (1998). *The Third Way: New Politics for the New Century*. London: Fabian Society.

Bouvet, L. and Michel, F. (2001). 'Pluralism and the Future of the French Left', in S. White (ed.), *New Labour: The Progressive Future?* Basingstoke: Palgrave.

Brown, G. (1995). *Fair is Efficient*. London: Fabian Society.

—— (1999). 'Equality—Then and Now', in Dick Leonard (ed.), *Crosland and New Labour*. Basingstoke: Macmillan.

Brown, M., Conaty, P., and Mayo, E. (2003). *Life Saving: Community Development Credit Unions*. London: New Economics Foundation.

Clift, B. (2003). 'New Labour's Second Term and European Social Democracy', in S. Ludlam and M. Smith (eds.), *Governing as New Labour: Policy and Politics under Blair*. Basingstoke: Palgrave.

Cohen, G. (1995). 'The future of a disillusion', in G. Cohen, *Self-Ownership, Freedom and Equality*. Cambridge: Cambridge University Press.

—— (2000). *If You're an Egalitarian, How Come You're So Rich?* Cambridge, MA: Harvard University Press.

Commission on Social Justice (1992). *The Justice Gap*. London: Institute for Public Policy Research.

—— (1994). *Social Justice: Strategies for National Renewal*. London: Vintage.

Crosland, A. (1956). *The Future of Socialism*. London: Jonathan Cape.

Davies, G. (1996). *From Opportunity to Entitlement: The Transformation and Decline of Great Society Liberalism*. Lawrence: University of Kansas Press.

Deacon, A. (2002). *Perspectives on Welfare*. Buckingham: Open University Press.

—— and Mann, K. (1999). 'Agency, Modernity and Social Policy', *Journal of Social Policy*, 28: 413–35.

Durkheim, É. (1992). *Lectures on Professional Ethics and Civic Morals*. London: Routledge.

Dworkin, R. (1985). 'Why Liberals Should Care about Equality', in R. Dworkin, *A Matter of Principle*. Oxford: Oxford University Press.

—— (2000). *Sovereign Virtue: The Theory and Practice of Equality*. Cambridge, MA: Harvard University Press.

Etzioni, A. (1992). *The Spirit of Community: The Reinvention of American Society*. New York: Touchstone.

—— (ed.) (1995). *New Communitarian Thinking: Persons, Virtues, Institutions, and Communities*. Charlottesville: University of Virginia Press.

—— (1996). *The New Golden Rule: Community and Morality in a Democratic Society*. New York: Basic Books.

—— (ed.) (1998). *The Essential Communitarian Reader*. Lanham, MD: Rowman and Littlefield.

Freeden, M. (1978). *The New Liberalism: An Ideology of Social Reform*. Oxford: Oxford University Press.

—— (1999). 'The Ideology of New Labour', *Political Quarterly*, 69: 42–51.

Gamble, A. (2003). *Between Europe and America: The Future of British Politics*. Basingstoke: Palgrave.

Giddens, A. (1998). *The Third Way: The Renewal of Social Democracy*. Cambridge: Polity.

—— (2000). *The Third Way and its Critics*. Cambridge: Polity.

—— (2002). *Where Now for New Labour?* Cambridge: Polity/Fabian Society/Policy Network.

Greenberg, S. (1995). *Middle Class Dreams: The Politics and Power of the New American Majority*. New York: Random House.

HM Treasury (2001). *Saving and Assets for All*. London: HMSO.
—— (2003). *Budget 2003*. London: TSO.
Hobhouse, L. (1912). *The Labour Movement* (3rd edn.). New York: Macmillan.
—— (1993 [1911]). *Liberalism*, in J. Meadowcroft (ed.), *Liberalism and Other Writings*. Cambridge: Cambridge University Press.
Hobson, J. (1996 [1902]). *The Social Problem*. Bristol: Thoemmes Press.
Jackson, B. (2003). 'Equality of Nothing? Social Justice on the British Left, c.1911–31', *Journal of Political Ideologies*, 8: 83–110.
Kelly, G. and Lissauer, R. (2000). *Ownership for All*. London: Institute for Public Policy Research.
King, D. (1999). *In the Name of Liberalism: Illiberal Social Policy in Britain and the United States*. Oxford: Oxford University Press.
—— and Wickham-Jones, Mark (1999). 'From Clinton to Blair: The Democratic (Party) Origins of Welfare to Work', *Political Quarterly*, 70: 62–74.
Klein, J. (2002). *The Natural: The Misunderstood Presidency of Bill Clinton*. London: Hodder and Stoughton.
Laski, H. (1925). *The Grammar of Politics*. London: Allen and Unwin.
Lea, R. and Mayo, E. (2003). *The Mutual Health Service: How to Decentralise the NHS*. London: Institute of Directors and New Economics Foundation.
Lukes, S. (2003). 'The Last Word on the Third Way', in S. Lukes, *Liberals and Cannibals*. London: Verso.
Mandelson, P. and Liddle, R. (1996). *The Blair Revolution: Can New Labour Deliver?* London: Faber and Faber.
Marshall, T. (1950). 'Citizenship and Social Class', in T. Marshall, *Citizenship and Social Class*. Cambridge: Cambridge University Press.
Marx, K. (1976 [1875]). *Critique of the Gotha Programme*. Peking: Foreign Languages Press.
Mead, L. (1986). *Beyond Entitlement: the Social Obligations of Citizenship*. New York: Free Press.
—— (1992). *The New Politics of Poverty: The Nonworking Poor in America*. New York: Basic Books.
Miller, D. (2000). *Principles of Social Justice*. Cambridge, MA: Harvard University Press.
Nagel, T. (1991). *Equality and Partiality*. Oxford: Oxford University Press.
New Economics Foundation (2001). *Time Banks: A Radical Manifesto for the UK*. London: New Economics Foundation.
Nissan, D. and Le Grand, J. (2000). *A Capital Start: Start-up Grants for Young People*. London: Fabian Society.
Piachaud, D. (1993). *What's Wrong with Fabianism?* London: Fabian Society.
Policy Network (2003). *Progressive Politics* 2 (1). London: Policy Network.
Powell, M. (2002). 'The Hidden History of Social Citizenship', *Citizenship Studies*, 6/3: 229–44.
Rawls, J. (1999). *A Theory of Justice* (rev. edn.). Cambridge, MA: Harvard University Press.
—— (2001). *Justice as Fairness: A Restatement*. Cambridge, MA: Harvard University Press.

Rosanvallon, P. (2000). *The New Social Question*. Princeton, NJ: Princeton University Press.

Tawney, R. (1948 [1920]). *The Acquisitive Society*. New York: Harcourt Brace Jovanovich.

—— (1964 [1931]). *Equality*. London: Allen and Unwin.

Tilton, T. (1990). *The Political Theory of Swedish Social Democracy*. Oxford: Oxford University Press.

Welshman, J. (2004). 'The Unknown Titmuss', *Journal of Social Policy*, 33: 225–47.

White, S. (1999). ' "Rights and Responsibilities": A Social Democratic Perspective', in A. Gamble and T. Wright (eds.), *The New Social Democracy*. Oxford: Blackwell.

—— (2000). 'Social Rights and the Social Contract: Political Theory and the New Welfare Politics', *British Journal of Political Science*, 30: 507–32.

—— (2001). 'The Ambiguities of the Third Way', in S. White (ed.), *New Labour: The Progressive Future?* Basingstoke: Palgrave.

—— (2003). *The Civic Minimum: On the Rights and Obligations of Economic Citizenship*. Oxford: Oxford University Press.

Young, M. (1958). *The Rise of the Meritocracy*. London: Thames and Hudson.

3

One Third Way or Several?

GIULIANO BONOLI AND MARTIN POWELL

Although use of the term 'Third Way' has declined in the UK, it still figures among other terms such as 'new social democracy' and 'progressive governance' in international debate (Cuperus, Duffek, and Kandel 2001; Etzioni 2000; *Journal of Policy History* 2003; Hale et al. 2004; Schmidtke 2002; *Social Policy and Society* 2002). New Labour and the Third Way are also often used as reference points or templates to examine the position of governments and policies on an Old Left–Third Way–New Right spectrum. Indeed, some British commentators have seen recent electoral defeats for social democrats in Europe in terms of failure to keep sufficiently to the Third Way path (Giddens 2002*b*; Mandelson 2003; Wintour 2003). One of the problems in the Third Way debate concerns different interpretations of the empirical evidence: for example, to what extent Jospin's privatization programme may be viewed as Old Left, New Right, or *'la gauche plurielle'* (cf. for example Bell 2003; Bergounioux 2001; Bouvet and Michel 2001; Clift 2003; Marian 2002; Sferza 2001).

However, our concern in this chapter focuses on the more fundamental problem that relates to the vague definition of the Third Way. As C. Pierson (2001: 130) puts it, it has been hotly contested but consistently underspecified. Similarly, Clift (2001*a*: 72) writes that the Third Way needs more rigorous definition before firm conclusions can be drawn about its compatibility with contemporary European social democracy. Two opposing routes appear to lead nowhere. At one extreme, it is possible to take a self-definition or nominalist route. On this line, very few countries proclaim themselves to be Third Way and, even in the best exemplar, Britain, the currency seems at the time of writing to be devalued. At the other extreme, it is possible to take a definition imposed by a third party. Taking this approach, writers such as Blair (1998) and Giddens (1998, 2001, 2002*a*) claim that many countries *are* Third Way, irrespective of the views of those countries. For example, Giddens (2001: 1–2) writes that the changes made by Left parties in Scandinavia, Holland, France, or Italy since the late 1980s are as much part of Third Way politics as those developed in

Anglo-Saxon countries. However, C. Pierson (2001: 19) points out that, for 'old' social democracy, at times social democratic strategies were pursued by governments that would never call themselves social democratic, and social democratic governments pursued non-social democratic programmes.

Although volumes have been written, there is still little agreement on a relatively consensual definition of the Third Way and whether there is *one* Third Way or different or multiple Third *Ways*. In the words of Przeworski (2001), how many ways can be third? At the risk of some oversimplification, conclusions vary from convergence towards one model (Thomson 2000; Giddens 2001), a Third Way with some variants (Green-Pedersen, van Kersbergen, and Hemerijck 2001), or different Third Ways (Gamble and Wright 1999; Clift 2000*a*; Merkel 2001; Driver and Martell 2002*a*, *b*; Cuperus, Duffek, and Kandel 2001). However, the evidence for these claims is not fully clear. This chapter aims to move this debate forward by examining recent social democratic party discourse and social policies in Europe. It begins by examining some basic concepts of the Third Way, and then discusses a method of analysing its main themes based on a 'policy process' model of discourse, values, policy goals, and mechanisms (Bonoli and Powell 2002, 2003; Powell and Barrientos 2004) to examine recent social policy developments in European social democratic party policies.

1. Conceptualizing the Third Way

The most obvious strategy to define a Third Way is to differentiate it from the First and Second Ways. The simplest method is to place a Third Way on a linear scale between the First and Second Ways. For example, if the Old Left favoured high 'tax and spend' and the New Right favoured low tax and spend, a Third Way might aim for a pragmatic medium level of tax and spend. However, some commentators have moved beyond a one-dimensional linear scale to suggest two intersecting dimensions, giving four quadrants. For example, White (1998; see also Chapter 2) sets out two main axes. The first opposes egalitarians to meritocrats, while the second opposes liberals and communitarians. New Labour is placed in the bottom left 'meritocratic communitarian' quadrant. However, this approach is not exhaustive as it is possible to consider other two-dimensional categorizations, and possible to imagine (if difficult to depict on paper) N-dimensional categorizations.

The Third Way is defined as being beyond (rather than between) the Old Left and the New Right (see Driver and Martell 2002*a*, *b*).

Giddens (1998: 44) claims that the shift from 'emancipatory politics' to 'life politics' cannot be captured by the traditional Left/Right divide. Similarly, Blair (1998: 1) argues that the Third Way is not an attempt to split the difference between Right and Left to form a 'middle way' or compromise, but aims to offer a novel synthesis between liberal and socialist thinking. In other words, the Third Way is a new politics that transcends the old categories, making them redundant. This is a bold claim, and much of it rests on the aim of reconciling themes that in the past have been wrongly regarded as antagonistic, such as social justice *and* economic efficiency or rights *and* responsibilities (Blair 1998; Fairclough 2000; see below). Driver and Martell (2002*a*, 2002*b*; cf. Leadbetter 1999) consider that the Third Way involves a combination rather than the more radical definition of a transcendence of these traditional foes. They claim that the novelty of the Third Way lies in a new mix of values and approaches.

The second problem concerns the 'dependent variable' of the Third Way. A number of commentators have suggested broad characteristics or themes of the Third Way or new social democracy (see Powell and Barrientos 2004 for a summary). Although the key source is often given as Giddens (1998), many elements of the Third Way were earlier flagged up in the report of the British Commission on Social Justice (CSJ 1994). It rejected the approaches to social and economic policy of the 'Levellers'—the Old Left—and the 'Deregulators'—the New Right—and advocated the 'middle way' of 'Investor's Britain'. This approach features much of the discourse which was to become central to New Labour: economic efficiency and social justice are different sides of the same coin; redistributing opportunities rather than just redistributing income; transforming the welfare state from a safety net in times of trouble to a springboard for economic opportunity; welfare should offer a hand-up not a handout; an active, preventive welfare state; a fair wage for paid work is the most secure and sustainable way out of poverty; and the balancing of rights and responsibilities. Giddens (1998: 70) suggests a 'third way programme' including the new democratic state; active civil society; the democratic family; the new mixed economy; equality as inclusion; positive welfare; and the social investment state. White's (1998) themes include the state as guarantor, not necessarily provider; receptivity to forms of mutualism; new thinking about public finance, including increased use of environmental taxes, hypothecation at the margin, new consultative procedures on tax and community fund; and asset-based egalitarianism. Vandenbroucke (1998) offers what Cuperus and Kandel (1998: 25) term 'the nine commandments of a post-pessimistic social democracy'. These are full employment for men and women; attention to new risks for the welfare state; an 'intelligent' welfare state; a revalorization of active labour market policies;

subsidizing low-skilled labour as a new redistribution target; preventing poverty traps; developing a competitive private service sector; finding non-dogmatic approaches to a fair distribution of burdens and benefits; and maintaining discipline with regard to growth of average wage levels. Blair and Schröder (1999) suggest a 'new programme for changed realities' that includes a new supply-side agenda for the Left; a robust and competitive market framework; a tax policy to promote sustainable growth; adaptability and flexibility; an active government that invests in human and social capital; and sound public finance. Ferrera, Hemerijck, and Rhodes (2001) list 'elements of an optimal policy mix' that consist of a robust macroeconomic strategy; wage moderation; employer-friendly and efficient tax and social policy; labour market flexibility and flexicurity; investment in education, training, and mobility; and new forms of fighting poverty and social exclusion. Thomson (2000: 159) contrasts six 'aims' of classic and new social democracy. However, these aims are not policy goals in our terms (see below), and are best considered as broad themes: fairness; individual rights; 'aid the market'; individual initiative to achieve enhancement; the state as enabler; and community. Finally, Bresser-Pereira (2001: 368) distinguishes the New Left from the Old Left and the New Right from the perspective of developing countries or 'the view from the south'. These characteristics are: party control by the new middle class; a complementary role for the state; managerial state reform; basic social services executed by public non-state organizations; financing of basic social services by the state; state-assured basic state security; neo-Keynesian macroeconomic policy; and globalization seen as a challenge.

However, these 'sound-bite' themes lack specificity, making it difficult to differentiate the Third Way from First and Second Ways. Concepts such as Giddens's 'social investment state' and 'positive welfare' tend to be broad and vague. If these mean investment in human capital, and supply-side employment policy, then it could be argued that this was a staple feature of the First Way of Swedish social democracy. Similarly, 'conditionality' is often said to be a feature of the Third Way, but it is also a feature of the Second Way of neo-liberalism. Moreover, it is unlikely that totally unconditional or fully decommodified welfare has ever existed in any time or place (see C. Pierson 2001; Kleinman 2002). There are many different variants of 'workfare' and 'active labour market policy', with different balances of 'carrots and sticks' ranging from the Rehn–Meidner model of Swedish social democracy to 'starving the poor back to work' in the English New Poor Law of 1834.

Moreover, these themes conflate different dimensions such as aims and mechanisms. For example, Marquand answers the question of whether New Labour are social democrats with 'Yes, if you read their lips. No, if you watch their hands' (in Giddens 2002*a*: 18). Cuperus, Duffek, and Kandel (2001: 245) suggest that that Third Way discourse consists of three levels or layers of analysis: a political-theoretical level; a programme-orientated level, the level of political projects; and the level of practical policy-making. We argue that it is necessary to separate the themes suggested above with reference to a loose 'policy process' model of discourse, values, policy goals mechanisms, and outcomes (Bonoli and Powell 2002, 2003; Powell and Barrientos 2004). As a heuristic device, this assumes a 'rational' policy-making process with different stages. The important point is that the policy process should be coherent. For example, an equality discourse should be matched by equality as a value, policy goals that are based on equality, mechanisms to achieve this, with a successful policy showing greater equality. In this account, we do not consider outcomes. For a successful policy, outcomes will match goals. Our concern here is not with policy success, and in many cases it is too early to evaluate policy success (but see Powell 2002). We also examine goals and mechanisms together. While the Third Way claims to separate means and ends (see Powell 1999), in practice this has not been clear. While this classification is far from watertight, it is conceptually useful. First, it is important to compare like with like. For example, a similar discourse can mean very different things (see Fairclough 2000). For example, Blair, Schröder, and Jospin all 'support a market economy, but reject a market society' and all endorse 'the active state'. However, evidence suggests all place very different interpretations on this. Second, it allows the degree of 'fit' or 'flow' between the dimensions to be examined. For example, are policy mechanisms congruent with discourse? Are there gaps between 'rhetoric' and 'reality' (Fairclough 2000; Clift 2001*a*). It is important not to compare, say, Blair's policy with Jospin's rhetoric .

2. Third Ways in Europe

This section examines recent social policies of social democratic parties in Europe. The analysis focuses on both discourse and actual policy decisions. Within the category of discourse, we further distinguish between rhetoric and values. Rhetoric refers to the words that are used in a given policy discourse, whereas values are the normative perceptions to which discourse makes reference. Within the category of policy, we focus on both the goals and the instruments that are adopted. Overall, the objective of our analysis is to uncover patterns of similarity or difference in social policy-making across social democratic Europe.

Rhetoric

In recent years, several commentators have put much emphasis on the role of discourse and rhetoric in policy-making. The labels and words that are used to designate political projects and policy goals can matter because they carry meanings that clearly go beyond their simple denotative value (Cox 2001; Hering 2003; Schmidt 2000, 2001).

At root, the Third Way claims to be new and distinct from both traditional social democracy and neo-liberalism. According to Fairclough (2000), the Third Way is a _rhetoric of reconciliation_ built out of elements from other political discourses of the Left and of the Right, such as 'economic dynamism as well as social justice' and 'enterprise as well as fairness'. They are not deemed antagonistic: while neo-liberals pursue the former and traditional social democrats the latter, the Third Way pursues both. The more radical claim is of 'going beyond' or transcending such contrary themes. It follows that it is important not just to identify the keywords of the Third Way, such as 'new', 'tough', 'deal', 'reform', and 'partnership', but also their relationship with the rest of the discourse. The discourse contains a mix of 'Old Left' words such as 'equality' linked with (_and_) New Right words such as 'efficiency', and words that attempt to stamp a Third Way identity such as 'partnership' or 'contract'.

The diffusion of this sort of Third Way rhetoric in Europe has not been totally unproblematic. This is understandable. First, in many European countries the label 'Third Way' is often associated with Britain, (post-) Thatcherism, and neo-liberalism. It is thus regarded as inappropriate terrain for the Left, however modern it aspires to be. Second, to openly adopt the Third Way label may be perceived as some form of acknowledgement of a leadership role for the UK and the British Labour Party in the international social democratic movement. This can make social democrats, proud of their own achievements in their respective countries, feel uneasy. It seems reasonable, then, not to expect European social democratic parties to rush into explicitly adopting the Third Way label.

In addition, the rhetoric of reconciliation that has so much characterized the politics of the British Third Way is to a large extent a by-product of Britain's electoral system and recent history. Governments in office can rule with few checks and balances, unlike many continental systems (Bonoli and Powell 2002: 63–4). The legacy of the Thatcher Conservative government left ample room in the centre that fits well with the rhetoric of reconciliation. Obviously, this kind of discourse cannot be presented as an innovative approach to social and economic policy in countries like Germany, the Netherlands, or Italy, which for most of the post-war years were ruled by centrist coalition governments and have practised this kind of mixed and balanced approach to policy on a daily basis.

The discourse developed by the British authors and politicians seems, understandably, to be tailor-made for that country, and it should not come as a surprise that it has made relatively few inroads in continental Europe and Scandinavia. As a matter of fact, explicit attempts to adopt the Third Way label or to identify with the political movement it represents are rare. Beside the British Labour Party, few other social democratic parties have openly embraced the Third Way label. The German SPD, with the publication of the Blair–Schröder paper in 1999, has taken some steps in that direction.[1] However, the reactions in Germany to the paper were so negative that they have discouraged the party leader from insisting in stressing its intellectual affinity with the Third Way. The Italian DS (reformed communists) under the leadership of the then Prime Minister Massimo D'Alema looked to align governments closely to the Third Way as a force of modernization that would constitute the centre point of a new Left. The Italian Left in government has embarked on the 'Third Way', at times making clear reference to the term and to other European experiences (Della Salla 2001: 124–8), including hosting a meeting in Florence in 1999. But this did not pay off, as D'Alema was forced to resign after a poor performance in regional elections (Della Salla 2001).

It is intriguing that one of very few governments that makes open reference to the Third Way movement is the Belgian purple coalition government, led not by a Social Democrat but by a Liberal, Guy Verhofstadt (Hoop 2003). Similarly, in Germany, the Blair–Schröder paper was greeted with much more approval by the liberal FDP than by any other political party, including of course Schröder's own SPD (FDP 1999). The Third Way label does not seem to attract the interest of social democrats as much as it does of liberals. This fits with the claims of White (1998) and Driver and Martell (2002*a*, *b*) that the Third Way is not *necessarily* a centre-left project (but see Giddens 1998, 2001, 2002*a*).

Other social democratic parties have tended to avoid both the Third Way label and the rhetoric of reconciliation. Most European social democrats are reluctant to openly declare themselves part of the Third Way political project (Bonoli and Powell 2003). Parties like the Dutch PvdA or the Portuguese PS, in spite of being clearly at the forefront of the process of social democratic renewal in Europe, carefully avoid any hint of association with the Third Way movement. The Swedish SAP has supported many key Third Way policies for several years (active labour market policies,

---

[1] It should also be noted that the choice to render Third Way as *Neue Mitte* (new centre) rather than its literal translation *Dritter Weg* suggests that the novelty in the German context does not consist so much in having found a middle way between extremes but in having developed a modern approach to centrist politics which is presented in contrast to the old centre dominated by the Christian Democrats.

gender equality, and so on) but to describe itself as a Third Way party would mean failing to acknowledge the contribution that the party has made to develop such policy ideas in the first place (Svensson 2001: 221). Cuperus, Duffek, and Kandel (2001: 243) write that some countries appear to have developed 'Third Wayish' strategies before the term was coined. Spain, Sweden, and the Netherlands may all rightfully claim to be 'Third Way *avant la lettre*'. Indeed, a quantitative content analysis of election manifestos (Volkens 2003) suggests that social democrats all over Europe entered the Third Way as early as the 1950s. Finally, the French Socialist leader Lionel Jospin has probably been the most vociferous critic of the Third Way, taking position against it publicly on several occasions (Bell 2003; Bergounioux 2001; Clift 2003; Marian 2002).

Values

The values of the Third Way remain problematic. This is mainly for two reasons. First, adequate understanding of values requires more than one-word treatments. Terms such as 'equality' are essentially contestable concepts, meaning different things to different people. More specificity is needed to explain more precise meanings. For example, neo-liberals emphasize some dimensions such as equality before the law and basic equality of opportunity, while old social democrats stressed dimensions such as equality of outcome, and new social democrats tend to emphasize equality of worth and 'real' equality of opportunity. It follows that values must be more clearly defined and linked with goals (see below).

   Second, and linked, it is not clear whether the Third Way is concerned with 'old' values, new or redefined meanings of old values, or new values (cf. Driver and Martell 2002*a*, *b*). The best-known accounts argue the first position. Blair (1998, 2001) and Blair and Schröder (1999) claim that the Third Way is concerned with linking traditional values with modern means. According to Blair (1998), these traditional values are equal worth, opportunity for all, responsibility, and community. Blair and Schröder (1999) write that fairness and social justice, liberty and equality of opportunity, solidarity, and responsibility to others are timeless values. Social democracy will never sacrifice them. Other commentators have suggested a range of values including opportunity, responsibility, and community. As Driver and Martell (2000: 151) sum up, there is broad agreement over Third Way values, but problems emerge over their interpretation and the extent to which they define a centre-left political project. However, critics point out that terms such as equality are redefined. For example, the old concern with equality of outcome is reinterpreted as a meritocratic equality of opportunity. Moreover, a few 'new' values appear to have been smuggled in. Positive mentions of values such as entrepreneurship (for example, Blair 1998; Blair and Schröder 1999) were rarely part of the repertoire of traditional social democracy.

In the 1990s, key Third Way values featured prominently in social democrats' election manifestos throughout the continent, but especially in Spain, the Netherlands, Germany, Belgium, and Portugal. According to Volkens's content analyses of party manifestos, social democratic parties in all the above countries score even higher than the British Labour Party in the extent to which they conform to Third Way values (Volkens 2003).

These findings have been confirmed by qualitative analysis of national political debates. In the Netherlands, even though there is no explicit mention of the Third Way as a guiding principle of policy, the government discourse is characterized by a strong emphasis on work for all and the idea that the policies they put forward go beyond traditional cleavages between labour and capital (Braun and Girod 2003; Hoop 2003). In Germany, the Schröder government had trouble developing a coherent discourse. Initially, internal divisions, most notably between Schröder himself and Oscar Lafontaine, prevented the government from speaking with one voice. Lafontaine's resignation in early 1999 was followed by a clumsy attempt to introduce the political discourse of the Third Way in the German context. More recently, and in particular after the rather poor showing in the 2002 general election, German Social Democrats seem to have abandoned the ambition of developing grand political ideas and have resorted to a more pragmatic discourse, justifying policy with reference not so much to values and notions of social justice but more to expected benefits in dealing with widely recognized problems (Hering 2003). In Portugal, the Socialists have swapped equality with solidarity and equity as the fundamental goals of the party. Election manifestos in the 1990s put substantial emphasis on employment promotion as an anti-poverty policy and on the acceptance of a role for the private sector in the delivery of public services (Costa-Lobo and Magalhaes 2003).

It is probably in the Nordic countries that traditional social democratic values of equality of outcomes and universality of welfare provision remain most influential. In Sweden, the dominant discourse has focused on how to preserve the Swedish model in an international economic context characterized by tight constraints, but there has not been, on the social democratic side, any deep questioning of the desirability and adequacy of such a model. The Danish Social Democrats have maintained a similar position, but have also incorporated typically liberal values like efficiency in the management of public services and equity in the welfare state (Braun and Girod 2003; Schmidt 2000: 259–67). Finally, the French Socialists have also been very reluctant to adopt Third Way values in their political discourse. In the late 1990s and early 2000s, Lionel Jospin insisted on traditional social democratic themes such as the superior status of politics over markets in democratic societies, and duties of solidarity towards the most disadvantaged in society.

The comparison of rhetoric and values of social democrats across Europe yields striking results. In spite of the deliberate avoidance of third way terminology by many Western European social democratic parties, the reference values that are used to structure political discourse and to 'sell' policies to their respective electorates are surprisingly similar. It appears that rhetoric and values do not necessarily go together.

3. Policy Goals and Mechanisms

Goals or objectives may be seen as a more specific operationalization of values. For example, 'equality' is often referred to as a value but this may result in very different policy objectives, such as equality of inputs or equality of outcomes. Taking a broad perspective on developments in social and economic policy, one can identify three salient objectives in policy-making in social democratic European countries: to expand employment, to contain public expenditure, and to strengthen the social investment component of welfare states. Virtually all left-of-centre governments have in the late 1990s and early 2000s adopted policies that clearly fall under these different themes. Finally, the mechanisms are the actual instruments and their settings that are used to implement a policy (and to achieve a given policy objective). Mechanisms are arguably the most important dimension (cf. Green-Pedersen, van Kersbergen, and Hemerijck 2001). After all, the essential point of the welfare state is to make a difference to the lives of citizens, and it is policies that make a difference 'on the ground'. Although conceptually different things, for ease of presentation objectives and mechanisms are dealt with together in the remainder of this section.

The Expansion of Employment

The maximization of employment is a policy objective that at first sight may resemble the traditional social democratic goal of full employment. In fact the two are very different. Full employment was about guaranteeing a job to anyone who wanted to work. In practice, based on the 'male breadwinner' model, the aim was generally to guarantee a job to all males who wanted to work. This policy had little intentional impact on labour supply, and the matching between supply and demand was to be achieved by adapting the latter to the former through state intervention in employment preservation and creation. On the other hand, employment maximization is, firstly, concerned with increasing in labour supply, to some extent regardless of the personal aspirations of the individuals concerned. Rather, the objective is to construe a set of incentives around non-working males and females (full-time parents, long-term unemployed, moderately disabled people) that are clearly pushing them in the direction of labour market participation. Secondly, employment expansion is also about promoting job creation, but as a result of private sector initiatives and not by direct state intervention using Keynesian demand management.

In practical terms, the expansion of employment relies on a large number of policy instruments. A widely used mechanism has been the tightening of conditions for receiving unemployment benefits. In general, in order to continue receiving a benefit, recipients must demonstrate efforts to obtain work. This may involve participation in labour market programmes, availability to attend a meeting with a case worker to evaluate work prospects, or simply accepting a job offer. Non-compliance may result in sanctions such as benefit suspensions or reductions.

This has been the standard approach in the Nordic countries for several years, even though work requirements are now being enforced more strictly than in the past (Goul-Andersen 2000). Most other countries moved in this direction during the 1990s under social democratic rule. The UK and the Netherlands have developed policies that target non-working people, including older workers, single parents, and disabled people, and encourage them to (re-)enter the labour market, although benefit conditionality is generally not enforced for these social groups. With the exception of the Netherlands and possibly Belgium,[2] continental European countries have been less inclined to introduce employment promotion mechanisms in their unemployment compensation systems. In France, the main income support programme (*Revenu Minimum d'Insertion*, RMI), introduced by the Socialists in 1988, does contain obligations for recipients, but this is seldom interpreted as an obligation to re-enter the labour market. Germany has not seen any significant expansion in work requirements and benefit conditionality over the last few years, but this seems to be to a large extent a result of the institutional structure of the German unemployment compensation system, which includes a strong entitlement-based contributory component and is based on shared responsibilities

---

[2] The Christian-Social governments that ruled Belgium during most of the 1990s did not develop such employment promotion policies to any significant extent (Hemerijck, Unger, and Visser 2000). However, the new Liberal-Social 'purple coalition' government seems considerably more oriented towards an 'activation' approach in policy towards non-working people (Hoop 2003).

between different levels of government (Clasen 2000). Southern European countries have not made significant moves in this direction but they generally lack developed unemployment compensation systems, so that the issue of benefit conditionality is not as pressing as in other parts of Europe.

A second instrument developed to reinforce work incentives has been subsidies for low-wage employment. The Netherlands, Portugal, France, and Belgium have introduced social insurance contribution reductions/ exemptions for low-paid workers. France and the UK have also introduced cash benefits that supplement the wages of low-paid workers. This instrument provides an additional incentive to take up employment for non-working people, but can also be seen as a redistributive social policy measure in so far as it boosts the purchasing power of low-income workers. The British version, the Working Families Tax Credit, was adopted soon after the 1997 general election and was part and parcel of a wider employment promotion policy package that included also a national minimum wage. In France, the *'prime pour l'emploi'* is paid to workers at a variable rate that is highest for a full-time worker at the minimum wage level.

Employment expansion has been pursued also in the field of labour legislation, often through the relaxation of employment protection laws. In the 1990s Italy took some limited steps in this direction by relaxing restrictions on employment agencies and by introducing new types of employment contracts that do not enjoy the full extent of Italian social and employment protection (Ferrera and Gualmini 1999). In the Netherlands, a reduction in employment protection for core full-time workers has been traded with an improvement for marginal temporary employees (Hemerijck, Unger, and Visser 2000). A similar course has been followed by Portugal and Spain. Apparent outliers here are Britain and the Nordic countries. However, in this part of Europe employment protection legislation was never particularly strong. The potential for additional jobs to be created thanks to the relaxation of employment protection rules is as a result rather limited. In Germany, the reform programme known as Agenda 2010 includes a relaxation of protection against dismissal rules and a reduction in benefits for long-term unemployed people (*Süddeutschezeitung* 2003*a*).

Employment expansion seems to be a common trait of social democratic economic policy. The instruments are a mix of negative and positive incentives, or of sticks and carrots: on the one hand, more benefit conditionality for recipients; on the other, wage supplements for those who agree to take up employment in the low-wage sector. In addition, employment expansion takes place also in the field of employment demand by creating an incentive structure for employers that is conducive to employment creation.

Contain Public Spending

A second ubiquitous theme in current social democrats' policy-making is that of containing public spending. Blair and Schröder (1999) argue that current levels of taxation have reached their limits, even though subsequently the Blair government has increased 'taxes' under the guise of National Insurance contributions, while Schröder is planning 18 billion euros of income tax cuts (*Süddeutschezeitung* 2003*b*). Arguably under pressure from international constraints (globalization, European monetary union, EMU, for Eurozone countries), social democratic parties have accepted fiscal discipline as an unavoidable constraint over policy-making (Aust 2003). For example, Della Salla (2001) shows how the Italian Left's conversion to fiscal discipline is inextricably linked with the EMU criteria. Under such circumstances, European social democrats have been left with no option but to adopt public expenditure cuts in some core areas of the welfare state, like pensions, unemployment, or disability insurance. These programmes (especially pensions) are generally the largest items of expenditure in public budgets, and in this respect they constitute an obvious target for cost containment initiatives. At the same time, however, retrenchment in these policy areas is a notoriously politically treacherous exercise (see for example P. Pierson 1994).

Pension reforms have been adopted in a number of countries, generally with the objective of containing the expected increase in public spending on old age pensions. Germany, Italy, and Sweden, under left-of-centre majorities, have adopted similar policy measures in this field. In all three countries, benefit formulas for public pensions have been modified so as to result in lower benefits. Often this has been done in a rather obscure way, and presented as an inevitable development to electorates. Together with these measures, however, all three countries have introduced a second pillar of private pension provision that is supposed to supplement the diminished state pensions. The acceptance of a role for the private sector is certainly something that distinguishes today's social democrats from their predecessors, to whom such a measure would most likely have sounded like anathema. However, it should be noted that the regulatory framework of the new private pensions is particularly stringent (especially in Sweden) and clearly geared towards social objectives, so that, for example, in Germany individuals who are not working because they are performing caring tasks full-time can see their private pensions subsidized by the state (Anderson and Mayer 2003).

Social democratic pension policies reveal an interesting and innovative approach in this area, which combines liberal ideas of public spending containment and preference for the private sector with social democratic goals like equality of access and vertical redistribution. It seems qualitatively different from both the standard liberal approach followed by Thatcher in the 1980s and the traditional social democratic policy of crowding out the market from pension provision (Anderson and Mayer 2003). In countries like the Netherlands or the UK, which had in the past been exceptional in the European context because of their large private pension sectors, left-wing governments took initiatives aimed at improving the 'social performance' of private pensions in terms of universality and benefit adequacy for low-income and atypical workers.

Cuts in public expenditure have tended to fall on income-transfer programmes or 'passive' expenditure, and within these programmes on those that seemed to be abused or those that provided benefits seen as over-generous. This was particularly the case in Italy with early retirement pensions and in the Netherlands with invalidity insurance. If cost containment is being pursued by social democratic governments, it seems not to be guided merely by expenditure considerations but to incorporate social concerns, as testified by the choice of targets for cost containment and by the inclination to regulate private alternatives with the objective of making them more suitable to those whose position in the labour market is weakest. Of course, whether this strategy will be successful in achieving the standard social policy objectives of poverty prevention and universality of coverage remains to be seen.

Strengthen the Social Investment Component of Welfare States

Even though the 1990s are considered to be a decade of 'hard times' for European welfare states, there are some social programmes that prospered in those years. In particular, we have seen the development in several European countries of policies that have a strong social investment dimension. Social investment policies are those that make individuals more successful in the labour market and link with the theme of maximizing employment that was discussed above. Typical social investment polices are training, particularly when related to employment policy, measures that help parents reconcile work and family life, and of course the emphasis that social democrats have been putting on education and health policies. Social investment is tightly related to one of the goals discussed above: employment maximization. The former, however, consists of a modification of the incentive structure faced by non-workers. Social investment, instead, means above all improving human capital. It does impact on employment, but more on quality than on quantity.

The UK is probably the country that has taken the most substantial steps in this direction, in view of the degree of underdevelopment of these policies before the accession to power of New Labour in 1997. Blair's three priorities were 'education, education, education'. It is intended to increase the proportion of the relevant age cohort entering higher education, with special emphasis on increasing the participation of traditionally under-represented groups (see Powell 1999, 2002). A significant effort has been made in active labour market policies that include training, job placements, or socially useful activities. Various 'New Deals' are targeted at different groups of the population, for example those associated with youth and long-term unemployment, single parents, or disabled people. There have been attempts to increase childcare provision. Childcare vouchers have also been made available to low-income parents so that they can more easily participate in the labour market and, finally, a wage supplement for low-paid workers has been introduced in the shape of a tax credit (Millar 2002).

Some of these measures have been adopted in several other countries, generally under social democratic leadership (for example, the Netherlands, Italy, France, Germany). Active labour market policies have been introduced or strengthened throughout the continent, although in some countries the focus on reintegrating the labour market is less strong than in others. For example, the French RMI includes a reinsertion component that is generally interpreted in terms of 'social insertion' rather the (re-)integration of the labour market. As a result, the sorts of measures that are offered to RMI recipients do not necessarily improve opportunities in the labour market. There are, however, other schemes in France that include a more work-oriented dimension.

Policies that aim at reconciling work and family life are also being stepped up in a number of countries. In Germany, new legislation on parental leave and benefits promised in the 1998 election campaign was adopted in 2000 by the Schröder government, with the result of increasing child benefit levels and introducing the right to part-time employment for young parents, though with some exceptions. The Netherlands has also introduced a legal right for parents to request, a part-time job. In Italy, the duration of parental leave has been extended to up to eleven months. But these developments are not found only in countries ruled by social democrats. In Austria, the ÖVP/FPÖ coalition government introduced, in 2001, a childcare voucher for low-income parents, and Spain has also recently improved parental leave coverage (Bertelsmann Foundation 2000, 2001). If the idea of a 'social investment' welfare state originated in social democratic thinking (Giddens 1998), it seems that today social democrats are not the only political force that is pursuing this course of policy.

4. Conclusion: One Third Way with Several Variants

Comparative studies of the Third Way have reached conflicting conclusions on the question of convergence among social democrats across the globe. Cuperus, Duffek, and Kandel (2001) suggest that there is greater similarity among social democratic parties at the level of political principles and political projects than at the level of policy design and policy-making, as concrete solutions differ because they depend on each country's specific employment patterns and welfare state structures. As Fernando Cardoso, the Third Way President of Brazil, put it, the Third Way has shown a convergence of ideas together with a diversity of policies. We agree that, whether termed the 'Third Way', 'new social democracy', or 'progressive governance', there have been changes in the discourse, values, policy goals, and mechanisms of social democratic parties in recent years that go in one similar direction, and that an examination of these different dimensions may tell different stories. However, we tend to take a different view in that we find much more similarity on the level of policy content than on values or rhetoric (Bonoli 2003). The impression is that, as we move from the abstract level of words, concepts, and morals to the more down-to-earth level of actual policies, similarities increase. In simpler words, there seems to be much more similarity in what social democrats across the globe are doing than in what they are saying.

While at first sight this conclusion may be surprising, there are in fact powerful reasons explaining it. Decisions taken by social democratic governments (or by governments of any other political persuasion) in the realms of discourse and actual policy-making are subjected to very different sets of constraints. When it comes to words, values, and social norms, constraints are mostly national: the discourse which provides the packaging of policy must resonate culturally and must be compatible with public expectations with regard to the appropriate role of the state in society and in the economy (Schmidt 2000). In the field of policy, especially economic and social policy, instead, key constraints are essentially international and are represented by global markets and the fiscal discipline imposed by international institutional arrangements such as the Maastricht Treaty upon EMU members. It is the presence of two distinct sets of constraints that in our view best explains the apparent inconsistency between social democratic discourse and practice over the last decade or so.

References

Anderson, K. and Meyer, T. (2003). 'Social Democratic Pension Politics in Germany and Sweden', in G. Bonoli and M. Powell (eds.), *Social Democratic Party Policies in Contemporary Europe*. London: Routledge.

Aust, A. (2003). 'From Eurokeynesianism to the "Third Way": The Party of European Socialists and European Employment Policies', in G. Bonoli and M. Powell (eds.), *Social Democratic Party Policies in Contemporary Europe*. London: Routledge.

Bell, D. (2003). 'French Socialists: Refusing the "Third Way" ', *Journal of Policy History*, 15/1: 46–64.

Bertelsmann Foundation (ed.) (2000). *International Reform Monitor: Social Policy, Labour Market Policy, Industrial Relations*. Issue 3. October. Gütersloh, Stuttgart Bertelsmann Foundation.

Besser-Pereira, L. (2001). 'The New Left Viewed from the South', in A. Giddens (ed.), *The Global Third Way Debate*. Cambridge: Polity Press.

Blair, T. (1998). *The Third Way*. London: Fabian Society.

—— and Schröder, G. (1999). *Europe: The Third Way/Die Neue Mitte*. London: Labour Party.

Bonoli, G. (2003). 'Conclusion: Towards a European Third Way?', in G. Bonoli and M. Powell (eds.), *Social Democratic Party Policies in Contemporary Europe*. London: Routledge.

—— and Powell, M. (2002). 'Third Ways in Europe?', *Social Policy and Society*, 1/1: 59–66.

—— —— (eds.) (2003). *Social Democratic Party Policies in Contemporary Europe*. London: Routledge.

Bouvet , L. and Michel, F. (2001). ' "La Gauche Plurielle": An Alternative to the Third Way?', in S. White (ed.), *New Labour: The Progressive Future?* Basingstoke: Macmillan.

Braun, D. and Giraud, O. (2003). 'Models of Citizenship and Social Democratic Policies', in G. Bonoli and M. Powell (eds.), *Social Democratic Party Policies in Contemporary Europe*. London: Routledge.

Busch, A. and Manow, P. (2001). 'The SPD and the Neue Mitte in Germany', in S. White (ed.), *New Labour: The Progressive Future?* Basingstoke: Macmillan.

Clasen, J. (2000). 'Motives, Means and Opportunities: Reforming Unemployment Compensation in the 1990s', *West European Politics*, 23/2: 89–112.

Clift, B. (2001a). 'New Labour's Third Way and European Social Democracy', in S. Ludlam and M. Smith (eds.), *New Labour in Government*. Basingstoke: Macmillan.

—— (2001b). 'The Jospin Way', *Political Quarterly*, 72/2: 170–9.

—— (2003). 'The Social and Employment Policies of the Jospin Government', in G. Bonoli and M. Powell (eds.), *Social Democratic Party Policies in Contemporary Europe*. London: Routledge.

Commission on Social Justice. (1994). *Social Justice: Strategies for National Renewal*. London: Vintage.

Costa-Lobo, M. and Magalhaes, P. (2003). 'The Portuguese Socialists and the Third Way', in G. Bonoli and M. Powell (eds.), *Social Democratic Party Policies in Contemporary Europe*. London: Routledge.

Cox, R. (2001). 'The Social Construction of an Imperative: Why Welfare Reform Happened in Denmark and the Netherlands but Not in Germany', *World Politics*, 53: 463–98.

Cuperus, R. and Kandel, J. (eds.) (1998). *European Social Democracy*. Freudenberg/Amsterdam: Friedrich Ebert Siftung/Wiardi Beckman Stiching.

—— Duffek, K., and Kandel, J. (eds.) (2001). *Multiple Third Ways: European Social Democracy Facing the Twin Revolution of Globalisation and the Knowledge Society*. Freudenberg/Amsterdam/Vienna: Renner Institut/Friedrich Ebert Siftung/Wiardi Beckman Stiching.

Della Sala, V. (2002). 'D'Alema's Dilemmas: Third Way, Italian Style', in O. Schmidtke (ed.), *The Third Way Transformation of Social Democracy*. Aldershot: Ashgate.

Driver, S. and Martell, L. (2000). 'Left, Right and the Third Way', *Policy and Politics*, 28/2: 147–61.

—— —— (2002a). 'Third Ways in Britain and Europe', in O. Schmidtke (ed.), *The Third Way Transformation of Social Democracy*. Aldershot: Ashgate.

—— —— (2002b). *Blair's Britain*. Cambridge: Polity.

Etzioni, A. (2000). *The Third Way to a Good Society*. London: Demos.

Fairclough, N. (2000). *New Labour, New Language?* London: Routledge.

FDP (1999). 'Gerhardt: Schröder's Wendepapier—auch ein Wendepunkt fuer die SPD?' (press release). Bonn, 9 June.

Ferrera, M. and Gualmini, E. (1999). *Salvati dall'Europa?* Bologna: Il Mulino.

—— Hemerijck, A., and Rhodes, M. (2001). 'Recasting European Welfare States for the 21st Century', in S. Leibfried (ed.), *Welfare State Futures*. Cambridge: Cambridge University Press.

Gamble, A. and Wright, A. (eds.) (1999). *The New Social Democracy*. Oxford: Blackwell.

Giddens, A. (1998). *The Third Way*. Cambridge: Polity Press.

—— (2000). *The Third Way and its Critics*. Cambridge: Polity Press.

—— (2002a). *Where Now for New Labour?* Cambridge: Polity Press.

—— (2002b). 'The Third Way Can Beat the Far Right', *Guardian*, 3 May.

Goul-Andersen, J. (2000). 'Welfare Crisis and Beyond: Danish Welfare Policies in the 1980s and in the 1990s', in S. Kuhnle (ed.), *Survival of the European Welfare State*. London: Routledge.

Green-Pedersen, C., van Kersbergen, K., and Hemerijck, A. (2001). 'Neo-Liberalism, the Third Way or What?', *Journal of European Public Policy*, 8: 307–25.

Hale, S., Leggett, W., and Martell, L. (eds.) (2004). The Third Way and Beyond. Manchester: Manchester University Press.

Hemerijck, A. and Visser, J. (2001). 'Dutch Lessons in Social Pragmatism', in S. White (ed.), *New Labour: The Progressive Future*? Basingstoke: Palgrave.

—— Unger B., and Visser, J. (2000). 'How Small Countries Negotiate Change. Twenty-Five Years of Policy Adjustment in Austria, the Netherlands and Belgium', in F. Scharpf and V. Schmidt (eds.), *Welfare and Work in the Open Economy. Volume 1: From Vulnerability to Competitiveness*. Oxford: Oxford University Press.

Hering, M. (2003). 'Turning Ideas into Policies: Implementing Modern Social Democratic Thinking in Germany's Pension Policy', in G. Bonoli and M. Powell (eds.), *Social Democratic Party Policies in Contemporary Europe*. London: Routledge.

Hoop, R. (2003). 'Social Policy in Belgium and the Netherlands: Third Way or Not?', in G. Bonoli and M. Powell (eds.), *Social Democratic Party Policies in Contemporary Europe*. London: Routledge.

Journal of Policy History (2003). Special Issue: The Future of the Democratic Left in Industrial Democracies, 15/1.

Jun, U. (2003). 'The Changing SPD in the Schröder Era', *Journal of Policy History*, 15/1: 65–93.

Kleinman, M. (2002). *A European Welfare State?* Palgrave: Basingstoke.

Leadbetter, C. (1999). *Living on Thin Air*. Harmondsworth: Penguin.

Levy, J. (1999). 'Vice into Virtue? Progressive Politics and Welfare Reform in Continental Europe', *Politics and Society*, 27: 239–73.

—— (2000). 'France: Directing Adjustment?', in Fritz Scharpf and Vivien Schmidt (eds.), *Welfare and Work in the Open Economy. Volume 2: Diverse Responses to Common Challenges*. Oxford: Oxford University Press.

—— (2001). 'Partisan Politics and Welfare Adjustment: The Case of France', *Journal of European Public Policy*, 8: 265–85.

Mandelson, P. (2003). 'We Need to Rethink the Welfare State', *Guardian*, 25 April.

Marian, M. (2002). 'France 1997–2002: Right-Wing President, Left-Wing Government', *Political Quarterly*, 73: 258–65.

Merkel, W. (2001). 'The Third Ways of Social Democracy', in R. Cuperus, K. Duffek, and J. Kandel (eds.), *Multiple Third Ways: European Social Democracy Facing the Twin Revolution of Globalisation and the Knowledge Society*. Freudenberg/ Amsterdam/Vienna: Friedrich Ebert Siftung/ Wiardi Beckman Stiching/Renner Institut.

Millar, J. (2002). 'Adjusting Welfare Policies to Stimulate Job Entry: The Example of the United Kingdom', in H. Sarfati and G. Bonoli (eds.), *Labour Market and Social Protection Reforms in International Perspective*. Aldershot: Ashgate.

Pierson, C. (2001). *Hard Choices. Social Democracy in the Twenty First Century*. Cambridge: Polity Press.

Pierson, P. (1994). *Dismantling the Welfare State? Reagan, Thatcher and The Politics of Retrenchment*. Cambridge: Cambridge University Press.

Powell, M. (ed.) (1999). *New Labour, New Welfare State?* Bristol: Policy Press.

—— (ed.) (2002). *Evaluating New Labour's Welfare Reforms*. Bristol: Policy Press.

—— and Barrientos, A. (2004). 'The Route Map of the Third Way', in S. Hale, W. Leggett, and L. Martell (eds.). *The Third Way and Beyond*. Manchester: Manchester University Press.

Przeworski, A. (2001). 'How Many Ways Can Be Third?', in A. Glyn (ed.), *Social Democracy in Neoliberal Times*. Oxford: Oxford University Press.

Schmidt, V. (2000). 'Values and Discourse in the Politics of Adjustment', in F. Scharpf and V. Schmidt (eds.), *Welfare and Work in the Open Economy. Volume 1: From Vulnerability to Competitiveness*. Oxford: Oxford University Press.

—— (2001). 'The Politics Of Economic Adjustment in France and Britain: When Does Discourse Matter?', *Journal of European Public Policy*, 8: 247–64.

Schmidtke, O. (ed.) (2002). *The Third Way Transformation of Social Democracy*. Aldershot: Ashgate.

Sferza, S. (2002). 'The Third Way in France: Tertium non datur?', in O. Schmidtke (ed.), *The Third Way Transformation of Social Democracy*. Aldershot: Ashgate.

Social Policy and Society (2002). Special theme on Social Democracy 1(1).

Süddeutschezeitung (2003*a*). 31 May.

—— (2003*b*). 26 June.

Svensson, C. (2001). 'Swedish Social Democracy and the Third Way: A Delicate Affair', in R. Cuperus, K. Duffek, and J. Kandel (eds.), *Multiple Third Ways: European Social Democracy Facing the Twin Revolution of Globalisation and the Knowledge Society*. Amsterdam/Berlin/Vienna: Friedrich-Ebert-Stiftung/Wiardi Beckman Stichting/Renner Institut.

Thomson, S. (2000). *The Social Democratic Dilemma*. Basingstoke: Macmillan.

Vandenbrouke, F. (1998). 'Globalization, Inequality and Social Democracy', in R. Cuperus and J. Kandel (eds.), *European Social Democracy*. Freudenberg/ Amsterdam: Friedrich Ebert Siftung/Wiardi Beckman Stichting.

Volkens, A. (2003). 'Changes in Policy Positions of European Social Democrats, 1945–1998', in G. Bonoli and M. Powell (eds.), *Social Democratic Party Policies in Contemporary Europe*. London: Routledge.

White, S. (1998). 'Interpreting the Third Way', *Renewal*, 6: 17–30.

—— (ed.) (2001). *New Labour: the Progressive Future?* Basingstoke: Palgrave.

Wintour, P. (2002). 'Jospin Blamed for Failure to Modernise', *Guardian*, 24 April.

II

Policy Areas, Goals, and Mechanisms

4

Modernizing the State: A New Style of Governance?

JANET NEWMAN

Talking about 'the state' is now somewhat unfashionable. The impact of the neo-liberal reforms in the US, UK, Australasia, and much of northern Europe has led to the partial dismantling of state institutions under the twin imperatives of marketization and decentralization (though this has taken different forms in different national and political contexts: Christensen and Laegreid 2002; OECD 2002; Pollitt and Bouckaert 2000). This has been accompanied by a panoply of new governmental strategies by which state power is exercised 'at a distance' through a plurality of agencies and practices. This reconfiguration of power—often described as a new form of governance—is fraught with tensions and contradictions, some of which are explored in this chapter.

The chapter draws mainly on sources describing governance shifts in Finland, Denmark, Sweden, the Netherlands, Germany, and the UK. Each of these nations has very specific institutions and political cultures, and they cannot be collapsed into a common trajectory of change. However, each appears to be grappling with questions about how to govern in changing social and economic conditions in which neither traditional social democratic/Christian democratic forms of governance nor neo-liberal solutions appear to be sustainable. My aim is to critically assess the potential contribution of theoretical work on governance from these countries to the analysis of Third Way formations. I argue that such theoretical work has much to contribute to the analysis of some aspects of Third Way governance in that it focuses on the problems of governing in societies in which power is dispersed across a range of agencies and groups both within and beyond the nation-state. Indeed, some of the literature implies that a Third Way approach is an inevitable consequence of such processes of dispersal rather than a political choice made by elected political leaders. Section 1 provides an overview of some of the processes associated with Third Way styles of governing: policy and practice networks, collaborative governance, new forms of citizen participation and involvement, all steered by processes of regulation and influence at the level of the state rather than direct state control. These are then explored in more detail in sections 2–5. The conclusion draws out critical questions and issues that need to be considered in any assessment of the Third Way, including the limits of network or collaborative governance in states in which power remains highly centralized and in which collaboration is accompanied by more coercive approaches to governing.

1. The Third Way and 'Governance'

The Third Way, as other chapters of this book emphasize, is not a singular, coherent political formation. This has several implications. First, it is necessary to treat it as a project, not a programme. That is, it is an attempt—no more than that—to forge a new social and political settlement, and as such its impact is unfinished, uneven, and contested. Even the language itself is subject to change, with a shift to the language of 'progressive governance' at an intergovernmental conference in London in 2003. Second, the Third Way is a loose assemblage of different ideas and policies rather than a tightly woven ideology—a soupçon of communitarianism here, a trace of public sector values there, and a lot of markets everywhere. Third, the form it takes is shaped by the national political and social contexts in which it occurs. This means that it is impossible to speak of the changes associated with the Third Way other than in very general, trans-national terms. The Third Way might be characterized as a term around which debates about future political directions became crystallized at a specific historical moment rather than a particular political or policy programme. That is, it works better as a piece of rhetoric than as a descriptor of a specific political settlement (Fairclough 2000). As a consequence, both academic and political commentators have long argued about what the substance of a Third Way politics might be.[1]

My aim in this chapter, then, is not to attempt to describe changes in specific nation-states but to identify assumptions about the changing character of economy and society on which Third Way forms of governance appear to draw. The Third Way is presented as offering an alternative to both the market individualism of neo-liberalism and the state-centred politics of social democracy. The contradictions inherent in such a project have been the focus of a series of political and academic critiques (Fairclough 2000; Finlayson 2003; Hay 1999; Rustin 2000). These have in

---

[1] See for example the 1998 NEXUS debate between leading commentators on the Left at www.newarkleft.org.uk/3way.htm

common a predominant focus on the political-economic tensions inherent in the combination of neo-liberalism and social democracy. Such assessments provide a backcloth against which attempts to 'modernize' the state itself can be discussed. However, something more is needed to analyse the intellectual and policy legitimizations that support Third Way approaches to modernization. The 'something more', I suggest, might be found by applying some of the concepts drawn from governance theory.

Governance theory starts from the proposition that we are witnessing a shift from government (through direct control) to governance (through steering, influencing, and collaborating with multiple actors in a dispersed system). The predominant focus is on the increasing significance of governance through networks as an alternative to markets and hierarchy (Rhodes 1997, 2000; Stoker 1998; Pierre and Peters 2000; Kickert 1997; Messner 1997). The state, it is argued, can no longer assume a monopoly of expertise or resources necessary to govern, and must look to a plurality of interdependent institutions drawn from the public, private, and voluntary sectors. So governments must seek new tools and techniques to guide, steer, and influence, albeit retaining to itself the role of 'meta governance' (Jessop 2000).

This proposition refers to a whole set of linked, but distinct, empirical phenomena. In the economy, attention has focused on the demise of the large, monolithic corporation and rise of the flexible, 'networked' company linked to others through strategic alliances and value-adding partnerships. At the same time processes of state modernization—especially the introduction of New Public Management strategies based on decentralization, contractualization, marketization, and so on—have produced a significant break-up of the large bureaucracies associated with the social democratic welfare state. This in turn has led to an extension of managerial power (Clarke and Newman 1997) and a proliferation of new regulatory mechanisms (audit, inspection, standard setting, and so on; Power 1997). The fragmentation has also, however, produced a need for new coordination strategies based on partnership working between public and private sectors ('public/private partnerships'), within the public sector ('multi-agency working'), and between public and third-sector organizations (sometimes termed 'social partnerships'). Such partnerships are a distinguishing characteristic of Third Way governance in that they seek to overcome the fragmentation produced by neo-liberal reforms and in that they draw on both public and private sector approaches. They thus apparently transcend the dualism of 'market versus hierarchy'.

Writings on governance also note the challenge to the nation-state as a unitary actor produced by the 'hollowing out' of its powers (Rhodes 1994), with decentralization and dispersal within the nation-state and the flow of governance powers both upwards to trans-national bodies such as the World Bank, IMF, European Parliament, and so on, and downwards to regions. Studies have described the ways in which individuals and institutions—public and private—engage in governance practices beyond the nation-state and showed how, while states remain significant actors, the growth of trans-national institutions has led to considerable power flowing beyond the democratic control of elected politicians serving in 'representative' institutions (e.g. Commission on Global Governance 1995). At the same time, the legitimacy of such institutions has been threatened as a result of declining trust between politicians and people and increasing social differentiation, leading to a rising interest in finding new ways of connecting state and citizen through public participation and new democratic forms of engagement.

There is now a rich tradition of writings from across Europe, Australasia, and North America that seeks to describe and analyse these shifts. These are influenced by the national cultures and political traditions of the countries from which writings have emerged. In highly simplified terms, writings from the UK, the US, and Australia tend to focus on economic and political networks while those from continental Europe, especially the Netherlands and Scandinavia, are more evidently 'social' in their orientation. Work from continental Europe in particular explores new governance processes and relationships as adaptations to changes in the social system that pose new demands on, and raise new possibilities for, the processes of governing (Klinj 2002; Kooiman 1993, 2000). The context for this lies in both the increasing complexity and intractability of social and economic problems (environmental concerns, public health, social welfare, crime control) and the growing importance of associations and institutions outside the state in solving them. Rather than governments acting alone, they are increasingly drawn into processes of co-regulation, co-steering, co-production, cooperative management, and other forms of governing that cross the boundaries between government and society as well as between public and private sectors. This model shifts the focus of attention towards a much broader concern with issues of citizen and community involvement in governance processes. In what follows I explore each of these themes in turn.

2. Beyond Markets and Hierarchies? The Shift to 'Network Governance'

Many of the arguments about network governance are derived from economic analyses of the conditions produced by global markets and competition. Amin and Hausner, for example, argue that the dominant models of economic governance associated with social democracy have been undermined both by internal contradictions and by a changing economic environment. In particular globalization, it is argued, produces forms of instability and uncertainty that challenge post-war models of economic governance based on regulated competition. In such conditions a 'third way' of interactive governance is proposed:

The history of modernity has been that of increasing complexity in the patterns of social and economic organisation, defiant of singular or all embracing solutions. . . . Yet, in much of our thinking, we continue to believe that society can somehow be governed or steered. Alternatively, at the other extreme, individual-centred . . . approaches hypothesise that market selection or autopoesis is the best you can hope for (Amin and Hausner 1997: 1)

In trying to transcend such 'dualistic' approaches, they argue that in conditions of complexity an 'interactive' model of governance—one that is neither the traditional conception of state nor market-based processes of governing—is required. This must be based on a form of collective agency, defined as 'the capacity to guide and shape existing networks through reflexive interaction and strategic guidance' (Amin and Hausner 1997: 10).

This has much resonance with the political rhetoric of the Third Way, a rhetoric that holds out the possibility of transcending both the bureaucratic disadvantages of 'old', monolithic state hierarchies and the fragmenting and individualizing consequences of neo-liberal, market-based models. The network model of economic coordination has particular implications for processes of state reform. What is envisaged is a mix of methods—decentralization, collaboration, partnerships—all coordinated by a state more focused on 'steering' (guiding, shaping, leading) than 'rowing' (intervening at the operational level of policy delivery).[2] We can see examples of this mix of models in many of the prescriptions of the 'New Public Management' (NPM) that has become institutionalized—albeit in different forms—across Europe, Australasia, North America, and beyond, and that can be traced in the models of governance imposed on nation-states by multilateral governance agencies such as the World Bank. There has been extensive discussion of the extent of 'convergence' that has been produced as a consequence of NPM hegemony and an emphasis on the continued importance of national institutions and cultures (Flynn and Strehl 1996; Pollitt and Bouckaert 2000). NPM has certainly been more extensively developed in the Anglo-Saxon countries of Australia, Canada, New Zealand, the UK, and the USA. Germany and France have followed rather

---

[2] The terms 'steering' and 'rowing' were brought to prominence in a highly influential US book (Osborne and Gaebler 1992) that influenced state reform in the US, the UK, and beyond.

different reform trajectories, while Finland, Sweden, and the Netherlands have been more disposed to a consensual style of governance that tends to 'blunt the sharper corners' of NPM (Pollitt and Bouckaert 2000: 61).

The basic features of the NPM model have included the dismantling of state hierarchies through market and contractual mechanisms coupled with the decentralization and devolution of services. This appears to be very similar to Third Way forms of governance but it is important to note that it is more usually associated with the neo-liberal phase of state reform that took place in the 1980s and 1990s—that is, with the dismantling of state power either by governments of the right or, in other nations, under the auspices of the IMF and World Bank. This produced a flow of power away from state institutions and towards private companies, new forms of public/private partnerships, and unelected and unaccountable agencies (the so-called quangos; Skelcher 1998: 20). One of the contradictions of the Third Way is that it seeks to continue these processes of state reform— the further dismantling of state institutions, the extension of market mechanisms, and so on—at the same time as creating new processes of coordinating and controlling the fragmented array of agencies and actors that are produced by the reform process itself.

The language used to describe these coordination processes varies, with Kauppi, Lahdesmacki, and Ojala (2002) describing the Finnish model as the 'network bureaucracy' while elsewhere the language is one of 'partnership'. The role of the state shifts to one of 'steering' through mechanisms such as regulating, inspecting, auditing, coordinating, and influencing. In the UK, for example, there has been an intense focus on regulating and managing the performance of public bodies: the setting of goals and targets, a proliferation of agencies concerned with audit and inspection, the publication of league tables, the removal of the power of 'failing' organizations, and the attempt to install preferred models of policy and delivery based on assessments of 'what works'. However, we can see different overlapping strategies of regulation and control, not all of which can be characterized as 'power at a distance': some are more directly interventionist, suggesting that any shift towards network governance is at best partial. I return to this point in the conclusion; here, I want to explore the idea of governance beyond the state a little further.

3. Beyond the Autonomous State? Governing Complex, Diverse, and Dynamic Social Systems

The idea of the networked economy and the dispersal of state power are, in many writings, inextricably linked to changes in society. Among writers on governance from continental Europe, networks are viewed not just as means of economic and political coordination but as a response to deep social changes. Writing on the German experience, Messner highlights the growing social as well as economic differentiation that poses problems of coordination in firms and societies alike. Networks are viewed as an implicit 'third way' solution:

. . . the network society is accordingly characterised by an organizational and governance pluralism that was not acknowledged in the dichotomist debate of the 1980s over the issue of 'market versus state'. Besides law, power and money as the classic governance media, the flow of information, the skills involved in communication and the development of a problem solving orientation shared by groups of social actors and policy arenas, and the ability to organise continuous social search and learning processes are gaining in significance for the governance capacity of societies. (Messner 1997: iv)

Here the contemporary focus on governance is understood as a response to the challenge of governing complex and fragmented societies. Emerging new governance processes and relationships are viewed as adaptations to changes in the social system that pose new demands on, and raise new possibilities for, the processes of governing. Growing social complexity, the development of greater access to information, and other social changes make the task of governing more difficult. Complex social issues (such as environmental protection) elude traditional approaches. Klinj (2002), exploring the implications of the 'network society' for the processes of governance, he links sociological work on individualization to the demise of social solidarities and the loss of attachment to political parties and concludes that

. . . the rise of the network society will make society more fluid, more horizontal, more pluralistic in values and less likely to be governed from above by public actors. At the same time, problems in this society will call for more integral solutions that have to be implemented with many different actors with different knowledge of the issues involved. (Klinj 2002: 30)

The conceptualization of 'collaborative' governance that is required in these conditions is perhaps most fully developed by the Dutch writer Jan Kooiman. Kooiman discusses the problem of governance in social systems characterized by complexity, diversity, and dynamic change: societies that are characterized by strong patterns of mutual dependence and long-established 'co-' governing arrangements rooted in a tradition of corporatism. The need for a 'third way', here, is viewed as an alternative to existing forms of governance failure:

Empirically we can see around us that the capacities of political/administrative governing systems either have crossed the threshold of diminishing returns (policies cancelling each other's effects) or are quite close to this boundary (implementation difficulties). In this situation governing systems try to reduce the need for governing (e.g. by deregulation) or shift the need (e.g. by privatisation). But a third way seems to be developed and not in terms of more 'neo-corporatist arrangements'. . . . In the new forms of governance one can see a shift from a unilateral focus (government or society separately) to an interactionist focus (government with society). (Kooiman 1993: 35)[3]

Rather than governments acting alone, he argues, they must increasingly engage in co-regulation, co-steering, co-production, cooperative management, public–private partnerships, and other forms of governing that cross the boundaries between government and society as well as between public and private sectors (Kooiman 1993: 1). These collaborative arrangements operate at different levels of governing (macro, meso, and micro) and Kooiman explores the complexity of their interaction rather than assuming that new governance processes displace the need for 'meta-governance' by the state. As a consequence, governance processes are depicted as 'heterarchical' in character, comprising diverse vertical and horizontal relationships (Kooiman 2000).

These governance shifts are reflected in policies based on 'partnership', widely recognized as a key discourse of Third Way governance. This is not just a case of neo-liberal preference for private sector involvement: partnership also offers a means of developing so called joined-up solutions to complex social, educational, and welfare problems-problems that require a coordinated approach and long-term investment. Solutions to such problems cannot be found by states acting alone, but depend on a wide range of actors working together across sectoral boundaries and drawing in community actors in a way that seems to dissolve the boundary between state and civil society. These dependencies are recognized not only in the academic governance literature but also in a wide range of policy documents: for example, EU and national policy documents on social exclusion. As a result there has been a proliferation of partnerships, across sectors and between different tiers of governance, as a means of delivering social and public policy.

However, assessments of partnership working have highlighted a number of different problems. Klijn and Teisman (2003) highlight institutional and strategic barriers in Dutch public–private partnerships; Roose, Taillieu, and Sips (2001) explore the difficulties of partnership working in the social service sector in Belgium produced by governmental policy and regulations; and Nauta and von Grumbkow (2001) focus on the socio-psychological

---

[3] The translation of this text is somewhat flawed and I have made small amendments to the grammar to clarify, I hope, the intended meaning.

problems of achieving trust in cooperative working between GPs and occupational therapists in the Netherlands. In the UK, Balloch and Taylor (2001), reviewing work across a range of policy fields, note a range of political, cultural, and technical challenges that together produce a privileging of statutory bodies over third-sector partners and user or community involvement. Other evaluations highlight the tensions between horizontal collaboration between partners and the hierarchical power represented in central-local relations: that is, between government bodies and local partnerships (Davies 2002). The continuance of quasi-markets alongside partnership working has also produced a tendency for partnership bodies to have to engage in competitive bidding for resources.

Together, these assessments suggest that the idea of a shift from hierarchy to collaborative governance offers a very partial and even flawed understanding of partnership working. Clarke and Glendinning concur that there is a lack of fit between the empirical complexity of Third Way partnerships and the formal model of network governance, and go on to suggest that 'the formalization of abstract models of governance—hierarchies, markets and networks—may have diverted attention away from more complex, compound and contradictory processes and systems' (2002: 45). Some of these contradictions arise from ambiguities and oscillations in the state's own role in partnerships: at some points it claims to be working 'in partnership' with a wide range of agencies and organ-izations, at others it draws back into its 'meta-governance' role of steering, and at yet others it acts in very hierarchical—even coercive—ways, directing, controlling, and regulating activity, monitoring performance, and bestowing or removing the powers of subsidiary bodies.

4. Governing Reflexive Societies? The Problem of Democracy

One of the consequences of the break-up of state institutions and the development of 'collaborative', network-based governance has been a flow of power away from elected bodies and the institutions of representative democracy on which they are based. The 'hollowing out' of the nation-state, the unsettling of hierarchical institutions, processes of globalization, and the development of more complex, differentiated societies have produced a number of democratic deficits. New forms of governance, then, are seen to require new forms of democracy:

. . . contrary to the classic form of 'government', contemporary governance is not imprisoned in closed institutions and is not the province of professional politicians. Though rarely defined with precision, it refers to patterns of decision-making taking place in a larger set of institutions, with a broader range of actors and processes. One of the ambitions of those who defend this new concept is indeed to enlarge the accepted notion of civic participation beyond the well established and constantly declining procedures of representative democracy. (Magnette 2003: 144)

Notwithstanding the attempts to enhance the role of elected representatives, it is now widely accepted that representative democracy is insufficient as a means of reconnecting citizens with governing institutions and processes (Scarrow, 2001). As a consequence there has been considerable interest, among both policy networks and academics, in alternative forms of public participation and experiments in deliberative democracy (Burns, Hambleton, and Hoggett 1994; Dryzek 2000; Elster 1998; Fishkin 1991). In a number of European countries there have been attempts to increase government consultation with citizens and enhance their participation in decision-making. Again, the forms this takes varies, reflecting specific national cultures and traditions: Finland is among the strongest example of foregrounding the use of new information technologies to enhance participation, reflecting the significance of such technologies to its economy (Turenan 2002).

New forms of participation—especially deliberative democracy—are viewed in the literature as having the potential to overcome some of the problems inherent in the limited capacity of the party system and representative democracy to accommodate public views on specific issues or to take account of social difference and diversity (Dryzek 2000; Young 1990). In part this is because representative democracy is too hierarchical, bureaucratic, and party-bound to be able to deal effectively and democratically with 'reflexive individuals' and questions of identity in a multicultural and global/local world (Bang 2002). Bang argues that the current dilemma arises not only because of the decline of formal political participation in mature democracies, but also because

. . . democratic states lack governance capacities simply because they are attuned more to coping with abstract problems . . . and conflicts of interests in the democratic regime . . . than to handling concrete policy and identity problems (project politics and politics of presence). (Bang 2002: 1)

Democratic innovations—such as public involvement in decision-making, experiments in deliberative democracy, and community self-governance— are, it is argued, better able to capture the differentiated needs and interests of citizens and to mobilize a range of different identities. They are viewed as integral to 'reflexive modernity' (Giddens 1994; Beck, Giddens, and Lash 1994) in that deliberation is a site in which decisions can be taken on the basis of 'a more or less continuous reflection on the conditions of one's own action' (Giddens 1994: 86). They are thus linked to what Giddens terms a 'generative' politics: one which 'seeks to allow individuals and groups to make things happen, rather than have things happen to them, in the context of overall social goals and concerns . . . generative politics is the main means of effectively approaching problems of poverty and social exclusion in the present day' (1994: 15). New opportunities for citizen engagement offer the possibility to challenge established power structures, acting back on those very institutions that sponsor them in the name of developing 'more responsive' services or getting more closely 'in touch with the people'.[4] They may be the site in which identities are 'discovered, constructed and actively maintained' (Giddens 1994: 82).

However, citizen participation initiatives, like partnership working, are situated precisely in the tension between hierarchical and collaborative governance. While nominally transcending hierarchy and the formal democratic structures associated with it, partnerships are shaped within institutional structures and processes that tend to constrain the extent to which they influence policy-making or service delivery. As a result, the capacity of public participation to transform state policies and practices has been questioned (Newman et al. 2004). Beresford (2002) notes a number of fundamental contradictions in public participation: for example, enhanced political interest but public dissatisfaction; official priority but very limited achievements and resourcing. Magnette argues that, as a strand of European Union governance, participatory mechanisms 'constitute extensions of existing practices, and are underpinned by the same elitist and functionalist philosophy' (2003: 144).

However, the proliferation of initiatives that seek to draw citizens and communities into decision-making processes may have other consequences. They produce the possibility of new subject positions and forms of identification for citizens and 'community' actors. They also potentially subject such actors to the possibility of new regulatory strategies (there is a fine line between asking citizens to engage in consultation exercises about the delivery of health services and constituting them as 'responsible' users of those same services). Participation, then, is not only designed to address the decline of electoral turnout and legitimize state institutions but also to enhance the social engagement of citizens. I explore this further in the next section.

5. Governing Citizens? 'Cultural Governance' and the Regulation of Conduct

Public administration and social policy literatures describe the ways in which governments—in the UK, the USA, and across much of Western

---

[4] Both phrases are used repeatedly in UK government policy documents on modernization: for example, DETR (1998).

Europe—have attempted to shift the focus towards various forms of co-production with citizens themselves through community and citizen involvement strategies. In the UK, such strategies underpin the Labour government's approach to the reform of the welfare state, including its focus on addressing social exclusion, by involving individuals, communities, parents, and families in solving social problems. They play a central role in policies designed to produce what one New Labour minister termed 'socially engaged citizens' (Blunkett 2003).

Writings on the network society highlight the new social and cultural characteristics that must be inculcated in the social actors concerned. As Messner puts it, 'It is not only institutional structures and organisations but also systems of social values and action orientations that will have to be cultivated, modernised and advanced' (1997: v). This has significant consequences for Third Way approaches to governance; so significant that some writers have characterized the core strategies of 'modernizing' states as a form of 'culture governance'. This takes a number of different inflections. One is to view cultural change as the aim of modern governance. Perri 6, for example, suggests that 'culture is now the centre of the agenda for government reform' in that it is 'the most important determinant of a combination of long-run economic success and social cohesion (1997: 173). Such an approach is traceable in a wide range of government documents generated by the EU and national governments. In the UK, the reports of the Social Exclusion Unit (1998, 2001) highlight cultural rather than material factors as the principal barriers to inclusion. But culture is also viewed as an increasingly important strategy of governance alongside, and partly displacing, more coercive strategies (Finlayson 2003). Bang (2002) uses the term 'culture governance' to denote the processes of politicized and culturalized steering that characterizes the governance of modern states.

This idea of cultural governance is more usually associated with poststructuralist theories of governmentality in which governance takes place through a range of strategies and technologies directed towards what Foucault terms the 'conduct of conduct' (Foucault 1991). Governmental power is concerned with disposing populations towards particular forms of self-governing action. It works by creating subjects and empowering them to act, rather than coercing or directing them (though governments continue to exercise coercive power alongside its strategies of 'empowerment', for example in welfare-to-work programmes and criminal justice policies). This alters the terrain on which governance shifts can be understood, highlighting the forms and flows of power involved in 'governing at a distance'. Rather than debating whether the power of the state has been 'hollowed out', this directs attention to the kinds of knowledge and power through which social activity is regulated and through which actors—citizens, workers, organizations—arc constitutcd as self-disciplining subjects. This is, if you like, thc obvcrsc of the Giddensian reflexive subject whose existence produces a need for new forms of collaborative governance.

A post-structuralist approach displaces, or decentres, government and/or the state within the analysis by insisting that governing takes place through multiple agencies, relations, and practices (Dean 1999; Petersen et al. 1999). Rather than the reduction of government promised by neo-liberal regimes, such changes can be understood as the dispersal of governmental power across new sites of action. The literature traces attempts to create new forms of governable subject: responsible con-sumers of scrvices in the 'modernized' welfare state, or communities taking responsibility of solving their own problems. For example, Dwyer (2000) highlights the strategies of 'responsibilization' through which citizens are newly constituted as responsible for their own welfare rather than as reliant on a wclfarc state, and Rose (1999) highlights the emer-gence of 'community' as a site for governmental strategies and tech-nologies. To these we might add the public service managers constituted by new managerial discourse as the coordinators of the fragmented array of organizations and services produced by the neo-liberal state reforms of Thatcherism (Clarke and Newman 1997). Such strategies might, in the governance literature, be regarded as evidence of a shift towards collaborative governance or co-governance. In political or managerial discourse, they might be described as the 'empowerment' of nations, regions, communities, and citizens. Post-structuralist theory, however, would view them not in terms of the empowerment of free actors but as part of an array of governmental strategies that draw actors into new fields and technologies of power. State practices of empowerment—of actors to participate in decision-making, of citizens to be responsible for their own health decisions, or households for the provision of their own welfare needs—can be understood in terms of new strategies of regulation and control.

As such, post-structuralist theory provides a sharp contrast with the normative view of networks as the preferred mode of governance, capable of overcoming the disadvantages of both market and hierarchy. However, it is necessary to question the effectiveness of strategies for governing populations and their conduct, in particular the assumption that discourses are necessarily effective in constituting new subjects. Post-structuralist theory may also produce an over-unified conception of governmentalities as coherent formations. We need to pay attention to the processes that shape the micro-politics of governance in specific sites. Actors are posi-tioned in compound and contradictory processes and in the interaction between different fields of power. The discourses associated with Third Way politics encounter a cultural and social terrain already replete with meanings and identities associated with earlier policies and practices and formed through struggles around them. So, for example, a voluntary organization or community group working in partnership with government, although subjected to governmental strategies of inclusion and incorporation, may also be likely to have strong identity-based attachments to the interests of particular groups, places, or 'communities'. Public service users, newly positioned as consumers, may carry with them older—and perhaps more collective—allegiances and identifications. Actors are constituted not only within governmental discourses but also through historical and geographically specific identities, each of which brings alternative sets of commitments and logics of appropriate action. The Third Way, then, can be characterized not as a new social and political settlement that transcends both neo-liberal governance and the social democratic state but as a site of instabilities and struggle.

6. Conclusion: The Third Way as an Unsettled Settlement

Governance theory takes many forms and itself suffers from a number of problems. In Newman (2001) I suggested that the narratives of change (from hierarchy or markets to networks) are both normative and tend to involve a misremembering of the past and an over-tidy view of the present. In highlighting shifts and changes it tends to gloss over the extension of neo-liberal strategies of state reform based on markets and competition, and to underestimate continuities in state power (see also Jessop 2002). Nevertheless, concepts drawn from governance theory provide a useful starting point for analysing some of the shifts associated with the Third Way. In this chapter I have highlighted the capacity of different strands of governance theory to link academic conceptions of a networked society to specific aspects of Third Way approaches to governance. In doing so I have discussed the tensions that arise in the shift towards the emphasis on partnership working, public participation, citizen engagement, and the 'responsibilization' of citizens in modernized social health and welfare systems. Governance theory has much to offer to the analysis of state modernization, and can offer fruitful points of development and critique of government policies and practices. For example, we can commend the governance literature for alerting us to the idea that networks require more than an economic calculus to make them work: 'The social functional logic of networks is based on reciprocity, trust, a willingness to compromise on the part of actors, voluntary restriction of one's own freedom to act, and fair exchange.' As a consequence, 'One thing is becoming clear: the ideal type of the egoistic homo economicus—stylised since the 1980s, in the context of neo-liberal hegemony, as the maxim, as it were, governing all activity—is no longer adequate to the demands posed by the network society' (Messner 1997: v). The governance literature also has much to contribute to analyses of the Third Way in that it shifts the focus of attention beyond economic structures or processes (for example, public–private partnerships) towards a much broader concern with issues of citizenship, concepts of community, and flows of power beyond the state.

However, across many of the writings cited in this chapter we can trace at least three assumptions that can be challenged. First, the Third Way becomes not just a specific political formation, closely linked to a few particular states at specific historical moments (the US under Clinton, the UK under Blair, and so on), but part of an inevitable set of consequences arising from globalization and the latest phase of modernization. In these conditions state power becomes dispersed across a wide range of actors whose actions must then be coordinated through new governance mechanisms based on a common set of prescriptions drawn from New Public Management coupled with a new rhetoric of partnership working and decentralization. However, the determining power of globalization on nation-states has been extensively criticized (see, for example, Clarke 2004; Massey 1999; Yates 2001).

Second, economic, social, and cultural processes are merged into a seamless, apolitical depiction of systemic change. That is, social change is not just seen to flow from economic shifts in a base-superstructure kind of model; social and economic discourses are collapsed into the same narrative. We can see this, for example, in the quotations from Messner, Klinj, and Kooiman cited earlier. The difficulty here arises from the systems theories that characterize much of the governance literature, in which economy and society are viewed as elements of an holistic system characterized by reflexivity. Economy and state are 'sub-systems' of a self-managing system that requires 'steering' at a meta-level towards the desired homeostasis. The close links with systems and cybernetic theory produce a tendency to view systems as inherently adaptive or self-balancing rather than as the sites of unresolved conflicts or tensions. There is little consideration of the political processes through which temporary alliances across conflicting interests might be forged. Questions of antagonism and contradiction in social formations and how these might become the focus of social and political mobilization are thus excluded from the analysis. As a result, such frameworks are ultimately limited in their capacity to illuminate Third Way politics, with its project of reconciling conflicting opposites into an apparent consensus.

Third, the model of change in much of the governance literature is one in which 'old' forms of governance—the hierarchies of the social democratic welfare state and the markets of neo-liberalism—are displaced by a new form of governance based on networks and collaboration. However, the process of change is much more ambiguous, uneven, and contradictory than such a model implies. The Third Way in practice works through multiple regimes of governance representing different flows of power and authority, forms of relationship, and conceptions of social action. The conceptualization of governance regimes as compound and contradictory means that change cannot be understood as a linear shift from, for example, hierarchies and markets to networks, or as a shift from unitary nation-states to multi-level or devolved governance. Change, then, can better be conceptualized as a process in which different—and not necessarily coherent—trends and tendencies interact in combination, producing fields of tension within the process of governing. The interaction between markets, hierarchy, and networks as regimes of power has often been analysed in terms of 'hybrid' systems that need to be reconciled. However, the concept of hybridity does not adequately capture the inherent contradictions in Third Way formations; in Newman (2001) I set out a framework through which the interaction between different governance regimes might be explored in relation to the UK Labour government, and used this to suggest points of instability and potential political, as well as governance, failure.

The Third Way can be understood as an attempt to install a depoliticized politics, based on consensual multiculturalism and post-feminist gender relations, in which class-based patterns of inequality are displaced by more culturally based forms of 'social exclusion'. It thus both incorporates and deflects the social movements of the late twentieth century that involved struggles around gender, sexuality, disability, race, and other exclusions. The disadvantaged are simply recast as 'hard-to-reach groups' who, with proper policies and governing strategies, can be drawn into the unity of a 'modernized' nation and people. However, the attempts by Third Way governments to build a consensual politics across conflicting interests are repeatedly unsettled by conflicts between different conceptions of citizenship, nationhood, and belonging, especially in the context of the growing significance of the EU and transnational processes of migration. Their efforts to build socially inclusive societies are proving unsuccessful in overcoming the economic inequalities linked to class, gender, race, age, and disability. Their efforts to forge multicultural consensual societies are being repeatedly challenged by the surfacing of conflicts around race and ethnicity and the resurgence of the racialized politics of the Right. The attempt to forge a new social settlement is, then, subject to multiple disruptions, refusals, and resistances.

All this means that, as a political project, the Third Way faces many difficulties. These include fiscal crises that challenge the capacity of states to pursue new policy programmes and that weaken governments' abilities to deliver social reform. Third Way states are also threatened by the crisis of representative democracy resulting from the weakened trust between citizens and elected politicians. As such, their governments may be undermined and sometimes displaced by the emergence of new political parties—often of the Right—claiming to fill this trust vacuum. Such processes are exacerbated by those unanticipated events (from fuel crises to Gulf wars) that challenge the capacity of states to govern effectively in a globalized political terrain. Each of these difficulties creates cracks along the lines of fissure between neo-liberal economic and social democratic politics and policies. This is a deeply unstable political formation.

References

Amin, A. and Hausner, J. (1997). *Beyond Market and Hierarchy: Interactive Governance and Social Complexity*. Cheltenham: Edward Elgar.

Balloch, S. and Taylor, M. (2001). 'Introduction', in S. Balloch and M. Taylor (eds.), *Partnership Working: Policy and Practice*. Bristol: Policy Press.

Bang, H. (2002). 'Opening Up the Political System via Cultural Governance'. Paper from the *Institute for Political Science*, University of Copenhagen.

Beck, U., Giddens, A., and Lash, S. (1994). *Reflexive Modernisation: Politics, Tradition and Aesthetics in the Modern Social Order*. Cambridge: Polity Press.

Benyon, J. and Edwards, A. (1999). 'Community Governance of Crime Control', in G. Stoker (ed.), *The New Management of British Local Governance*. Basingstoke: Macmillan.

Beresford, P. (2002). 'Participation and Social Policy: Transformation, Liberation or Regulation?', in R. Sykes, C. Bochel, and N. Ellison, *Social Policy Review*, 14: 265–87.

Blunkett, D. (2003). Interview. *Guardian*, 11 June: 10.

Burns, D, Hambleton, R., and Hoggett, P. (1994). *The Politics of Decentralisation*. Basingstoke: Macmillan.

Clarke, J. (2004). *Changing Welfare, Changing States?* London: Sage.

—— and Glendinning, C. (2002). 'Partnerships and the Remaking of Welfare Governance', in C. Glendinning, M. Powell, and K. Rummery (eds.), *Partnerships, New Labour and the Governance of Welfare*. Bristol: Policy Press.

Clarke, J. and Newman, J. (1997). *The Managerial State: Power, Politics and Ideology in the Remaking of Social Welfare*. London: Sage.

Commission on Global Governance (1995). *Our Global Neighbourhood: The Report of the Commission on Global Governance*. Oxford: Oxford University Press.

Davies, J. (2002). 'Regeneration and partnerships under New Labour: a case of creeping centralisation', in C. Glendinning, M. Powell and K. Rummery (eds.), *Partnerships, New Labour and the Governance of Welfare*. Bristol: Policy Press.

Dryzek, J. (2000). *Deliberative Democracy and Beyond: Liberals, Critics, Contestations.* Oxford: Oxford University Press.

Dwyer, P. (2000). *Welfare Rights and Responsibilities: Contesting Social Citizenship.* Bristol: Policy Press.

Elster, J. (ed.) (1998). *Deliberative Democracy.* Oxford: Oxford University Press.

Fairclough, N. (2000). *New Labour, New Language.* London: Routledge.

Finlayson, A. (2003). *Making Sense of New Labour.* London: Lawrence and Wishart.

Fishkin, J. (1991). *Deliberative Democracy.* Cambridge: Cambridge University Press.

Flynn, N. and Strehl, F. (1996). *Public Sector Management in Europe.* London: Harvester Wheatsheaf.

Foucault (1991). 'Governmentality', in G. Burchell, C. Gordon, and P. Miller (eds.), *The Foucault Effect: Studies in Governmentality.* Hemel Hempstead: Harvester Wheatsheaf.

Giddens, A. (1994). *Beyond Left and Right: The Future of Radical Politics.* Cambridge: Polity Press.

Hay, C. (1999). *The Political Economy of New Labour: Labouring under False Pretences?* Manchester: Manchester University Press.

Hughes, G. and Lewis, G. (eds.) (1998). *Unsettling Welfare: the Reconstruction of Social Policy.* London: Routledge.

Jessop, B. (2000). *The Future of the Capitalist State.* Cambridge: Cambridge University Press.

Kaupi, U., Lahdesmacki, K., and Ojala, I. (2003). 'Modernising Public Services: The Possibilities and Challenges of Electronic Services in the Finnish Public Sector', in A. Salminon (ed.), *Governing Networks.* Amsterdam: IOS Press.

Klinj, E. (2002). 'Networks and Governance: A Perspective on Public Policy and Public Administration', in A. Salimon (ed.), *Governing Networks.* Amsterdam: IOS Press.

—— and Teisman, G. (2003). 'Institutional and Strategic Barriers to Public–Private Partnership: An Analysis of Dutch Cases', *Public Money and Management*, 23/3: 137–46.

Kooiman, J. (ed.) (1993). *Modern Governance: Government–Society Interactions.* London: Sage.

—— (2000). 'Societal Governance: Levels, Models and Orders of Social-Political Interaction', in J. Pierre (ed.), *Debating Governance: Authority, Steering and Democracy.* Oxford: Oxford University Press.

Lewis, G. (2000). *'Race', Gender and Social Policy: Encounters in a Post-Colonial Society.* Cambridge: Polity Press.

Magnette, P. (2003). 'European Governance and Civic Participation: Beyond Elitist Citizenship?', *Political Studies*, 51: 144–60.

Massey, D. (1999). 'Imagining Globalisation: Power-Geometries of Time-Space', in A. Brah, M. Hickman, and M. Mac an Ghiall (eds.), *Global Futures: Migration, Environment and Globalisation.* Basingstoke: Macmillan.

Messner, D. (1997). *The Network Society: Economic Development and International Competitiveness as Problems of Social Governance*. London: Frank Cass and Berlin: German Development Institute.

Nauta, N. and von Grumbkow, J. (2001). 'Cooperation of General Practitioners and Occupational Physicians: Identity, Trust and Responsibility', in T. Taillieu (ed.), *Collaborative Strategies and Multi-organisational Partnerships*. Leuven–Apeldoorn: Garant.

Newman, J. (2000). 'The Dynamics of Partnership'. Paper presented to the Seventh *International Conference on multi-organisational partnerships and strategic collaboration*. Leuven, July.

—— (2001). *Modernising Governance: New Labour, Policy and Society*. London: Sage.

—— Barnes, M., Sullivan, H., and Knops, A. (2004). 'Public Participation, Citizenship and Governance', *Journal of Social Policy*, 33/2: 203–23.

OECD (Organization for Economic Cooperation and Development) (2002). 'Public Sector Modernisation: A New Agenda'. Paper presented to the *26th session of the Public Management Committee*. Paris, October.

Osborne, D. and Gaebler, T. (1992). *Reinventing Government: How Entrepreneurship is Transforming the Public Sector*. Reading, MA: Addison Wesley.

Perri 6 (1997). 'Governance by Culture', in G. Mulgan (ed.), *Life After Politics*. London: Fontana.

Pierre, J. (ed.) (2000). *Debating Governance: Authority, Steering and Democracy*. Oxford: Oxford University Press.

—— and Peters, G. (2000). *Governance, Politics and the State*. Basingstoke: Macmillan.

Pollitt, C. and Bouckaert, G. (2000). *Public Management Reform: A Comparative Analysis*. Oxford: Oxford University Press.

Rhodes, R. (1994). 'The Hollowing-out of the State', *Political Quarterly*, 65: 138–51.

—— (1997). *Understanding Governance*. Buckingham: Open University Press.

—— (2000). 'Governance and Public Administration', in J. Pierre (ed.), *Debating Governance: Authority, Steering and Democracy*. Oxford: Oxford University Press.

Roose, H., Taillieu, T., and Sips, K. (2001). 'The Reverse Effects of Governmental Policy and Regulations in the Social Service Sector in Flanders', in T. Taillieu (ed.), *Collaborative Strategies and Multi-organisational Partnerships*. Leuven–Apeldoorn: Garant.

Rose, N. (1999). *Powers of Freedom: Reframing Political Thought*. Cambridge: Cambridge University Press.

Rustin, M. (2000). 'The New Labour Ethic and the Spirit of Capitalism', *Soundings*, 14/Spring: 111–26.

Scarrow, S. (2001). 'Direct Democracy and Institutional Design: A Comparative Investigation', *Comparative Political Studies*, 34: 651–65.

Skelcher, C. (1998). *The Appointed State: Quasi-Governmental Organisations and Democracy*. Buckingham: Open University Press.

Social Exclusion Unit (1998). *Bringing Britain Together: A National Strategy for Neighbourhood Renewal*. London: Stationery Office.

Janet Newman

—— (2001). *A New Commitment to Neighbourhood Renewal: National Strategy Action Plan*. London: Stationery Office.

Stoker, G. (1998). 'Governance as Theory: 5 Propositions', *International Social Science Journal*, 155.

Turenen, J. (2003). 'Networking Central Government', in A. Salminen (ed.), *Governing Networks*. Amsterdam: IOS Press.

Yates, N. (2001). *Globalisation and Social Policy*. London: Sage.

Young, I. (1990). *Justice and the Politics of Difference*. Princeton, NJ: Princeton University Press.

5

Does the Third Way Work? The Left and Labour Market Policy Reform in Britain, France, and Germany

JOCHEN CLASEN AND DANIEL CLEGG

An ambiguity underpins much of the debate about the Third Way and welfare state reform in Europe. It stems from the very different manners in which the term itself is employed and the multiplication of various 'dependent variables' for the Third Way (cf. Bonoli and Powell 2002: 60). The Third Way referred originally to the self-conscious 'rebranding' of the centre-left, as advocated by Tony Blair and some of his close advisers in Britain (Blair 1998; 2003; Giddens 1998). However, in more scholarly debates about welfare states and their reform, the term is also increasingly employed as shorthand for the policy mix perceived to be best suited to reconciling economic performance and social justice in a transformed international economy (Green-Pedersen, et al. 2001; Rhodes 2001; Vandenbroucke 2001). The perhaps unintended consequence of this double usage is the tendency to conflate a particular political *strategy* or *discourse* with the emergence of a specific set of public *policies*, leading to the rarely tested but widespread assumption that the former begets the latter.

The international 'evangelism' (Driver and Martell 2002) of Blair suggests that he, at least, is quite convinced that encouraging the centre-left elsewhere in Europe to be more rhetorically 'centre' and less 'Left' is a prerequisite for the generalization of economically and socially virtuous structural reform. This chapter will subject this claim to closer scrutiny on the crucial empirical terrain of reforms at the interface of the welfare state and the labour market, and in particular around the theme of 'activating' welfare states. The point of departure is the welfare-to-work policy of New Labour, which Blair presents as one of the greatest achievements of Third Way politics (Blair 2003). But how crucial has the centrist discourse of New Labour really been to the promotion of the welfare-to-work agenda in Britain? More importantly, would centre-left parties elsewhere in Europe have progressed further with similar reforms if they had reinvented and repositioned themselves as comprehensively as New Labour? In short, does the Third Way really 'work' as a conduit for a centre-left welfare state reform agenda articulated around work?

The cases of France and Germany offer interesting parallels and contrasts with that of Britain. In all three countries, Left-led governments came to power in the late 1990s, governing simultaneously until the defeat of the French Socialists in the spring 2002 parliamentary elections. In opposition, all three centre-lefts had put a more active response to unemployment at or near the centre of their eventually successful electoral programmes. Their broader discourse while in government differed more significantly, however, with the German Social Democratic Party (SPD) under Schröder vacillating somewhere between the often blunt traditionalism of the French Socialist Party (PS) under Jospin and the strident centrism of New Labour under Blair. Some years down the line, the three governments' records on social welfare and labour market reform are also, as we will discuss, rather different. In the field of activation, the succession of 'New Deal' after 'New Deal' under the first Blair administration contrasts with the near two-year-long wrangle over a seemingly modest activation measure in France during the 'plural left's' tenure. Meanwhile, the SPD in Germany has long appeared to be at best fumbling towards a more coherent activation policy with neither great conviction nor much success. Finally, Britain has the lowest open unemployment for a generation, while French and German rates continue to hover around the 10 per cent mark. The details of these thumbnail sketches of the three cases could probably be arranged to support a causal link between a centrist political discourse, successful labour market and welfare reform, and even the contemporary electoral viability of the Left.

This chapter suggests, however, that the apparent correlation is spurious. Looking more closely at reform dynamics in the three cases principally serves, on the contrary, to demonstrate the limits of the Third Way as a reformist discourse in labour market policy. It is necessary to better appreciate the mediating role played by differing national contexts for the viability of any discursive strategy. Germany and France are usually regrouped within the 'Continental' welfare model (Scharpf and Schmidt 2000; Ferrera et al. 2000). Their 'institutional', middle-class welfare states should be, in principle, more solidly entrenched than Britain's. Equally, the political economies of the two countries are very different from the liberal market economy model of Britain (Hall 2002). Arguably of greatest importance, however—albeit partially correlated with the above variables—are the models of social governance (cf. Ebbinghaus, 2002) that characterize social and labour market policy in the two countries. In France, the otherwise powerful state has historically been reticent to intervene in many domains of social policy, where it has conventionally delegated competencies to social actors (Ashford 1991; Palier 2001). Germany, the original 'semi-sovereign state' (Katzenstein 1987), has paradoxically a little more leverage over social policy, but continues to be characterized by a multi-actor social policy-making framework that has been called 'welfare corporatism' (Streeck 2003).

Patterns of policy-making are in both cases very different from Britain, where social reforms 'are fought out on an ideological front with party leaders manipulating the ideological and moral issues associated with benefit provision' (Daly and Yeats 2003: 95). The rhetorical leverage offered by a Third Way discourse, it is suggested here, is probably limited to those governance contexts that resemble Britain's. In France and Germany, in any event, the Third Way has been at best a sideshow and at worst a hindrance in the more intricate process of crafting reforms in complex governance systems. This is not meant to imply that French and German social democracies have not undergone significant changes in their general position towards labour markets and social policy over time. The modern German SPD, for example, is certainly more market-oriented and more guided by the notion of equality of opportunity (rather than out-come) than it was a few decades ago. However, this process of 'Christian democratization' of social democracy (Seeleib-Kaiser 2002) can be traced back to the 1970s, and needs to be distinguished from the more recent notion of Third Way policy (and politics). The relationship between the latter and more general modernizing trajectories of Lefts elsewhere in Europe is an issue to which we will return in the conclusion.

The chapter up to that point is organized in four sections. Section 1 discusses the actual welfare-to-work reforms of New Labour in Britain, characterizing them as one variant of a broader supply-side agenda for the Left emerging in contemporary Europe. Section 2 argues that New Labour developed its Third Way discourse principally to 'sell' these (and similar) reforms to recalcitrant or sceptical sections of the British public. A causal link, then, can in the British case be made between the Third Way discourse and pragmatic supply-side reforms. Sections 3 and 4 then extend this line of enquiry to the French and German cases respectively, sequentially examining the policies enacted and the political debates that accompanied them in each state. With respect to France, it is shown how the societal interests institutionalized in the governance of social protection tend to act as a bulwark against political intervention of *any* kind in existing arrangements, however it may be justified. Such depoliticization effects at the heart of the social welfare system are somewhat less present in the German case. Here, though, other institutional factors severely limit the potential for the centre-left to either develop a single structuring discourse or to fuse historically separate policy domains, as much of the current activation agenda supposes. To the extent that efforts have advanced in this latter respect, ad hoc exploitation of contingencies and crises has proved more effective than a Third Way discourse.

1. Policies: New Labour's 'Welfare to Work' and the Emergent Supply-Side Agenda for the European Left

In a context of an increasingly integrated economic and financial system and the nearly complete transition to service-based economies, the demand-management policies traditionally employed by many centre-left parties in Europe are widely recognized as ineffective. This realization has seen the European Left begin to converge, albeit haltingly, on an alternative strategy, centred on the supply side of the economy. Space considerations prevent the present chapter from expanding on its details or national variants, which have in any event been documented extensively elsewhere (for example, Esping-Andersen and Regini 2000; Green-Pedersen et al. 2001; Nickell and van Ours 2000; Vandenbroucke 2001; Merkel 2000). The important point is that this agenda accepts increasing labour market flexibility in the interests of employment-rich growth, but seeks—in contrast to neo-liberalism—to preserve an active role for political intervention to correct some of the worst inequities and failures of more deregulated labour markets. This policy agenda has been referred to as 'compensated recommodification' (Pierson 2001) or 'flexibility plus' (Blair 2003).

The Britain inherited by Tony Blair's first administration in 1997 had, after eighteen years of Conservative rule, already travelled much farther down the road of labour market deregulation than any of its European neighbours. It is in part as a result of this legacy that the British model remains more heavily biased in favour of flexibility than most other European states. While New Labour has not attempted to reverse most Thatcherite labour market reforms, many of its best-known policies can be read as an attempt to rebalance flexibility with a bit of 'plus'. A national minimum wage, for example, was introduced, albeit set at a comparatively moderate level and with a lower rate for the young. Labour costs and wages at the bottom end of the labour market have been kept low, but are now subsidized more generously than before, mainly through a new system of tax credits targeted at different groups in low-paying employment. That the number of low-wage families in receipt of tax credits had increased to over 1.2 million by November 2001, a rise of some 67 per cent since 1997 (Brewer et al. 2002: 23), reflects the vastly increased emphasis of the government on 'making work pay' in this manner.

Alongside this, the New Labour governments have progressively developed their various New Deals. These seek to tackle unemployment and labour market exclusion with a mixture of training measures, socially useful work opportunities, and yet more targeted subsidies to private employers. At first reserved for the young unemployed, the New Deals have since been expanded, on differing terms, to other groups of unemployed and, more recently still, to other economically inactive groups such as partners of the unemployed, the disabled, and single parents (for details, see Walker and Wiseman 2003). The financial commitment to these measures is certainly dwarfed by the sums devoted to tax credits: in 2001/2, for example, the government planned to spend £900 million on the former compared with more than £5 billion on the latter (Brewer et al. 2002: 23). UK expenditure on active labour market policy remains, moreover, resolutely low in comparison with most other OECD countries (OECD 2002). The New Deals can nonetheless be related to wider calls for the development of 'active' strategies of 'social investment' which should be, in a context of limited resources, privileged if necessary over the 'passive' measures of income maintenance that have long formed the bulk of social expenditure in Europe. Furthermore, the expansion of the New Deals to groups such as the disabled may suggest the beginning of more serious attempts to tackle the problem of non-employment (see also HM Treasury and DWP 2001), which has been on an upward trend since the 1980s, even in periods of falling unemployment.

Another challenge for the European Left has been to manage the collision of this increasingly flexible—if partially decommodified—labour market with the social security and welfare systems that they did so much to build in the post-war era. As the relative rewards and security offered by work have declined, so the incentive problems potentially posed by the availability of income maintenance have been thrown into sharper relief. In Britain, these problems have been compounded by the massive reliance on means-tested forms of income support for those out of work, which the New Labour governments have done little to reverse directly. Rather, they have preferred to seek to enforce market discipline for recipients of social security, making individual benefit receipt far more conditional than before on active job-search in the normal labour market or offers of special assistance under programmes such as the New Deals. As in other countries, the welfare-to-work agenda of the New Labour governments has involved an increasing number of offers to the unemployed and inactive, both in the formal labour market and (far more modestly) in training or sheltered employment. These, however, are now 'offers they can't refuse' (cf. Lødemel and Trickey 2001).

The so-called activation agenda of the European Left can be characterized as a functional and distributive restructuring of existing social commitments to make these accord with the social risks of the flexible labour market. The functional dimension refers to the attempts to recycle 'passive' expenditures into 'active' social investment measures, often by building employment promotion mechanisms into existing unemployment benefit schemes. The distributive dimension concerns the expressed desire to concentrate a greater share of resources on previously neglected groups, those for whom participation in the flexible labour market carries greatest risks and who are at greatest risk of 'social exclusion'. These two dimensions come together theoretically in what Powell (2001) has characterized as a shift from 'patterned to process-based distributions', in which there is a shift of attention from 'what you are' to 'what you do'. In Britain, they have come together administratively in the development of 'one stop shops' ('ONE', the single work-focused interview), in which all benefit recipients are in principle assessed, counselled, and treated individually according to capacities, situation, and behaviour rather than in terms of their benefit status or other broad categorical traits. Similar trends towards dedifferentiation (for example, the merging of social assistance and unemployment insurance administration) and reindividualization of social security delivery have been seen elsewhere in Europe, for example in the Netherlands (Clasen et al. 2001).

In sum, then, New Labour's welfare-to-work strategy can be seen as a variant of the labour market reform agenda that has been developed more widely, both in other nations' policies and in policy-oriented research. There is certainly some British specificity: a particularly strong emphasis on early job entry, low benefits, and an unusually modest commitment to skill formation. But the range of policy instruments—combinations of social benefits, work subsidies, and labour market programmes, delivered through an integrated administrative structure—are conventional features of the programmes of all those who advocate a pragmatic, supply-side approach to improving social justice under radically changed economic conditions. It arguably owes its notoriety less to its inherent originality than to the aggressive international promotion of the political discourse with which it was 'marketed' domestically: the Third Way.

2. Politics: New Labour's Third Way as Domestic Political Strategy

Always one of the most conventionally Keynesian centre-left parties in Europe, the Labour Party began to update its social and economic programme somewhat later than many of its European homologues. Although Blair's predecessors as Labour leader had successfully achieved a good part of this painful process, it was not until the advent of New Labour that a successful way of promoting it electorally was found. For Thatcherism had also bequeathed a peculiar political context. On the one hand, 'middle England' had become increasingly tax-resistant, and particularly resistant to providing resources to the unemployed and other groups repeatedly characterized as 'undeserving poor'. On the other hand, repeated attacks on the welfare state over the previous eighteen years had if anything galvanized the progressive electorate and their representatives in the Parliamentary Labour Party in defence of social rights. The explicit centrism of New Labour's Third Way should be seen as an attempt to woo the ones without completely alienating the others.

As developed by the Blairite sociologist Anthony Giddens, the Third Way contained clear messages to reassure conservative parts of the electorate who might be concerned even about the limited amount of redistribution towards the unemployed that would be possible within Tory spending limits (albeit supplemented by the one-off windfall tax). Proving that they would be tough on welfare recipients was a ploy New Labour borrowed from Clinton's Democrats (King and Wickham-Jones 1999). To this end, 'no rights without responsibilities' was pencilled in as the first 'rule of thumb' of the Third Way (Giddens 1998: 64). Transposed to practical policies, it meant that 'unemployment benefits, for example, should carry the obligation to look actively for work, and it is up to governments to ensure that welfare systems do not discourage active search' (Giddens 1998: 65). Similarly, Giddens' concept of 'positive welfare' supposed that 'benefit systems should be reformed where they induce moral hazard, and a more active risk-taking attitude encouraged, wherever possible through incentives, but where necessary through legal obligations' (Giddens 1998: 122). In short, the Third Way seemed deliberately to draw attention to, and stress in policy, the inevitable collision of parts of the flexible labour market with the welfare system in an attempt to claim some credit from conservative voters for some functional and distributive restructuring of social protection.

This inevitably risked antagonizing a progressive public opinion that, data suggest, is among the most supportive of unconditional social rights in Europe (Olm et al. 2000: 34–5). In part, New Labour strategists could to a certain extent rely on voters having nowhere else to take their votes in the bipolar British Party system. But to head off the residual potential for voter migration to the Liberal Democrats, the Third Way in any event developed other themes that allowed Blair to claim to 'reunite' liberalism and social democracy (Blair 1998: 1). Giddens's second rule of thumb— 'no authority without democracy'—saw the New Labour project itself as the champion of some radical-sounding and perennially popular political motifs, such as decentralization, devolution, and 'the fostering of an active civil society' (Giddens 1998: 72, 78–9). These reinforce the Third Way's 'claim to stand for political emancipation and a more meaningful form of democracy in terms of involving citizens in the political process' (Schmidtke 2002: 13). Giddens suggested that these general ideas, no less than 'balancing rights and responsibilities', also informed the Third Way agenda of 'positive welfare': 'we should recognise that the reconstruction of welfare provision has to be integrated with programmes for the active development of civil society' (Giddens 1998: 117–18).

In a number of respects, the Third Way has been a relatively useful rhetorical device for New Labour in pursuing its labour market and welfare reform agenda. New Labour's reiteration of the rights and responsibilities discourse seems, on the evidence of social attitudes data, to be reconciling progressive public opinion with more restrictive administrative treatment of the unemployed (Hills 2001), although this effect has probably been strongly mediated by the economic conditions of recent years (Clasen 2000). It may also, simultaneously, have played a role in persuading more conservative voters of the acceptability of the moderately redistributive policies New Labour has implemented since 1997. On the other hand, it is far from clear that this latter effect could ever stretch to legitimizing the more significant transfer of resources to the unemployed and inactive that would be the condition for a more skill-based labour market policy.

Nor, it should be noted, has the Third Way really been asked to help in promoting a genuinely radical institutional reform agenda in Britain. Most aspects of the positive welfare agenda related to Giddens's second 'rule of thumb' have been quietly ignored, at least as they could apply to the domain of labour market and welfare policy. There has been no decentralization of social security; indeed, it can be argued that centralization has increased in this policy area under New Labour (Daly and Yeats 2003: 95). Nor has there been any serious attempt to use welfare provision or labour market policy to 'develop civil society'.[1] This is not least, no doubt, because such efforts would interfere with the pursuit and implementation of the government's more substantive policy aims. A job-entry centred, administratively integrated welfare-to-work policy works largely with the grain of the existing centralized institutional set-up of social protection, and has

---

[1] The story in other social policy sectors is perhaps more complex. In health care, for example, the battle between those interested in promoting self-management in hospitals and those interested in performance and cost-effectiveness is still being waged within New Labour. In Britain, these conflicts serve to highlight some of the contradictions of the Third Way that might otherwise, in the absence of a comparative perspective, remain submerged.

benefited from there being 'few alliances, social pacts and social partners to stand in the way' of government projects (Bonoli and Powell 2002: 64). The very absence of collective social actors from the social welfare arena explains, furthermore, why the political debate over these issues tends in Britain to be reduced to a 'partisan-adversarial' conflict in which context, ironically, a well-deployed centrist discourse can appear (fleetingly) radical and create some (temporary) margins for manoeuvre.

Giddens states in the introduction to his 1998 essay that he conceptualizes the Third Way as an attempt to put 'theoretical flesh' on the bones of already existing centre-left policy programmes, to 'endorse what they are doing', and to 'provide politics with a greater sense of purpose' (Giddens 1998: 2). To criticize the Third Way as an *ex post* legitimization strategy thus seems rather to miss the point. A more telling question is whether it is a *useful* and *coherent* legitimization strategy for welfare and labour market reform. The British experience might suggest that its utility—convincing public opinion of the probity of New Labour's policies—was real, but only because its coherence was never, in the highly centralized British policy context, rigorously tested. The implicit counterfactual on which this argument rests suggests a need to consider whether the Third Way was or could have been an 'endorsement' of governments endeavouring to craft similar reforms in quite different contexts.

3. The Left, Labour Market Policies, and Politics in France

Policies

The 'plural left' coalition, headed by Jospin's PS, was returned by the French electorate in May 1997, a month after New Labour's accession to power. Comparisons between the two parties and their policies were thus inevitable, and tended to oppose Blair 'the modernizer' to Jospin 'the traditionalist'. It has been widely argued that the PS has a quite different vision of 'modernization' from New Labour (for example, Clift 2001). When in office, Jospin himself said so (Jospin 1999), and proudly pointed to 'the most left-wing policies of any western democracy' (Jospin 2001).

Some of the labour market policies implemented by the coalition in government (1997–2002) do support this. The so-called law on social modernization, which *inter alia* greatly increased the cost and difficulty of redundancies in larger firms and placed stricter limits on the use of 'precarious' employment contracts, is perhaps the best example of a policy diametrically opposed to the strictures of 'flexibility plus'. Better known still are the laws on the reduction of working time (*les 35 heures*) and a programme for the creation of 350,000 jobs for young people in the public and para-public sectors (*les emplois jeunes*). Although each of these policies was conceived as a response to unemployment, each was in many respects out of step with the broader centre-left supply-side agenda, the former because it greatly increased the burdens on business and the latter because it expanded the scope of the public sector.

The '35-hours' and the *emplois jeunes* programme, however, did have features that at least nodded to the supply-side agenda pursued elsewhere. The former, for example, was premised upon a significant generalization of the subsidization of employers' social contributions which had been developed by earlier French governments, of both Left and Right, from the late 1980s. It was intended, furthermore, that a transfer of contributions from the unemployment insurance scheme finance these subsidies, thereby putting expenditure otherwise earmarked for 'passive' use (unemployment benefits) to a more 'active' purpose (effective reduction of the marginal cost of labour). As for the *emplois jeunes*, they generalized fixed-term (five-year) contracts in the public sector, and were widely suspected of being a way of reducing the number of tenured *fonctionnaires*. For the more irascible critics, they were even seen as 'a weapon of war against the status of civil servants' (Collin and Cotta 2001: 24).

Furthermore, the Jospin government's policies contributed to what can be seen as a French variant of British-style activation (Clasen and Clegg 2003). Although the *emplois jeunes* were not compulsory for unemployed young people, this must be seen in the context of the near-absence of any formal unemployment *or* social assistance for the under-25s in France (cf. Enjorlas et al. 2001). The fact that they were implicitly intended as an alternative, and not a complement, to benefit receipt can be seen in their extension to unemployed 25–28-year-olds not eligible for unemployment benefits. When the unemployed mobilized in the winters of 1997 and 1998 to protest against the absence of minimum income protection for young people and other marginal groups in the labour market, Jospin responded that he wanted 'a society of work and not a society of assistance'. Similarly, the 1998 'law on exclusions' explicitly resisted calls to extend the minimum income programme to the under-25s, concentrating instead on measures to ease the transition into work for current recipients by reducing rates of benefit withdrawal. 'Making work pay' more than inactivity was also behind the Socialists' introduction of an in-work tax credit, the *prime pour l'emploi*. At the same time, though, it was designed in such a way as to avoid subsidizing 'very' part-time work, thus expressing a somewhat critical perspective as to excessive flexibilization of the labour market and a strong emphasis on 'quality in work' (Coron and Palier 2002: 126–30).

There thus seems to have been a certain ambiguity in the attitude of the French Socialists to the supply-side labour market reform agenda. Their stance on the reform of unemployment insurance provides the single best example of this. Jospin himself had argued that the activation of unemployment benefits was necessary as far back as his 1995 presidential election manifesto (Jospin 1995: 19). It was under the Socialist-led coalition that the main unemployment insurance benefit was renamed the 'return to work' benefit (*allocation de retour à l'emploi*, ARE), and its full receipt made conditional on the signature of an individual return to work plan (*plan d'aide au retour à l'emploi*, PARE). At the same time, though, the reform in question, which had been negotiated between the social partners, was long opposed by the government, and agreed by them only in a considerably watered down version. The reason is that there was more at stake in the reform proposal than the treatment of the unemployed alone. The politics of this reform, in fact, offers a valuable perspective on the difficulties of supply-side reform for the centre-left in France and the role a Third Way discourse could play in this context.

Politics

It could be imagined that being in coalition with parties to their left, including Communists, would have been the major constraint on the PS in negotiating a reform of a public policy as ideologically charged as unemployment benefit. What was arguably at stake, however, in the seven-month tussle over activation of unemployment policy was not activation itself but rather the respective role of the state and the social partners in controlling this public policy. Certainly, the employers' confederation, the *Mouvement des Entreprises de France* (Medef), which was responsible for launching the reform, had at first argued that they were more interested in ends than in means. But the reform was, much like the supply-side agenda in the Third Way, framed as part of a much broader 'social reconstruction' (*refondation sociale*) that sought to define a new substantive and procedural basis for the French welfare state. As this whole programme was conceived by the Medef as a rebuke to the government after their anger at the 35-hours, it was somewhat over-determined that the procedural settlement they proposed would leave little role for the state.

This had considerable implications for the way they developed their propositions for activating unemployment benefits. In France, the social partners have always managed unemployment insurance on a bipartite basis, while the public employment service is under state control. In this governance context, the principal obstacle to activation policies in France has long been the jealous defence of institutional prerogatives by the respective parties. But rather than suggesting a negotiated redefinition of roles, the activation policy the Medef proposed was instead premised on a maintenance and even reinforcement of the autonomy of the unemployment insurance system from the state. If there was to be greater functional integration between unemployment benefit policy and labour market policy, it would be on the basis of the administrative council of the unemployment insurance system—a formally private institution—having a greater say in the operation of the public employment service, as well as being free to dispose of any financial savings that might result. The government's steering capacity and margin of manoeuvre in labour market policy would thus be further circumscribed rather than enhanced.

It was almost certainly on these grounds rather than out of principled opposition to activation that the government at first objected to the reform. If they didn't say so openly, it was probably less to do with the PCF than because openly challenging the autonomy of social insurance from the state would have been politically risky. Across the political spectrum, there is widespread (if rhetorical) agreement that reducing the role of the state in social and economic life is the key to France's modernization. This ties in to a wider obsession, also cutting across political cleavages, with reinvigorating civil society that draws on a critical reading of the peculiar history of state–society relations in France (Laborde 2000). Even on the Left, many would concur with conservative President Chirac's judgement that the nationalization (*étatisation*) of unemployment insurance would be 'an extraordinary step backward' (Chirac 2000). The *Confédération Française Démocratique des Travailleurs* (CFDT) union had, after all, been driven to embrace the Medef's social reconstruction precisely because of the 'affront' of the government in suggesting that contributions to the unemployment insurance system might be recycled into the financing of the '35-hours' (see above). It was mainly to placate this constituency that the PS was ultimately forced to accept a watered down version of the reform, which allowed everyone to save face but ultimately did little for a more genuinely coherent activation policy.

The CFDT is the standard bearer of the so-called second Left (*deuxieme gauche*), widely perceived to be the 'modernizers' on the French Left and, as such, in the words of Bouvet and Michel (2001: 25), 'the group closest to the Third Way position advocated by Tony Blair'. This observation underscores perfectly why the self-consciously centrist discourse of the Third Way would have been of so little use to Jospin in taking the lead on a more satisfactory unemployment insurance reform, even if he had chosen to adopt it. In France, themes like 'fostering the active development of civil society' cannot be used lightly, for they reinforce those who are simply opposed to political intervention—for whatever ends—in domains like unemployment insurance, where the social partners have carved out a real, if somewhat precarious, autonomy. In this context, moreover, the theme of 'balancing rights and responsibilities' is strictly redundant, as many social rights (and responsibilities) are not even seen to be the proper business of politicians.

It was suggested that the abortive reform of unemployment insurance was symptomatic of the broader political difficulties facing the PS in developing a strong supply-side agenda for labour market policy. It is probably more accurate to see it as being at or near the centre of a vicious circle. While the inability for a government of the Left (or, indeed, the Right) to intervene legitimately and effectively in domains such as unemployment insurance doesn't at first glance explain their extremely interventionist policies of, say, working-time reduction or 'taxing' redundancies, on closer inspection these phenomena are plausibly linked. For the heaping of social functions on to the economy is far more explicable when it is politically impossible to adapt 'the social' to changing economic conditions. The more French governments intervene in the economy, the more social actors defend their role in the social security system, requiring the government—if it wants to have any strong policy at all—to intervene once more in the economy. Hardly an economically and socially virtuous spiral, the Socialists' electoral debacle in 2002 suggests that it is far from politically optimal for the centre-left either. But when the knot of political strategy, social security, and the economy is this involved, it would certainly take rather more than the one-size-fits-all solutions of the Third Way to cut through it.

4. The Left, Labour Market Policies, and Politics in Germany

Policies

The SPD was elected at the head of a governing coalition in 1998. Since that time, there have been frequent changes to German labour market policy, in some contrast to the perceived immobility of the German welfare state. In an initial period, policies owed more to the demand-side agenda pursued to an extent in France than the supply-side agenda pursued by New Labour. Job-creation schemes were expanded, especially in eastern Germany, while the protection of workers in the formal economy was reinforced. Gradually, however, policies have moved towards a supply-side orientation, with an increasing emphasis on raising the employability of job-seekers and the structural reform of benefits and labour market administration (cf. Blancke and Schmid 2003; Heinelt 2003).

The notion of the need to shift from an 'active' to an 'activating' labour market policy developed gradually in the early period of the Schröder government's tenure, emanating not from the government itself but rather from the 'benchmarking' group which was attached to the corporatist Alliance for Jobs (*Bündnis für Arbeit*). This group was responsible for coining the idea that labour market policy must 'promote and oblige' (*fördern und fordern*), which can be seen as an equivalent of the 'rights and responsibilities' concept of the Third Way. Although many of their more specific proposals were rather too controversial to be implemented, a certain number—individual labour market reintegration agreements, promoting temporary jobs, and short-term training courses—did find their way into the 'Job-Aqtiv' Act implemented in January 2002.

More controversial measures were, however, proposed by a commission which was set up to investigate the reform of labour market policy and particularly the role of the Federal Labour Office (BA). In the run-up to the general election in autumn 2002, the left-wing coalition (and indeed the conservative opposition) pledged to fully implement the proposals of the commission, and after its narrow electoral victory the Hartz Recommendations—named after the chairman of the commission—were introduced in January 2003. These aimed mainly at organizational changes intended to make placement and labour market services more effective, to promote private job services, and to facilitate small-business start-ups. There were some moves towards promoting the development of a network of 'one-stop-shops' for all working-age benefit claimants, while geographical and suitable work-related aspects of job-search rules were more strictly defined (Schmid 2003).

While none of the above measures altered benefit structures or benefit entitlement, this will change in due course as a result of Schröder's so-called Agenda 2010. Against stubbornly high unemployment and low growth, this latest government proposal was passed by Parliament in October 2003, but only after some concessions had been made by the SPD leadership in order to secure a parliamentary majority for the ruling red–green coalition. These concessions, made to the Left of the party, would apply to recipients of means-tested unemployment benefit (guaranteeing minimum wage rates for job seekers, making the means test less extensive, and allowing higher disregards for retirement savings). However in December 2003 all of the concessions were removed again in response to the position of the CDU/CSU and their solid majority within the second chamber (*Bundesrat*). The most substantial change brought about by the reform will be the merging of general social assistance and unemployment assistance into a new 'unemployment benefit II' in 2005 which, in principle, has been welcomed by all major parties. For the vast majority of current claimants of unemployment assistance this would represent a substantial decline of income maintenance and a shift towards a stronger benefit activation approach. Furthermore, the maximum duration of first-tier unemployment insurance benefits will be reduced from thirty-two months currently (for older claimants with long contribution records) to twelve months for most claimants, and eighteen for those over fifty-five. In his speech to Parliament in March 2003, Schröder claimed that this 'is the only way to both improve the incentive to take up employment and also be able to reduce non-wage labour costs'.

Politics

When Schröder came to power, his first step was to reinvigorate the corporatist Alliance for Jobs that, as mentioned above, was responsible for some of the proposals that would eventually find their way into the Job-Aqtiv legislation. The Alliance had in fact been set up under the previous Christian Democratic government, and broke down only when Kohl started pursuing more aggressively liberal policies from around 1997 (Busch and Manow 2001: 182). This shows how in Germany there is an expectation that labour market policy should emerge from a somewhat more complex, multi-actor process of political exchange than the simple British-style face-off between elected governments and public opinion. As the stalling of negotiations and eventual collapse of the alliance (under both Kohl and Schröder) also shows, this expectation places considerable constraints upon the ease with which radical reforms can be formulated and implemented (Hassel 2001).

The institutionalization of existing social protection and labour market policy adds to the difficulties of pursuing a coherent supply-side reform agenda. Vocational training and employee relations fall within the consti-tutionally guaranteed sphere of collective labour relations. As Wood (2001) has demonstrated, preserving the autonomy of this system has often led employers to resist statutory intervention, even if it is in the name of enhanced flexibility. The German social insurance system is cer-tainly less autonomous from the state than unemployment insurance in France, but nonetheless integrates non-state actors into its administration, whose consent must therefore be secured for significant reforms. The BA was long organised on a similar tripartite basis, underpinned by a widely accepted principle of auto-administration (*Selbstverwaltung*). When the Hartz Commission proposed increasing the government's control over the BA to help promote a more coherent and ostensibly 'liberal' supply-side policy, this idea was resisted not only by the unions but also by the employers (Rehfeldt 2002: 132–3).

Another problem is that certain social policies (notably social assistance) have traditionally been under the financial and administrative control of local government, and their administrative integration with contribution-financed or federal state-financed measures raises thorny issues regarding the repartition of the financial benefits and burdens of any such reform. As constraining legislation must be approved by the upper house, 'veto players' can use their influence to block measures that go against their interests. It is plausibly for this reason that, although cooperation between social assistance offices and employment services has long been promoted, it has until recently remained something that local offices are free to negotiate on an ad hoc basis with each other rather than being systematically enforced (Clasen et al. 2001: 7).

The complexity of the German reform context also derives from the nature of the party system and its interaction with the layered institutional structure of the German polity. It has been pointed out that one of the reasons that the German SPD failed to reinvent itself more comprehensively while in opposition at federal level was that it remained in power at *Land* level (Busch and Manow 2001). The federal structure of the German state not only makes the costs of failure in national elections less high for political parties but also fosters heterogeneous interests within them. The differences between Schröder and his former finance minister Oskar Lafontaine were far more starkly ideological than any conflicts close to the centre of gravity of New Labour. With respect to labour market policy specifically, a 2001 report by a working group (*Projektguppe 'Zukunft der Arbeit'*) highlighted the SPD's internal divisions perfectly. In this, 'traditionalists' advocated the further development of a 'second labour market', while 'modernizers' emphasized the need for more placement, training, and initiative on the part of job-seekers themselves to find unsubsidized employment in the normal labour market (Heinelt 2003). The Christian Democrats, too, are internally differentiated, with a long prominent social wing as well as a more conventionally liberal business wing (Wood 2001: 392). Elements from within the Christian Democrats—notably Horst Seehofer, a former social affairs minister—were reported to be opposed to certain propositions made by the Hartz Commission for being too liberal (Rehfeldt 2002: 133). A social democratic party that adopts a more centrist discourse is unlikely to reap as much electoral benefit in this context as in the more polarized British one.

Given these contextual conditions, it might seem all the more surprising that Schröder actually *did* endeavour to develop an explicitly centrist discourse and strategy, which he referred to as the 'new middle' (*Neue Mitte*). He even went as far as jointly publishing a paper on centre-left politics in Europe with Tony Blair (Blair and Schröder 1999). But the papers reception was predictably, much cooler in Germany than in Britain. Schröder's new middle was fiercely contested and remains highly controversial long after the heated, but brief, discussion it provoked (Jeffrey and Handl 1999). Whereas in Britain the Third Way was a rhetoric with which Blair could sell his domestic policies, in the German context it more likely inflamed opposition to current and ongoing changes. It no doubt played, however, a subtler agenda-setting role by propagating certain ideas and themes that could be attached to more radical policy ideas in the future.

For the present, though, contingency and crisis (persistently high levels of unemployment, low economic growth, soaring public deficits) appear to be better allies to would-be reformers in Germany than a discourse like the Third Way. Contingencies such as the scandal surrounding the misrepresentation of placement figures at the BA in early 2002—which gave rise to the Hartz Commission—can be exploited to float policy reforms which are difficult to place on the agenda at other times. More recently, the gloom surrounding the economic situation in Germany has rendered radical reform proposals possible, as with the current Agenda 2010, whereas the improving economic situation in the first part of the first Schröder government probably acted as a brake on reform (Blancke and Schmid 2003). In the current environment, themes such as the immediate need to reduce non-wage labour costs or to reduce Germany's budget deficit are more plausible points of consensus than calls for an ideological *aggiornamento*.

5. Conclusions

Reforms at the frontier of the welfare state and the labour market that have been pursued by recent or current centre-left governments in Britain, France, and Germany are less dissimilar than their political rhetoric would often suggest. All have sought to recast the work–welfare interface in the pursuit of a renewed balance between economic dynamism and social justice, in response to a common set of changes in the environment of the contemporary welfare state. The changes are sometimes overstated, but some very real developments do oblige centre-left parties to adapt their policy programmes. The transition from an industrial to a service economy, and the accompanying need for flexibility to ensure that this transition is compatible with high rates of employment, are trends that go beyond national borders. So too are processes of population ageing, which drive governments, including those of the centre-left, to think increasingly about how to optimize the utilization of the potentially active population or at least minimize its flagrant under-utilization. As has been pointed out before (Bonoli and Powell 2002; Hall 2002), though, it is inevitable that the efforts and preferred policy paths of social democratic parties in different countries will be mediated by distinctive institutional legacies and political economy traditions.

In this spirit, the different policies pursued by the British, French, and German centre-left have sometimes been presented as local *variants* of a broader Third Way (Hall 2002). This, however, only perpetuates the conflation of particular policies and a particular style of political discourse and, ultimately, unduly dignifies the proselytizing tendencies of the current British administration. Promoting the Third Way abroad may serve Blair's international and European ambitions well but, this chapter has suggested, does not necessarily do much to help the centre-left elsewhere in Europe as it grapples with difficult reforms. Though some manifestly progressive reforms have not been adopted in France or Germany, this is not because of the ideological blinkers or the ignorance of their centre-left parties. It is rather because it is simply more difficult politically to recast social compromises that, in countries like France and Germany, are far more complex and institutionalized than in Britain. In such contexts, a Third Way political discourse may ideologically antagonize opponents of reform, reinforce the legitimacy of the status quo, or both.

This chapter has particularly emphasized the role played by different models of governance in determining both the viability and the helpfulness of a Third Way discourse in contemporary welfare and labour market reform. In the British governance context such a discourse is both viable, because it is expected that governments will take a lead in the development of social policy, and to an extent helpful, because it can play a role in cementing an at least temporary coalition behind supply-side labour market reform. In the French or German context it is far less viable, because it is not generally expected or approved of that elected governments will go over the heads of established policy-making partners in an appeal to public opinion. Nor, in any case, would it be likely to be helpful. The Third Way's utility to Blair in Britain seems to have been in broadening the appeal of essentially pragmatic policies by simultaneously paying lip-service to the more radical-sounding ideas of decentralization or of debureaucratization. But in the governance context of the French and German welfare states—long characterized by an elaborate interweaving of the public and the private, and in which the key to reform appears to be enhancing the autonomy of elected governments to act in the social sphere (cf. Jobert 1996; Palier 2001; Streeck 2003)—such a discourse can only be counter-productive. To the extent that the centre-left in these countries has long been pursuing a particular brand of centrism—as the idea of the 'Christian Democratization' of social democracy in Germany and elsewhere suggests (for example, Seeleib-Kaiser 2002; see also Navarro 1999)— then the real challenge is probably not to justify the principle of a more active labour market policy but to legitimize the statism on which its more coherent development and deployment depends.

Schmidt (2002) has argued that the careful exploitation of discourse can play a role in promoting progressive reform, but also that different discourses are needed in different contexts. We should therefore not expect very structurally different welfare states to be responsive to the same political rhetoric. This is all the more true if one of the key dimensions of welfare state variation is precisely their degree of embeddedness and depoliticization or, inversely, of vulnerability to political conflict. Accordingly, aggressively promoting a single reform discourse in very different contexts is likely to be of little help in promoting policy convergence, and may even inadvertently have the opposite effect. Only analysis that is sensitive to the institutional differences between welfare states, to the diversity of their ideological embeddedness, and to their variable links to party politics can hope to identify the differing roads to centre-left modernization in general and more precisely to the various context-specific recipes for the development of a coherent and virtuous social and labour market policy for the centre-left.

References

Ashford, D. (1991). 'In search of the *Etat providence*', in J. Hollifield and G. Ross (eds.), *Searching for the New France*. New York: Routledge.

Blair, T. (1998). *The Third Way: New Politics for a New Century*. London: Fabian Society.

—— (2003). 'Where the Third Way Goes from Here'. Launch speech at the Progressive Governance Conference, www.progressive-governance.net/php/article.php?sid=9&aid=35

—— and Schröder, G. (1999). *Europe: The Third Way/Die Neue Mitte*. London: Labour Party.

Blancke, S. and Schmid, G. (2003). 'Bilanz der Bunderegierung im Bereich der Arbeitsmarktpolitik 1998–2002: Ansätze zu einer doppelten Wende', in C. Egle, T. Ostheim, and R. Zohlnhöfer (eds.), *Das rot-grüne Projekt: Eine Bilanz der Regierung Schröder 1998–2002*. Wiesbaden: Westdeutscher Verlag.

Bonoli, G. and Powell, M. (2002). 'Third Ways in Europe?', *Social Policy and Society*, 1/1: 59–66.

Bouvet, L. and Michel, F. (2001). '"La gauche plurielle": An Alternative to the Third Way?', in S. White (ed.), *New Labour: The Progressive Future?* Houndmills: Palgrave.

Brewer, M., Clark, T., and Wakefield, M. (2002). *Five Years of Social Security Reform in the UK* (Working Paper WP02/12). London: Institute for Fiscal Studies.

Busch, A. and Manow, P. (2001). 'The SPD and the Neue Mitte in Germany', in S. White (ed.), *New Labour: The Progressive Future?* Houndmills: Palgrave.

Chirac, J. (2000). *Le Monde*, 16 July, p. 8.

Clasen, J. (2000). 'Motives, Means and Opportunities: Reforming Unemployment Compensation in the 1990s', in M. Ferrera and M. Rhodes, (eds.), *Recasting European Welfare States*. London: Frank Cass.

—— and Clegg, D. (2003). 'Unemployment Protection and Labour Market Reform in France and Great Britain in the 1990s: Solidarity versus Activation?', *Journal of Social Policy*, 32: 361–81.

—— Duncan, G., Eardley, T., Evans, M., Ughetto, P., van Oorschot, W., and Wright, S. (2001). 'Towards "Single Gateways"—A Cross-National Review of the Changing Roles of Employment Offices in Seven Countries', *Zeitschrift für ausländisches und internationales Arbeits- und Sozialrecht*, 15/1: 43–63.

Clift, B. (2001). 'Jospin's Alternative to the Third Way', *Political Quarterly*, 72/2: 170–9.

Collin, D. and Cotta, J. (2001). *L'Illusion plurielle*. Paris: JC Lattes.

Coron, G. and Palier, B. (2002). 'Changes in the Means of Financing Social Expenditure in France since 1945', in C. de la Porte and P. Pochet (eds.), *Building Social Europe through the Open Method of Co-ordination*. Brussels: Peter Lang.

Daly, M. and Yeats, N. (2003). 'Common Origins, Different Paths: Adaptation and Change in Social Security in Britain and Ireland', *Policy and Politics*, 31/1: 85–97.

Driver, S. and Martell, L. (2003). 'Third Ways in Britain and Europe', in O. Schmidtke (ed.), *The Third Way Transformation of Social Democracy*. Aldershot: Ashgate.

Ebbinghaus, B. (2002). 'Varieties of social governance: Comparing the Social Partners' Involvement in Pension and Employment Policies', Max Planck Institute for the Study of Societies Working Paper. Cologne: MPIfG.

Enjorlas, B., Laville, J.-L., Fraisse, L., and Trickey, H. (2001). 'Between Subsidiarity and Social Assistance—The French Republican Route to Activation', in I. Lødemel and H. Trickey (eds.), *An Offer You Can't Refuse—Workfare in International Perspective*. Bristol: Policy Press.

Esping-Andersen, G. and Regini, M. (eds.) (2000). *Why Deregulate Labour Markets?* Oxford: Oxford University Press.

Ferrera, M., Hemerijk, A., and Rhodes, M. (2000). 'Recasting European Welfare States for the 21st Century', *European Review*, 8: 427–46.

Giddens, A. (1998). *The Third Way: The Renewal of Social Democracy*. Cambridge: Polity Press.

Green-Pedersen, C., Hemerijck, A., and Van Keesbergen, K. (2001). 'Neo-liberalism, Third Way or What?', *Journal of European Public Policy*, 8: 307–25.

Hall, P. (2002). 'The comparative political economy of the "third way" ', in Schmidtke, O. (ed.) *The Third Way Transformation of Social Democracy*. Aldershot: Ashgate.

Hassel, A. (2001). 'The Problem of Political Exchange in Complex Governance Systems: The Case of Germany's Alliance for Jobs', *European Journal of Industrial Relations*, 7: 307–26.

Heinelt, H. (2003). 'Abeitmarktpolitik—von "versorgenden" wohlfahrsstaatlichen Interventionen zur "aktivierenden" Beschäftigungsförderung', in A. Gohr and M. Seeleib-Kaiser (eds.), *Sozialpolitik unter Rot-Grün*. Wiesbaden: Westdeutscher Verlag.

Hills, J. (2001). 'Poverty and Social Security: What Rights? Whose Responsibilities?', in A. Park et al. (eds.), *British Social Attitudes: Public Policies, Social Ties*. London: Sage.

HM Treasury and DWP (2001). *The Changing Welfare State: Employment Opportunity for All*. London: HM Treasury/Department for Work and Pensions.

Jeffery, C. and Handl, V. (1999). 'Blair, Schröder and the Third Way', in L. Funk (ed.), *The Economics and Politics of the Third Way: Essays in Honour of Eric Owen Smith*. Münster: Lit Verlag.

Jobert, B. (1996). 'Le retour tâtonnant de l'Etat', in F. d'Arcy and F. Rouban (eds.), *De la Ve République à l'Europe*. Paris: Presses de Sciences Po.

Jospin, L. (1995). *1995–2000: Propositions pour la France*. Paris: Stock.

——— (1999). *Modern Socialism*. London: Fabian Society.

——— (2001). *Le Monde*, 12 June, p. 1.

Katzenstein, P. (1987). *Policy and Politics in West Germany: The Growth of a Semisovereign State*. Philadelphia: Temple University Press.

King, D. and Wickham-Jones, M. (1999). 'From Clinton to Blair: The Democratic (Party) Origins of Welfare to Work', *Political Quarterly*, 70/1: 62–74.

Laborde, C. (2000). 'The Concept of the State in British and French Political Thought', *Political Studies*, 48: 544–57.

Lødemel, I. and Trickey, H. (2000). *An Offer You Can't Refuse: Workfare in Comparative Perspective*. Bristol: Policy Press.

Merkel, W. (2000). 'Die dritten Wege der Sozialdemokratie ins 21. Jahrhundert', *Berliner Zeitschrift für Soziologie*, 10: 99–124.

Navarro, V. (1999). 'Is There a Third Way? A Response to Giddens' "The Third Way"', *International Journal of Health Services*, 29: 667–77.

Nickell, S. and van Ours, J. (2000). 'Falling Unemployment: The Dutch and British Cases', *Economic Policy*, April: 137–80.

OECD (Organization for Economic Cooperation and Development) (2002). *Employment Outlook 2002*. Paris: OECD.

Olm, C., Le Queau, P., and Simon, M-O. (2000). *La perception de la pauvreté en Europe* (Cahier de Recherche no. 144). Paris: Credoc.

Palier, B.(2001). 'Reshaping the Social Policy-Making Framework in France', in P. Taylor-Gooby (ed.), *Welfare States under Pressure*. London: Sage.

Pierson, P. (2001). 'Coping with Permanent Austerity: Welfare Restructuring in Affluent Democracies', in P. Pierson (ed.), *The New Politics of the Welfare State*. Oxford: Oxford University Press.

Powell, M. (2001). 'Third Ways in Europe: Concepts, Policies, Causes and Roots'. Paper presented to 29th ECPR Joint Sessions. Grenoble, 6–11 April.

Rhefeldt, U. (2002). 'Allemagne: Une réforme radicale de la politique de l'emploi avec consentement syndical', *Chronique Internationale de l'IRES*, 78: 129–41.

Rhodes, M. (2001). 'Globalization, Welfare States and Employment: Is There a European Third Way?', in N. Bermeo (ed.), *Unemployment in the New Europe*. Cambridge: Cambridge University Press.

Scharpf, F. and Schmidt, V. (2000). *From Vulnerability to Competitiveness: Welfare and Work in the Open Economy*. Oxford: Oxford University Press.

Schmid, G. (2003). *Moderne Dienstleistungen am Arbeitsmarkt: Strategie und Vorschläge der Hartz-Kommission, Aus Politik und Zeitgeschichte*, 3B6–7. Bonn: Bundeszentrale für politische Bildung.

Schmidt, V. (2002). *The Futures of European Capitalism*. Oxford: Oxford University Press.

Schmidtke, O. (2002). 'Transforming the Social Democratic Left: The Challenges to Third Way Politics in an Age of Globalisation', in O. Schmidtke (ed.), *The Third Way Transformation of Social Democracy*. Aldershot: Ashgate.

Seeleib-Kaiser, M. (2002). 'Neubeginn oder Ende der Sozialdemokratie? Eine Untersuchung zur programmatischen Reform sozialdemokratischer Parteien und ihrer Auswirkung auf die Parteiendifferenzthese', *Politische Vierteljahresschrift*, 43: 478–96.

Streeck, W. (2003). *From State Weakness as Strength to State Weakness as Weakness: Welfare Corporatism and the Private Use of the Public Interest*. Max Planck Institute for the Study of Societies Working Paper 03/2, Cologne: MPIfG.

Vandenbroucke, F. (2001). 'European Social Democracy and the Third Way', in S. White (ed.), *New Labour: The Progressive Future?* Houndmills: Palgrave.

Walker, R. and Wiseman, M. (2003). 'Making Welfare Work: UK Activation Policies under New Labour', *International Social Security Review*, 56: 3–29.

Wood, S. (2001). 'Labour Market Regimes Under Threat? Sources of Continuity in Germany, Britain and Sweden', in P. Pierson (ed.), *The New Politics of the Welfare State*. Oxford: Oxford University Press.

6

Third Sector–Third Way: Comparative Perspectives and Policy Reflections

HELMUT ANHEIER

The purpose of this chapter is to present a comparative overview of non-profit or third-sector organizations in the context of welfare policies and the wider civil society of which they are a part. In doing so, we will address the social, economic, and political developments that have made this set of institutions more central to policy debates in developed market economies, and particularly as providers of health, social, educational, and cultural services of many kinds. Of special interest throughout is the role of the non-profit, voluntary, or third sector (used synonymously) in a broad policy framework of what has come to be known as the Third Way. Indeed, in contrast to both neo-liberal policy approaches and traditional social democratic policies, Third Way thinking pays the greatest and most systematic attention to the third sector. To explore what this attention means for the voluntary sector, and how possible implications might differ from other policy scenarios, is the main objective of this chapter.

The Third Way rose to prominence in the mid- to late 1990s, with a succession of influential speeches, pamphlets, and books (see Blair 1998; Giddens 1998; The White House 1999; Blair and Schroeder 1999), and political successes in the US, the United Kingdom, Germany, France, Italy, and the Netherlands. While some of these successes were cut short when conservative politicians came to power (United States, France, Italy, the Netherlands), the influence of the Third Way continues, despite much criticism (see review by Giddens 2000), in large measure because it is the only major ideological challenger to neo-liberal policies.

At the same time, it is difficult to identify what the Third Way is, in particular its ideological core. In many ways, it is still an emerging political vision to modernize 'old-style social democracy' that rested on solidarity and state-led welfare, and seeks to develop a comprehensive framework for a renewal of both state and society to counteract neo-liberal policies that are regarded as socially blind, simplistic, and unsustainable. The Third Way calls for decentralized forms of government based on transparency, efficient administration, more opportunities for direct democracy, and an environmentally friendly economy. The role of the state changes from welfare provider to risk manager and enabler—a fundamental redefinition from the social democratic welfare state, and one that is complemented by a change in the notion of citizenship that stresses individual rights and responsibilities alike (Giddens 2000; Mulgan 2000).

The Third Way foresees a reorganization of the state that requires a renewal and activation of civil society, social participation, the encouragement of social entrepreneurship, and new approaches to public–private partnerships in the provision of public goods and services. Specifically, the framework involves a renewal of political institutions to encourage greater citizen participation; a new relationship between government and civil society that involves an engaged government as well as a vibrant set of voluntary associations of many kinds; a wider role for busineses as socially and environmentally responsible institutions; and a structural reform of the welfare state away from 'entitlement' towards risk management (Giddens 1998, 2000).

Clearly, the Third Way and the third sector are in close policy vicinity of each other, especially in the areas of civil society and welfare reform. In Tony Blair's words, a 'key challenge of progressive politics is to use the state as an enabling force, protecting effective communities and voluntary associations and encouraging their growth to tackle new needs, in partnership if appropriate' (Blair 1998: 4). Mulgan (2000: 18) is explicit in spelling out the principles that guide Third Way policies toward the voluntary sector:

First, a good society is founded on a balance between the interests of business, government and the voluntary sector. Second, institutions of the third sector are insulated from the immediate pressures of the market and electoral democracy and are, therefore, not only able to identify and anticipate needs, but also to act as guardians of much longer-term value. Third, institutions of the third sector can play a crucial role in fostering habits of responsibility and cultures of co-operation, self-control and self-expression.

The clearest policy expression of the relationship between government and third sector in Third Way policies comes in the form of the Compact (Home Office 1998). It is a common platform which rests on four principles:

1. an independent voluntary sector with its own agenda is good for society;
2. government and the voluntary sector have complementary roles in delivering social services;
3. there is added value in public–private partnership; and

4. government and the voluntary sector have different forms of accountability but similar values and commitments to public benefit.

How does the policy programme envisioned by the Third Way line up
with third-sector realities and changes in developed market economies?

As we will see, the answer to this question is at first perplexing.
Even though the United Kingdom stands out in setting out a systematic
voluntary sector policy, we find that Third Way types of policies are at
work in most developed market economies, though rarely under that
name. In essence, the various policy developments, which we will review
below, expect third-sector organizations to be efficient providers of services in the fields of health care, social services, humanitarian assistance,
education, and culture, *and* agents of civic renewal by forming the infrastructure of burgeoning civil society. The fact that Third Way and neo-
liberal approaches alike harbour such expectations basically suggests
that the growing economic and political role of the third sector is somewhat independent of 'new politics' and part of more fundamental changes
taking place in post-industrial societies.

1. A Growing Economic Force

To be sure, heightened policy attention, be it Third Way or neo-liberal, comes
at a time of significant third-sector growth. In the course of the last decade,
most developed market economies in Europe, North America, and the Asia-
Pacific region have seen a general increase in the economic importance of
non-profit organizations as provider of health, social, educational, and cultural
services of many kinds. On average, the non-profit sector accounts for about
6 per cent of total employment in OECD countries, or nearly 10 per cent with
volunteer work factored in (Salamon, Anheier, and Associates 1999).

Indeed, the non-profit sector has experienced significant economic
expansion, with rates of employment generation well above that of the
economy as a whole (Salamon, Anheier, and Associates 1999), and growth
in its full-time equivalent paid employment averaged 24 per cent for the
five-year period 1990–5 in the United States, United Kingdom, Germany,
Belgium, France, Israel, and Japan. By contrast, overall employment
growth in these countries was 6 per cent for the same period. In some
countries such as Germany, the expansion of the non-profit sector extends
back to the 1960s (Anheier and Seibel 2001). As we will suggest below,
the high growth rates in non-profit employment in developed market
economies are closely related to systems of welfare financing, in particular patterns of government social welfare spending, and higher demands
for human services such as health, education, and welfare.

In developed market economies, as Salamon, Anheier, and Associates (1999) show, two-thirds of all non-profit employment is concentrated in the three traditional fields of welfare services: education (accounting for 28 per cent of total non-profit employment), social services (27 per cent), and health (22 per cent). Western Europe in particular displays a significant concentration of non-profit employment in welfare services, in large part a reflection of the historic prominence of organized religion traditionally maintained in this particular field (see Esping-Anderson 1990).

The major sources of non-profit income in developed market economies are fees and public support. Fees and other commercial income alone account for over half of all non-profit revenue (42 per cent), whereas public sector payments amount to 49 per cent of the total. By contrast, private philanthropy—from individuals, corporations, and foundations combined—constitutes only 9 per cent of total non-profit income (Salamon, Anheier, and Associates 1999). This pattern varies somewhat, however, by country, but what these findings suggest is that, in all developed market economies, the non-profit sector is an integral part of a mixed economy of welfare.

2. Increased Policy Relevance

Parallel to the increase in economic importance is the greater policy recognition non-profits enjoy at national and international levels. Prompted in part by growing doubts about the capacity of the state to cope with its own welfare, developmental, and environmental problems, analysts across the political spectrum (Giddens 1998; Dilulio 1999; Chaves 2003) have come to see non-profits as strategic components of a middle way between policies that put primacy on 'the market' and those that advocate greater reliance on the state. This is a central tenet of Third Way thinking, but the basic argument for a greater non-profit role is based on conventional public administration (Salamon 1995), which suggests that non-profits are efficient and effective providers of social and other services that governments may find costlier and more ineffectual to offer themselves. As a result, cooperative relations between governments and non-profits in welfare provision have become a prominent feature in countries such as the United States (Salamon 2002), Germany (Anheier and Seibel 2001), France (Archambault 1996), or the United Kingdom in the field of social services (Kendall and Knapp 1996).

Indeed, Salamon and Anheier (1996) suggested that the presence of an effective partnership between state and non-profits is one of the best predictors for the scale and scope of non-profit activities in a country. Where such partnerships exist—for example, the Netherlands (Burger and

Dekker 2001), Israel (Gidron and Katz 2001), or Australia (Lyons, Hoking, and Hems 1999)—the scale of the non-profit sector is larger than in countries where no such working relationship is in place in the delivery of welfare, health, and education, as is the case in Japan or Italy. From an institutional perspective, the presence of a sizeable non-profit sector is contingent on collaboration with the state—another central element of Third Way thinking.

Salamon's (1987) analysis of the workings of the United States non-profit sector identified institutional patterns of third party government in many policy fields, which suggested that strengths and weaknesses of both government and the non-profit sector complement each other, leading to interdependent structures of service delivery and finance over time. Yet in both the Third Way and in neo-liberalism this partnership, based on interdependence, is now seen much more broadly and in the context of privatization and 'market-building' under the heading of 'New Public Management' (NPM). It stresses the role of non-profits as providers of services, typically as contractors of services paid for, at least in part, by government (Ferlie 1996; McLaughlin, Osborne, and Ferlie 2002). As a broad label, NPM includes several related aspects that draw in the non-profit sector specifically:

- from third party government (Salamon 1995), where non-profits served as either extension agents or partners of governments in service delivery, to a mixed economy of social care and welfare that includes businesses and public agencies next to non-profit providers (Knapp, Hardy, and Forder 2001); and
- from simple contracts and subsidies to 'constructed markets' (Le Grand 1999), particularly in health care and social services, with a premium on managed competition. For example, long-term care insurance in Germany and services for the frail elderly in Britain are based on competition among alternative providers through competitive bidding for service contracts.

With the rise of New Public Management, particularly in Europe, the emphasis on non-profits as service providers and instruments of privatization casts non-profit organizations essentially in a neo-liberal role, irrespective of Third Way intentions. Examples are Germany's efforts to modernize its subsidiarity policy by introducing competitive bidding into social service contracting (Anheier and Seibel 2001), the New Deal in Britain (Mulgan 2000), or France's unemployment policy of 'insertion' (Archambault 1996). The key here is that non-profits are no longer seen as the 'poor cousin' of the state or as some outmoded organizational form as conventional welfare state literature describes them (see Quadagno 1987; Esping-Anderson 1990). To the contrary, they have become instruments of welfare state reform guided by the simple equation of 'less government = less bureaucracy = more flexibility = greater efficiency' (see Kettl 2000). What New Public Management has done is to change the established role of non-profit organizations from provider of services and quasi-public goods that complement state provision (see Weisbrod 1988) to that of an equal partner (or competitor) along with other organizational forms.

3. Social Capital and Civil Society

Yet while their economic function, particularly in terms of service provision, has been a common though often overlooked feature of non-profits in most developed countries, a emphasis on non-profits as civil society institutions is new, and reflects profound changes in the wider political environment. Under the Third Way, the political discourse about the non-profit sector has expanded from the welfare state paradigm that long characterized the field to include what we call pronounced neo-Tocquevillian elements, that, again, figure in Third Way approaches but also among neo-conservative perspectives. In the 2000 presidential election in the United States and the 2002 parliamentary elections in the United Kingdom, the major political parties—be they Democrat or Republican, Labour or Conservative—favoured a greater role for voluntary associations, including faith-based communities, in local social policy.

In contrast to the basically quasi-market role non-profits assume under New Public Management, the neo-Tocquevillian approach emphasizes their social integrative and participatory function as well as their indirect contributions toward community building. Non-profit institutions are linked to the perspective of a 'strong and vibrant civil society characterised by a social infrastructure of dense networks of face-to-face relationships that cross-cut existing social cleavages such as race, ethnicity, class, sexual orientation, and gender that will underpin strong and responsive democratic government' (Edwards, Foley, and Diani 2001: 17). Norms of reciprocity, citizenship, and trust are embodied in networks of civic associations. Put simply, the essence of the neo-Tocquevillian approach is: civil society creates social capital, which is good for society and the economy (Putnam 2000). Thus, civil society is not only a bulwark against a state that could become too powerful, or a mechanism that creates social cohesion; it is much more than that: a general principle of societal constitution based on individualism and communal responsibility as well as self-organization.

Communitarianism is a variant of the United States as a society of self-organizing communities, rooted the American political tradition of a moral community of virtuous citizens (Etzioni 1996). Communitarianism is a social philosophy that views community as a voluntary grouping of individuals who come together to identify common goals and agree to rules governing the communal order. The community is created in part by recognizing common policies, or laws, that are set to meet legitimate needs rather than having been arbitrarily imposed from 'above' and 'outside' the groups. Members of such communities—for example, neighbourhood, city, or nation—accept responsibilities, both legal and moral, to achieve common goals and greater collective well-being.

In contrast to neo-Tocquevillian thinking, which views the non-profit or voluntary sector as the social infrastructure of civil society, communitarian thinking had less of a direct policy impact. According to the former, non-profits are to create as well as facilitate a sense of trust and social inclusion essential for the functioning of modern societies (for example, Putnam 2000; Anheier and Kendall 2002; Halpern 1999; Offe and Fuchs 2002). The link between non-profits and social trust was first suggested in Putnam's 1993 book *Making Democracy Work*, in which he shows that dense networks of voluntary associations are the main explanation for northern Italy's economic progress over the country's southern parts. Putnam (2000) looks at participation in voluntary associations in the United States and argues that a dramatic decline in both membership rates and other forms of civil engagement led to lower levels of trust in society and, consequently, to general increases in social ills such as crime. Fukuyama (1995), making a more general argument in his book *Trust*, shows that differences in economic success among US, Germany, or Japan are predicated on reservoirs of 'sociability' and social trust which, in turn, depend on some kind of 'associational infrastructure'.

Indeed, as Anheier and Kendall (2002) report, the relationship between interpersonal trust and membership in voluntary associations is a persistent research finding cross-nationally. The 1999–2000 wave of the European Value Survey (Halman 2001) shows that, for twenty-eight of the thirty-two participating countries, a positive and significant relationship exists between the number of associational memberships[1] held and interpersonal trust.[2] The data of the European Value Survey reveal a striking pattern: respondents with three or more memberships were twice as likely to state that they trust people as those holding no memberships. Overall,

---

[1] This includes memberships in health and social welfare associations, religious/church organizations, education, arts, music or cultural associations, trade unions and professional associations, local community groups and social clubs, environmental and human rights groups, youth clubs, women's groups, political parties, peace groups, sports and recreational clubs, among others.

[2] Measured by the following question: 'Generally speaking, would you say that most people can be trusted or that you need to be very careful when dealing with people?'

Helmut Anheier

there is almost a linear relationship between increases in membership and the likelihood of trusting people.

Nor is this finding limited to the specific question about interpersonal trust used in the European Value Survey. In the United States, a similar pattern emerges in relation to the question 'Do you think that most people would try to take advantage of you if they got a chance, or would you say that most people try to be fair?'[3] Results show that every second (46 per cent of) respondents with no memberships felt that people would try to take advantage, as opposed to every third (37 per cent) for those with three memberships, and nearly every fourth (29 per cent) for those with five and more memberships. Vice versa, 70 per cent of respondents with five or more memberships felt that people tend to be fair, compared with only 54 per cent for those with no membership.[4]

The main argument, which becomes important for the Third Way framework, is that participation in voluntary associations creates greater opportunities for repeated 'trust-building' encounters among like-minded individuals, an experience that is subsequently generalized to other situations such as business or politics. Thus, the neo-Tocquevillian case for non-profits is largely an argument based on the positive and often indirect outcomes of associationalism. The genius of Putnam (2000) was to link de Tocqueville's nineteenth-century description of a largely self-organizing, participatory local society to issues of social fragmentation and isolation facing American and other modern societies today (Hall 2002). This made his work very attractive to policy-makers in the United States and elsewhere. It identified a problem (erosion in social capital) and offered a solution from 'the past' (voluntary associations, community), suggesting tradition and continuity to an unsettled presence. This connection 'clicked' not only in the United States (Sirianni and Friedland 2000), but also in Britain (for example, the establishment of a social capital working group in the Cabinet Office in 2000) and countries like Germany (Enquettekommission des Deutschen Bundestages 2002).

4. Growing Policy Agenda

What the Third Way suggests is that the voluntary sector can be both agent of efficient and effective service delivery and institution of civil society enforcing civic virtue, social cohesion, and participation. Yet this

[3] World Value Survey (2000). United States Survey conducted by Gallop for Virginia Hodgkinson, Helmut K. Anheier, and Ronald Inglehart.
[4] See also Putnam's analysis (2000: 139) of trust in the United States.

assumption goes well beyond countries with left-of-centre governments in power; rather, it seems to apply across a wide range of political ideologies, agendas, and programmes.

At the *local* level, non-profit organizations are becoming part of community-building and empowerment strategies. Numerous examples show how policy-makers and rural and urban planners use non-profit and community organizations for local development and regeneration. These range from organizations among slum dwellers in Marseilles and neigh-bourhood improvement schemes in Berlin or Los Angeles to social invest-ment strategies in London or Bradford.

At the *national* level, non-profit organizations are engaging in the fields of welfare, healthcare, education reform, and public–private partnerships. Prominent cases are the establishment of private foundation hospitals as a means to modernize the National Heath Service in the United Kingdom; the transformation of state-held cultural assets into non-profit museums in former East Germany; and the privatization of social service agencies in the United States. In a number of countries, the greater role of non-profits in welfare reform is aided by laws that facilitate their establishment and operations, such as the Nonprofit Law of 1998 in Japan, which began to reverse a long history of state tutelage of civil society institutions.

At the *international* level, we observe the rise of non-governmental organizations (NGOs) and an expanded role in the international system of governance. The number of known international non-governmental organ-izations (INGOs) increased from about 13,000 in 1981 to over 47,000 by 2001. The number of INGOs reported in 1981 would make up just under 28 per cent of the stock of INGOs twenty years later. What is more, for-mal organizational links between NGOs and international organizations like the United National Development Program (UNDP), the World Health Organization (WHO), or the World Bank increased by 46 per cent between 1990 and 2000 (Glasius, Kaldor, and Anheier 2002: 330; Kaldor, Anheier, and Glasius 2003).

At the *global* level, we observe the emergence of a global civil society and trans-national non-profits of significant size with complex organiza-tional structures that increasingly span many countries and continents (Anheier and Themudo 2002). Examples include Amnesty International with more than one million members, subscribers, and regular donors in over 140 countries and territories. The Friends of the Earth Federation combines about 5,000 local groups and one million members. The Coalition against Child Soldiers established partners and national coalitions engaged in advocacy, campaigns, and public education in nearly forty countries. Care International is an NGO with over 10,000 professional staff. Its United States affiliate alone has an annual income of around $450 million.

All these developments suggest that the greater role for non-profit organizations is part of the transformation of societies from industrial to post-industrial, and from a world of nation-states to one of trans-national, even globalizing, economies. The Third Way is part of the policy reaction to these developments, and the full recognition of the immensely elevated position and role of non-profit organizations at the beginning of the twenty-first century is the main difference from the latter part of the previous century, in which non-profits were '(re)discovered' as providers of human services in a welfare state context.

5. The Continued Importance of Institutional Patterns

Let's take a closer look at the political and institutional context in which these developments are taking place to get a better understanding of how Third Way policies might fit in. Anheier and Seibel (2001) compare the United States with the German experience and identify critical differences in the embeddedness and role of the non-profit sector historically. These differences continue to reflect in individual mobility and a general mistrust of central state power so that, in the United States, voluntarism and associational life evolved as a compromise between individualism and collective responsibility (see Lipset 1996). Greatly simplified for purposes of comparison, this Tocquevillian pattern evolved into the system of third-party government and a patchy welfare state. By contrast, the German development and resulting state–society relations are strikingly different. Three different principles emerged separately in the complex course of the last two centuries of German history, but combined in shaping the country's state–society relations and its non-profit sector well into the late twentieth century:

- the principle of self-administration or self-governance, originating from the nineteenth century conflict between the state and citizens, allowed parts of the non-profit sector to emerge and develop in an autocratic society, in which the freedom of association had only partially been granted (see Schuppert 1981); the principle allowed for a specific civil society development in Germany that emphasized the role of the state as grantor of political privilege and freedom over notions of spontaneous self-organization;
- the principle of subsidiarity, originally formulated in the work of the Jesuit scholar von Nell-Breuning (1976), related to the settlement of secular–religious frictions and fully developed after the Second World War, assigns priority to non-profit over the public provision of social

services (Sachße 1994); this created a set of six non-profit conglomerates that today rank among the largest non-profit organizations worldwide (Anheier and Seibel 2001); and finally,

• the principle of *Gemeinwirtschaft* (communal or social economy), based on the search for an alternative to both capitalism and socialism, and linked to the workers' movement, led to the cooperative movement and the establishment of mutual associations in banking, insurance, and housing industries.

To varying degrees, the three principles continue to influence state–society relations in Germany. Though not exclusively, each is linked institutionally to specific areas and sectors of society: self-administration to a highly decentralized system of government; subsidiarity to service provision and welfare through non-profit organizations; and *Gemeinwirtschaft* to a (until recently) vast network of mutuals and cooperatives. However, in contrast to the United States' experience, what these principles neither cover nor address is the area of self-organized, autonomous associational life. They leave, in modern parlance, Tocquevillian elements aside. These were picked up by the Schröder government as part of the German equivalent to the Third Way, the *Neue Mitte*, and resulted in a high-level parliamentary committee to explore ways towards what German Social Democrats call 'citizen society' (Enquettekommission des Deutschen Bundestages 2002).

This example demonstrates the importance of different traditions, patterns, and 'cultures' in the third sector. While there may be 'non-profit organizations' and 'non-profit sectors' as defined by the structural operational definition, they nonetheless exist in very different contexts, and are linked to distinct histories and cultural as well as political developments. Indeed, taking Europe as a regional example, very different non-profit sector models or patterns exist—and in each the Third Way framework would take a different starting point and involve different emphasis:

• the French notion of the *économie sociale*, which emphasizes economic aspects, mutualism, and the communal economy. It groups non-profit associations together with cooperatives and mutual organizations, thereby combining the underlying notions of social participation, solidarity, and mutuality as a contrast to the capitalist, for-profit economy (see Defourny and Develtere 1999);

• the notion of associationalism in Italy, seen as a countervailing force against both church and state powers at the local level (Barbetta 1997);

• the German tradition of subsidiarity, described above, which provides a comprehensive framework for the relationship between state and third sector in the provision of social services (Sachße 1994);

- the Swedish model of democratic membership organizations in the form of broadly based social movements whose demands are picked up by the state and incorporated into social legislature (Lundström and Wijkström 1997); or
- the pragmatic patchwork of the British welfare system with a national-ized healthcare system and a decentralized, largely private system of charities in social service provision (Kendall and Knapp 1996; Glennerster 2000; Plowden 2001).

What these various models have in common is that they emerged in their current form during the industrial era and typically responded to the social questions at that time. Because they developed at a time when the role of the state was different, and when the constitution of society was not that of an emerging post-industrial, globalizing economy with a shrinking working class and an affluent middle class, we frequently find significant mismatches between reality and potential. For example, in France restrictive laws prevent the full development of private non-profit action, particularly foundations. The French state continues to find it difficult to accept the notion of private charity and private action for the public good, sticking to the nineteenth-century notion that the state is the clearest expression of the common weal (Archambault 1996). In Britain, chronic weakness in local governments combined with centralizing funding tendencies from Whitehall make it difficult for genuine local partnerships to develop in efficient and effective ways.

Indeed, it is in non-profit sector models in developed market economies that we find a significant need for policy innovation and modernization (see Strategy Unit 2002 for the United Kingdom). In the next section, we will explore different national patterns and 'non-profit regime types' in more detail, and show that a formal approach to defining non-profits can be combined with a comparative-historical approach to increase our cross-national understanding of this set of institutions in terms of Third Way–third sector relationships.

6. Cross-National Patterns and Trends

A major step forward for comparative non-profit research has been the basic insight from neo-institutionalism that institutional context matters (Powell and DiMaggio 1991). Based on modifications of Esping-Andersen's analysis of the welfare state (1990; see also Huber, Ragin, and Stephens 1993) to incorporate the non-profit sector, Salamon and Anheier (1998) identified four more or less distinct models of non-profit development and four types of 'non-profit regime'. Each of these types is characterized not only by a particular state role but also by a particular position for the third sector; and, most importantly, each reflects a particular constellation of social forces.

Table 6.1 differentiates these regimes in terms of two key dimensions: first, the extent of government social welfare spending; and second, the scale of the non-profit sector. Let's look at the regime types in a historical perspective first, before bringing in more recent developments.

In the *liberal* model, represented by the United States and the United Kingdom, a lower level of government social welfare spending is associated with a relatively large non-profit sector. This outcome is most likely where middle-class elements are clearly in the ascendancy, and where opposition from traditional landed elites or strong working-class movements has either never existed or been effectively held at bay. This leads to significant ideological and political hostility to the extension of government social welfare protections and a decided preference for voluntary approaches instead, a pattern that is more pronounced in the United States than in the UK, however. The upshot is a relatively limited level of government social welfare spending and a sizeable non-profit sector. As Table 6.2 shows, both the service delivery and the civil society component of the non-profit sector are well developed.

The *social democratic* model is very much located at the opposite extreme. In this model, exemplified by Sweden, state-sponsored and state-delivered social welfare protections are extensive and the room left for

TABLE 6.1. *Non-profit regime type*

Public sector social welfare spending	Non-profit sector size	
	Small	Large
Low	Statist (Japan)	Liberal (US)
High	Social democratic (Sweden)	Corporatist (Germany)

Source: Salamon and Anheier (1998).

TABLE 6.2. *Third sector models and emphasis*

Importance of social service component	Importance of civil society component	
	Lower	Higher
Lower	Statist	Social democratic
Higher	Corporatist	Liberal

service-providing non-profit organizations is quite constrained. Historically, this type of model emerged most likely where working-class elements were able to exert effective political power, albeit typically in alliance with other social classes. This is particularly true in the case of Sweden, where working-class political parties were able to push for extensive social welfare benefits as a matter of right in a context of a weakened, state-dominated church and a limited monarchy. While the upshot is a limited service-providing non-profit sector, however, it is not necessarily a limited non-profit sector overall, as shown above. Rather, the non-profit sector performs a different function in social democratic regimes, as a very substantial network of volunteer-based advocacy, recreational, and hobby organizations exists alongside a highly developed welfare state. Thus, to refer to Table 6.2, while the service delivery function of the Swedish non-profit sector is less pronounced, the civil society component, indicative of Tocquevillian aspects, is much more so.

In between these two models are two additional ones, both of which are characterized by strong states. However, in the *corporatist* model, present in France and Germany, the state has been either forced or induced to make common cause with non-profit institutions, so that non-profit organizations function as one of the several 'pre-modern' mechanisms that are deliberately preserved by the state in its efforts to retain the support of key social elites while pre-empting more radical demands for social welfare protections. This was the pattern, for example, in late nineteenth-century Germany when the state, confronting radical demands from below, began to forge alliances with the major churches and the landed elites to create a system of state-sponsored welfare provision that over time included a substantial role for non-profit groups, many of them religiously affiliated (Anheier and Seibel 2001; Seibel 1990). In the corporatist regime, as Table 6.2 shows, we find an emphasis on service delivery but less on the civil society function of the non-profit sector.

The *statist* model is the fourth possible model. In this model, the state retains the upper hand in a wide range of social policies but not as the instrument of an organized working class, as in the social democratic regimes. Rather, it exercises power on its own behalf or on behalf of business and economic elites, but with a fair degree of autonomy sustained by long traditions of deference and a much more pliant religious order. In such settings, in our analysis Japan, limited government social welfare protection does not translate into high levels of non-profit action, as in liberal regimes. Rather, both government social welfare protection and non-profit activity remain highly constrained and both components of the non-profit sector remain relatively under-developed (Table 6.2).

IIow do current developments and non-profit sector policies differ across the four regime types, and how does Third Way thinking come into play? In the liberal regime, in which non-profit organizations rely less on public sector payments, the pressures to seek additional and alternative revenue in the 'private market' are strongest. Observers point to the commercialization of the non-profit sector, a trend that is particularly acute in the United States healthcare industry (Weisbrod 1998). At the same time, popular political programmes such as the 1997 welfare reform emphasize the importance of private charity in solving the social problems of a rapidly changing society. While private giving, as we have seen above, contributes a significant share toward the financing of non-profit activities, actual giving levels have stagnated in recent years and are unlikely to offset any reductions in government funding. As a result, competition for donation dollars is likely to intensify.

The situation in the United Kingdom is somewhat different when it comes to commercialization, but it differs in terms of the 'moving force' behind it—amplified by Third Way policies. Unlike the United States, however, it is less the for-profit sector moving into non-profit domains like health and education and also less the internalization of market-like ideologies among non-profit managers. Rather, what seems to have happened in recent years is a more or less conscious but highly centralized government attempt to enlist the voluntary sector in social service delivery while reducing public sector provision. One result of this policy is the emergence of competitive contract schemes and engineered quasi-markets, which will lead to an expansion of the United Kingdom non-profit sector via larger flows of both public sector funds and commercial income. As a result, the United Kingdom third sector shows initial increases in public sector payments on route to greater fee income in the future. Importantly, however, the significant changes affecting non-profit organizations in both countries as a result of New Public Management come on top of greater expectation in their capacity as civil society institutions. Thus, in both countries emphases on the role of the voluntary sector in community building and generating social capital are very pronounced.

The situation in social democratic countries is very different. A broad public consensus continues to support state provision of basic healthcare, social services, and education. The role of non-profit organizations in service provision, while likely to increase somewhat, will happen at the margins and typically in close cooperation with government, leading to the emergence of public–private partnerships and innovative organizational models to reduce the burden of the welfare state. These expansions into service delivery, however, are likely to push the sector away from public sector funding, encouraging non-profit organizations to seek commercial forms of income, on the assumption that giving is already fairly high with 14 per cent for those working in health and social services (Lundström and Wijkström 1997). For the other parts of the Swedish non-profit sector, any significant expansion seems unlikely. With the great majority of Swedes already members of some of the country's very numerous associations, and with a revenue structure that relies 74 per cent on fee income, Swedish civil society is more likely to restructure rather than expand in its organizational underpinning. Specifically, the country is undergoing a significant secularization trend that is likely to lead to a reduction of church-related organizations and an expansion of cultural and recreational activities (Lundström and Wijkström 1997). Third Way policies in Sweden, if they seem relevant in that country at all, are more likely to come in the form of calls for civil renewal rather than greater roles for non-profits in service delivery.

One would be tempted to summarize the current policy situation in corporatist countries with the French adage '*le plus ça change, le plus ça reste la même.*' The French government is channelling massive sums of public sector funds to the non-profit sector to help reduce youth unemployment, while keeping some of the same restrictive laws in place that make it difficult for non-profit organizations to operate more independently from government finances. In Germany, too, the non-profit sector continues to be a close tool of government policies, not only in the area of unemployment policies but also more generally in the process of reunification (Anheier, Priller, and Zimmer 2001). It is only a slight overstatement to conclude that the German government is trying to build the eastern German non-profit sector with the help of public funds. Yet, given increased strains on public budgets, reunification will most likely result in greater flexibility in how the subsidiarity principle is applied. In policy terms, these developments are shifting the focus of subsidiarity away from the provider of the service and towards the concerns of the individual as consumer, thereby introducing market elements in an otherwise still rigid corporatist system (Zimmer 2001). There are now first moves in this direction, and it is likely that the German non-profit sector will rely more on private fees and charges in the future. In contrast, growth in volunteering and private giving will remain modest. Like in France, however, current tax laws prevent non-profit organizations from utilizing their full potential in raising private funds. At the same time, changing demographics and secularization continue to call established corporatist institutions and arrangement into question.

Thus, it is in corporatist countries that calls for more effective service delivery on behalf of government and non-profits will be rather pronounced, as will be attempts to modernize the social infrastructure of these countries towards more citizen participation and greater local involvement. The Third Way agenda, therefore, falls on fertile ground in these countries, particularly as they attempt to overcome the inertia of corporatism.

Finally, in statist countries like Japan there may be the first signs of change in the government's posture toward the non-profit sector. Today, the Japanese government speaks more favourably about the role non-profit organizations can play in policy formulation. The state grudgingly acknowledges the non-profit sector's abilities in addressing emerging issues that confront Japan, such as the influx of foreign labour, an ageing society, and environmental problems. In general, if the state shares a common interest with a particular non-profit, it will provide financial support but also exert great control over the organization. By contrast, if the state does not share common interests with a non-profit, the non-profit may be ignored, denied non-profit legal status, not considered for grants or subsidies, and not given favourable tax treatment. Overall, however, Japan's non-profit policies have not changed much, and changes have been incremental and not a fundamental shift. Though considered more mainstream than ever before, the state still regards non-profits as subsidiaries of the state. As subsidiaries, non-profits are subject to extensive and burdensome bureaucratic oversight. In sum, unless major reforms take place, Japan's non-profit sector will continue to exist and grow under close state auspices. Third Way thinking, it seems, may still be somewhat too early for Japan, but is likely to become important over the next few years.

7. Fundamental Questions

The Third Way approach to the voluntary sector seems instrumental and oriented to a societal vision that remains unspecified. While the need for modernization seems clear, as does the policy framework such as the Compact, the wider long-term vision does not. Indeed, a puzzling aspect of current policy debate about welfare and governmental reform, as well as civil renewal and community building, is the absence of a wider vision of what kind of future society we have in mind when we discuss the role of the third sector. What kind of society did the Clinton and the current Bush administrations have in mind with an emphasis on faith-based communities as part of welfare reform? What future British society does New Labour envisage when it links devolution with a greater reliance on the voluntary sector? Or what future German society does the governing coalition of Social Democrats and Greens have in mind as a blueprint when they discuss the renewal of civic engagement and the introduction of competitive bidding in social care markets at the same time?

In the absence of such a wider debate, including explicit policy blueprints, we suggest the following scenarios as markers to chart the deeper policy visions that government, opposition, and voluntary sector representatives may hold for the future:

- *NPM scenario*: non-profits and the third sector as the set of well-organized, corporate entities that take on tasks and functions, previously part of the state administration but now delivered through competitive bidding processes and contractual arrangements that try to maximize the competitive advantages of non-profit providers in complex social markets under state tutelage.
- *Social capital scenario*: non-profits and the voluntary sector as the self-organizing 'quasi-state' apparatus of the twenty-first century, as part of a benign civil society, with high levels of individualism, participation, and 'connectivity', that prevents social ills and detects and corrects them before they become 'social problems', well coordinated, at arm's length with, and by a minimalist, technocratic state.
- *Liberal scenario*: the voluntary sector as a source of dissent, challenge, and innovation, as a countervailing force to government and the corporate business world—a sector that serves as a social, cultural, and political watchdog keeping both market and state in check, a sector that creates and reflects the diversity, pluralism, and dynamism of modern society.
- *The corporate scenario*: this is what Perrow (2001) calls the 'corporatization' of NGOs and the expansion of business into civil society; corporations use extended social responsibility programmes to provide, jointly with non-profits, services previously in the realm of government (for example, healthcare, childcare, pensions, and so forth but also community services more widely).
- *The mellow weakness scenario*: non-profits are encouraged to operate in areas or problem fields that politicians find either too costly relative to pay-offs (actual, opportunity costs) or inopportune to tackle themselves, which allows them to pretend that 'something is being done' (Seibel 1994). Non-profits are the fig leaf for a political world unwilling to solve social problems in a serious way, and remain under mild state tutelage.

Importantly, the various scenarios imply different roles for the state. Schuppert's (2003) four types of state orientations and actions in relation to the public good in modern societies are very useful in this respect. Each of the four types involves a different role for the non-profit sector and points to different scenarios:

- *The constitutional state* is based on democratically legitimized decision-making about public good preferences, which the state implements through legislative and administrative procedures and enacts through specific programmes. Non-profits become parallel actors that may complement or even counteract state activities, very much in the sense of classical liberalism, or the liberal scenario and non-profit regime model suggested above.
- *The cooperative state*, which designs and implements public good policies in close collaboration with organized private interests, and carries out programmes via contractual arrangements; this is akin to the New Public Management scenario and also relevant to the social democratic model, whereby non-profits become part of public–private partnership with the state and typically work in complementary fashion with other agencies, public and private.
- *The guarantor state*, which is also close to the NPM scenario, views serving the public benefit as part of a division of labour between state and private actors, but under state tutelage and with primary state funding, as in the case of the corporatist non-profit model; and, finally, in this case, non-profits can become part of the overall division of labour, although their resourcing role will be less pronounced, but they can also form alternative mechanisms of serving the public good.
- *The active state* regards contributions to public benefit (other than pure public goods) as a task of civil society, as part of a self-organizing, decentralized, and highly connected modern society. The direct state contribution to public benefit will be limited, and non-profits, along with other private actors, are called upon to make substantial efforts to mobilize monetary and other resources for the common good. This is suggested by the social capital and the corporatist scenarios above.

Traditional notions of public benefit and public responsibilities have shifted from the state to other actors, which bring in the role of non-profit organizations as private actors for the public good. In particular, the role of the state as 'enabler' and 'animator' of private action for public service has increased, which heightens the role of the third sector. Third Way thinking includes two state orientations—the cooperative state and the active state—whereas neo-liberalism combines the constitutional state perspective with that of the active state. Perhaps because of these overlaps and the different scenarios that are possible under the Third Way perspective, analysts have found it easy to point to inconsistencies and a lack of coherence (see Giddens 2000 for a review of Third Way critiques).

8. Conclusion

Non-profit organizations and the third sector more generally are part of a complex dual transition: from industrial to post-industrial society and from national state to trans-national policy regimes. This transition shows the beginnings of a new policy dialogue in addressing the future role of non-profit organizations and involves two broad perspectives that have become prominent in recent years: on the one hand, non-profits are increasingly part of New Public Management and a mixed economy of welfare; on the other, they are seen as central to 'civil society–social capital' approaches, specifically the neo-Tocquevillian emphasis on the nexus between social capital and participation in voluntary associations. Both approaches make strong and specific claims about the role of non-profits, NGOs, and third sector institutions generally; both occupy key positions in current policy debates; both have major implications for the future of non-profits; and both could amount, in the end, to a highly contradictory set of expectations that push and pull these institutions in very different directions.

The strength of the Third Way stance towards the voluntary sector is closely related to its weakness. Because its basic perspective towards the voluntary sector and civil society overlaps significantly with those of neo-liberalism on the one hand and the reform-minded post-corporatists in countries like France and Germany on the other, its distinct policy thrust is hard to fathom. Indeed, many countries practise some form of 'quasi-Third-Wayism' in searching for new policy approaches and ways to modernize the welfare state. As we have seen, the basic characteristics of the Third Way can, to varying degrees and with the partial exception of statism, be found in all non-profit regime types:

- under the Third Way, policy-making and governance are no longer the primary responsibility of government but shared with other agencies: citizenship, voluntary associations, and business interests;
- third sector organizations are vehicles for social participation, cohesion, and innovation. At the same time, the third sector needs the encourage-ment of the state and the active participation of the citizenry to function as a cohesive force;
- the Third Way emphasizes the public responsibility of private economic action, and with it the role of the social economy and 'non-profitness'. Many of the organizations in the third sector have been part of this social economy that emphasizes aspects of social needs and equity over financial return on investments;
- the Third Way implies a redefinition of social welfare and a reorganization of welfare financing away from tax-based to fee-for-service revenue, and a greater incorporation of the voluntary sector in a mixed economy of care.

Unfortunately, the eminence of the Third Way in current policy debates leaves one of the distinct roles of the non-profit sector at the margins. In societies with different views of the public good, the third sector creates institutional diversity, contributes to innovation, and prevents monopolistic structures by adding a sphere of self-organization to those of state administration and the market. Indeed, Weisbrod (1988) and others (see for example Hansmann 1987; James 1989) have suggested that the very origin of the non-profit sector is found in demand heterogeneity for quasi-public goods—yet it is only now that we begin to understand the policy implications of such theorizing. The non-profit or third sector can become a field of experimentation, an area for trying out new ideas that may not necessarily have to stand the test of either the market or the ballot box. In this sense, non-profits add to the problem-solving capacity of modern societies.

References

Anheier, H. and Kendall, J. (2002). 'Trust and the Voluntary Sector', *British Journal of Sociology*, 53: 343–62.

—— and Themudo, N. (2002). 'Organizational Forms of Global Civil Society: Implications of Going Global', in M. Glasius, M. Kaldor, and H. Anheier (eds.), *Global Civil Society 2002*. Oxford: Oxford University Press.

—— and Seibel, W. (2001). *The Nonprofit Sector in Germany*. Manchester: Manchester University Press.

—— Priller, E., and Zimmer, A. (2001). 'Civil Society in Transition: East Germany Ten Years after Unification', *East European Politics and Society*, 15/1: 139–56.

Archambault, E. (1996). *The Nonprofit Sector in France*. Manchester: Manchester University Press.

Barbetta, P. (1997). *The Non-profit Sector in Italy*. Manchester: Manchester University Press.

Blair, T. (1998). *The Third Way: New Politics for a New Century* (Fabian Pamphlet 588). London: Fabian Society.

—— and Schröder, G. (1999). *Europe: The Third Way—die Neue Mitte*. London: Labour Party and SPD.

Burger, A. and Dekker, P. (eds.) (2001). *Noch Markt, Noch Staat. De Nederlandse Non-Profitsector in Vergelijkend Perspectief*. Den Haag: Sociaal en Cultureel Planbureau.

Chaves, M. (2003). 'Religious Authority in the Modern World', *Society*, 40/March–April: 38–40.

Defourny, J. and Develtere, P. (1999). *The Social Economy: The Worldwide Making of a Third Sector*. Liège: Centre d'Economie Sociale.

Dilulio, J. (1999). 'Congregations, the Government, and Social Justice'. *Sacred Paces, Civic Purposes: Crime and Substance Abuse*. Washington, DC: Brookings Institution.

Edwards, B., Foley, M., and Diani, M. (2001). *Beyond Tocqueville: Civil Society and the Social Capital Debate in Comparative Perspective*. Hanover: University Press of New England.

Enquettekommission des Deutschen Bundestages. (2002). *Zivilgesellschaft und buergerschaftliches Engagement*. Berlin.

Esping-Andersen, G. (1990). *The Three Worlds of Welfare Capitalism*. Princeton, NJ: Princeton University Press.

Etzioni, A. (1996). *The New Golden Rule*. New York: Basic Books.

Ferlie, E. (ed.) (1996). *The New Public Management in Action*. Oxford: Oxford University Press.

Fukuyama, F. (1995). *Trust: The Social Virtues and the Creation of Prosperity*. London: Hamish Hamilton.

Giddens, A. (1998). *The Third Way*. Cambridge: Polity Press.

—— (1999). *The Third Way: The Renewal of Social Democracy*. Cambridge: Polity Press.

—— (2000). *The Third Way and its Critics*. Cambridge: Polity Press.

Gidron, B. and Katz, H. (2001). 'Patterns of Government Funding to Third Sector Organizations as Reflecting a De-Facto Policy and their Implications on the Structure of the Sector in Israel', *International Journal of Public Administration*, 24: 1133–60.

Glasius, M., Kaldor, M., and Anheier, H. (eds.) (2002). *Global Civil Society*. Oxford: Oxford University Press.

Glennerster, H. (2000). *British Social Policy Since 1945* (2nd edn.). Oxford: Blackwell.

Hall, 2002 (Peter Hall at kennedy school or Michael Hall from Canada?)

Halman, L. (2001). *The European Values Study: A Third Wave* (source book of the 1999/2000 European Values Study surveys). Tilburg: Tilburg University Press.

Halpern, D. (1999). *Social Capital. The New Golden Goose?* London: Institute for Public Policy Research.

Hansmann, H. (1987). 'Economic Theories of Non-profit Organisations,' in W. Powell (ed.), *The Nonprofit Sector: A Research Handbook*. New Haven, CT: Yale University Press.

Home Office (1998). *Getting it Right Together: Compact on Relations between Government and the Voluntary Sector in England*. London: Stationery Office.

Huber, E., Ragin, C., and Stephens, J. (1993). 'Social Democracy, Christian Democracy, Constitutional Structure and the Welfare State', *American Journal of Sociology*, 99: 711–49.

James, E. (1989). *The Non-Profit Sector in International Perspective*. New York: Oxford University Press.

Kaldor, M., Anheier, H., and Glasius, M. (2003). 'Global Civil Society in an Era of Regressive Globalisation', in M. Glasius, M. Kaldor, and H. K. Anheier (eds.), *Global Civil Society 2003*. Oxford: Oxford University Press.

Kendall, J. and Knapp, M. (1996). *The Voluntary Sector in the UK*. Manchester: Manchester University Press.

Kettl, D. (2000). *The Global Public Management Revolution: A Report on the Transformation of Governance*. Washington, DC: Brookings Institution.

Knapp, M., Hardy B., and Forder J. (2001). 'Commissioning for Quality: Ten Years of Social Care Markets in England', *Journal of Social Policy*, 30: 283 306.

Le Grand, J. (1999). 'Competition, Collaboration or Control? Tales from the British National Health Service', *Health Affairs*, 18: 27–37.

Lipset, S. (1996). *American Exceptionalism: A Double-Edged Sword*. New York: Norton.

Lundström, T. and Wijkström, F. (1997). *The Nonprofit Sector in Sweden*. Manchester: Manchester University Press.

Lyons, M., Hoking, S., and Hems, L. (1999). 'Australia', in L. Salamon, H. Anheier, R. List, S. Toepler, S. Sokolowski, and Associates, *Global Civil Society*. Baltimore, MD: Institute for Policy Studies, Johns Hopkins University.

McLaughlin, K, Osborne S., and Ferlie, E. (eds.) (2002). *New Public Management: Current Trends and Future Prospects*. London: Routledge.

Mulgan, G. (2000). 'Government and the Third Sector: Building a More Equal Partnership', in H. Anheier (ed.), *Third Way—Third Sector. Report No. 1*. London: Centre for Civil Society, London School of Economics.

Nell-Breuning, O. von (1976). 'Das Subsidiaritätsprinzip', *Theorie und Praxis der sozialen Arbeit*, 27: 6–17.

Offe, C. and Fuchs, S. (2002). 'A Decline of Social Capital? The German Case', in R. Putnam (ed.), *Democracies in Flux: The Evolution of Social Capital in Contemporary Society*. New York: Oxford University Press.

Perrow, C. (2001). 'The Rise of Nonprofits and the Decline of Civil Society,' in H. Anheier (ed.), *Organizational Theory and the Nonprofit Form. Report No.2*. London: Centre for Civil Society, London School of Economics.

Plowden, W. (2001). *Next Steps in Voluntary Action*. London: Centre for Civil Society, London School of Economics, and NCVO.

Powell, W. and DiMaggio, P (eds.) (1991). *The New Institutionalism in Organizational Analysis*. Chicago: University of Chicago Press.

Putnam, R. (2000). *Bowling Alone: The Collapse and Survival of American Community*. New York: Simon and Schuster.

Quadagno, J. (1987). 'Theories of the Welfare State', *Annual Review of Sociology*, 13: 109–128.

Sachße, C. (1994). 'Subsidiarität: Zur Karriere eines sozialpolitischen Ordnungsbegriffes', *Zeitschrift für Sozialreform*, 40/1: 717–31.

Salamon, L. (1987). 'Partners in Public Service: The Scope and Theory of Government–Nonprofit Relations', in W. Powell (ed.), *The Nonprofit Sector: A Research Handbook*. New Haven, CT: Yale University Press.

—— (1995). *Partners in Public Service*. Baltimore, MD: Johns Hopkins University Press.

—— (2002). *The State of Nonprofit America*. Washington, DC: Brookings Institution.

—— and Anheier, H. (1996). *The Emerging Nonprofit Sector*. Manchester: Manchester University Press.

———— (1998). 'Social Origins of Civil Society: Explaining the Nonprofit Sector Cross-Nationally', *Voluntas: International Journal of Voluntary and Nonprofit Organizations*, 9: 213–47.

Salamon, L., Anheier, H., and Associates (1999). *The Emerging Sector Revisited: A Summary—Revised Estimates*. Baltimore, MD: Institute for Policy Studies, Johns Hopkins University.

Schuppert, G. (1981). *Die Erfüllung öffentlicher Aufgaben durch verselbständigte Verwaltungseinheiten*. Göttingen.

—— (2003). 'Gemeinwohlverantwortung und Staatsverständnis', in H. Anheier and V. Then (eds.), *Zwischen Eigennutz und Gemeinwohl: Neue Formen und Wege der Gemeinnützigkeit*. Gütersloh: Bertelsmann.

Seibel, W. (1990). 'Government/Third-Sector Relationship in a Comparative Perspective: The Cases of France and West Germany', *Voluntas*, 1: 42–60.

—— (1994). *Funktionaler Dilettantismus. Erfolgreich scheiternde Organisationen im 'Dritten Sektor' zwischen Markt und Staat*. Baden Baden.

Sirianni, C. and Friedland, L. (2000). *Civic Innovation in America: Community Empowerment, Public Policy, and the Movement for Civic Renewal*. Berkeley, CA: University of California Press.

Strategy Unit (2002). *Private Action, Public Benefit: A Review of Charities and the Wider Not-For-Profit Sector*. London: Cabinet Office.

The White House (1999). *The Third Way: Progressive Governance for the 21ˢᵗ Century*. Washington, DC (April 25).

Weisbrod, B. (1988). *The Nonprofit Economy*. Cambridge, MA: Harvard University Press.

World Values Survey (2000). Michigan: University of Michigan Press.

Zimmer, A. (2001). 'Corporatism Revisited: The Legacy of History and the German Nonprofit Sector,' in H. Anheier and J. Kendall (eds.), *Third Sector Policy at the Crossroads: An International Nonprofit analysis*. London: Routledge.

7

Changing Conceptions of Family and Gender Relations in European Welfare States and the Third Way

MARY DALY

In this chapter I want to demonstrate the value of interrogating recent developments in social policy in Europe through the lens of family and gender relations. Family-related reform in European welfare states raises a very interesting set of issues for what we understand as the trends in contemporary policy development and the influence of factors such as the philosophy and politics of the Third Way. We shall see that a new view of the relationship between family, state, and market is emerging in Europe. This is not entirely attributable to the Third Way, however. Like other philosophies of the welfare state, the Third Way has no coherently worked out position on the role of the family and how it should be configured in and by social policy. For this and other reasons, the relationship between the family and Third Way policy and politics makes for an interesting case study.

The chapter proceeds in two steps. The first identifies the broad trends in how welfare states across a range of European countries view and attempt to shape contemporary family life. The second part analyses how these developments are to be interpreted, especially in the context of what they reveal about how the Third Way approaches and understands the family.

This analysis draws in part on a recently published report (Daly and Clavero 2002). I would also like to acknowledge the helpful comments received from the editors of this volume—Jane Lewis and Rebecca Surender—and from Professor Herman Schwartz of the Department of Politics at the University of Virginia at Charlottesville.

1. Overview of Trends in Europe in Social Policy in
Relation to the Family

This section turns to some of the most significant changes to have been
made in social policy as it has affected the family in European countries
in the last decade or so. By surveying Western Europe (and especially the
EU member countries), the intention is to identify broad trends and
processes rather than to pinpoint the detail of policy reform. It should be
pointed out in advance that, while this kind of exercise runs the risk of
overemphasizing cross-national similarities and implies convergence, it
affords a breadth of comparative scope that is indispensable. It should
also be borne in mind that broad-brush comparisons allow us to identify
parallel and varying discourses and policy responses as well as striking
cross-national trends.

For the purposes of the chapter, 'family' is conceived in a relatively
broad way, as involving not just a structure or form but sets of practices
and relations as well. The actual policies considered include those that fall
under the general rubric of 'welfare state support for families'. The focus,
therefore, is on policies covering cash support for families (including
benefits and tax reliefs or credits), provisions for working parents (such as
leaves from employment), services for families with children (such as
childcare), and benefits and services for families with other care needs
(including those related to illness and old age).

The historical context is important. Europe is the home of family benefits. However, such provisions, while institutionalized in most countries in
the form of cash payments during the pre- and post-Second World War
periods, were slow to mature and remained relatively unchanged for quite
a long period in most countries once they had been introduced. It was
really only in the last two decades that family provisions and support
came to the active attention of policy-makers. As Ginsborg (2000: 413)
observes: 'The end of the century sees the family higher up on the political agenda of most European governments than at any previous time'.
When designing their family policy, European countries have had a number of key considerations. Most countries initially attached conditions to
their family benefits so as to guard against moral laxity and disincentives
to take up employment (Wennemo 1994). Population replacement concerns were also to the fore. These three sets of concerns—population,
morality, and employment—continue to influence the way public authorities approach the family but they have been joined by concerns about
gender equality. While Europe has adopted no singular approach to finan-
cially supporting families, there are some particularities of family policy

across countries. Most European countries began by supporting 'the family' (rather than families) and did so by developing particular sets of cash benefits for families within the general social security system. Once introduced, child benefits tended to be unique and indeed innovative among cash transfers in that they are the only universal measure in most welfare states (Montanari 2000: 309). There is some evidence that state support for families constitutes a separate domain of social policy within and across nations (Gauthier 1999). The periods of expansion and contraction of family benefits do not generally conform to more general trends in the development of welfare state benefits. Introduced later than social insurance, family benefits have generally been less affected than other benefits by the cutbacks and retrenchment which took root in Europe in the 1980s and 1990s.

To focus on the contemporary period, there are some key trends to be observed in the last ten years in Europe in how welfare states relate to family and family relations. This was in fact a period when governments were, if not actively experimenting with family supports, then more conscious of this domain of policy as requiring intervention and offering leverage in fulfilling economic and, to a lesser extent, social objectives.

A Redefinition of Family Obligation

There is taking place a general redefinition of the meaning of family obligation. This is in itself nothing new; we already had a redefinition of adult children's obligations to their parents early in the twentieth century, and in more recent times divorce laws have been actively rewriting the meaning of conjugal ties. What is new, however, is the strong focus on the obligations of parenthood. These are being if not rewritten then reconstructed.

There are a number of aspects or dimensions to this redefinition/ reconstruction of parenthood. In a general sense, family relations are being reinterpreted and redefined to refer to parental responsibility rather than spousal solidarity (Eekelaar and Maclean 2000). With the weakening of marriage ties and the diversification of forms of family life, parental obligations assume greater importance because of their potential to outlast the breakup of marriage. Given the relative constancy of motherhood, it is fatherhood that is especially targeted. Policy in many countries is active in constructing the obligations of fatherhood as being independent of the man's relationship with the mother of the child or children. It is in this light that actions around emphasizing and enforcing the responsibilities of absent fathers (to be found in many European countries) should primarily be read. While this is a development that extends beyond social policy, it is to be seen especially in increased efforts to utilize welfare to enable or force fathers to take financial responsibility for their children. In the UK, for example, the Child Support Agency, established in 1992 by the Conservative government and continued with some modifications by New Labour under Tony Blair, is testimony to a specific concern with fathers' obligations to their children. One could say that states nowadays are seeking stability through the paternal link.

Contemporary state interest in families is broader than the obligations of parenthood, however. It extends also to family relations and practices, especially the performance of parental roles. As Hobson and Morgan (2002: 2) put it, in policy discourse the question of who pays for the kids is now paired with that of who cares for the kids. Interestingly, this policy objective tends to be framed in terms of incentives rather than penalties. Quality, what one might term 'grade A', parenthood is being fostered by policy, law, and provision. Third Way thinking tends to conceive of the social exigency here in terms of a more professional form of parenting and so the role of the state as a provider of training and expertise is underlined. This kind of thinking is very advanced in the UK, the government there actively engaging in offering educational advice and support to parents about how to be 'good' parents. One could argue that it is the practice of fatherhood that is the subject of most reconstruction, however. As evidence, consider the general growth across Europe in paternity leave. In Spain, for example, fathers have been given entitlement to over half the period of maternity leave (on the assumption, presumably, that mothers and fathers are substitutable and that six weeks of leave is sufficient for the mother to recover from the effects of childbirth). An even more suggestive example of a policy that seeks to activate and reconstruct the practice of fatherhood is the 'daddy leave' introduced by the Swedish and Norwegian governments during the 1990s. This measure sets aside a certain proportion of the parental leave specifically for the father which, as a mandated period, is lost to the family if he does not take it. The significance of the change in the view of the father role should not be underestimated. Whereas fathers have always been expected to provide cash for their families, fatherhood in some European countries today is also defined around providing care (or, rather, demonstrating a readiness to care). Moreover, it seems to be accepted that it is a legitimate role for public policy to encourage fathers to care. The significance of such social engineering is noteworthy: it spells increasing state intervention in the distribution of labour, roles, and responsibility within the family. Hence, as law is becoming less regulatory (in its treatment of divorce, for example—see Lewis 2001), social policy appears to be increasingly regulatory.

Women's roles are also the subject of reconstruction by social policy. Whereas the family of a lone woman and her child(ren) appeared to have established a legitimate claim on public resources, welfare states are now more restive in regard to the financial and moral implications of supporting such families. European countries are certainly drawing back from unqualified support for families without a male head (witness the cutbacks in benefits for lone-mother families and the growing assumption across Europe—but especially in the Netherlands and the UK—that such mothers should be at least part-time if not full-time workers). This sits easily with a Third Way understanding of social inclusion to mean inclusion in the labour market. The developments are also in line with the 'activation' thrust of Third Way social policy in that they are part of a trend away from supporting workless families. As this process is played out in relation to lone-mother families, the legitimacy of care as a full-time component of motherhood is devalued.

A Strong Move Towards Children's Rights

If fathers are being targeted so as to improve the quality of their children's lives, and this is at least part of the rationale, children are also increasingly being treated as individuals. The second large trend that I identify in contemporary European countries is towards treating children as objects of social policy.[1] This involves a move away from the principle of subsidiarity (which, even though it was not always formally expressed in such terms, governed much of the state's attitude to family life across European countries) and a move towards granting children autonomous rights. While this can be interpreted as a manifestation of a trend towards individualization, it has three other roots: a more general recognition of children as agents, an interest in the well-being of children, and concerns about social sustainability.

There are many examples of the unfolding of a 'children's social policy'. Consider the recent introduction of a guarantee to each child of a place in childcare in the UK, Finland, Germany, and Sweden. This constitutes a reframing of the prevailing view of children, and regards the child as having an individual right to certain goods and services and, indeed, to a personal relationship with the state. This is in stark contrast to earlier

---

[1] Children are also increasingly the focus of academic work. A new sociology of childhood has emerged in recent years for example which is described by Lavalette and Cunningham (2002: 12) as 'committed to an engaged approach to studying the worlds of children and emphasising children's rights, needs and interests'.

social policies which familialized children, defining them as 'minors' and 'dependants' of adults and granting them derived rights only (in a similar manner to how wives gained derived rights through the link to husbands or breadwinners) (Makrinioti 1994; Lansdown 2001). The dominance of such a child protection perspective helps to explain why most countries have been caught unawares by the scale of child abuse and why it has to be perceived as a 'crisis' once it is discovered. Given that social policy has always been most comfortable in regarding the family as a haven, once the knowledge of child abuse is absorbed into policy a far-reaching change of approach is required: children have to be conceived of as persons separate from adults, as having interests of their own which are, in principle anyway, different from and potentially conflicting with those of adults. The role of public policy in this scenario is to lay out minimum requirements for the child's independent well-being (Whyness 2000: 40). The implications can be quite far-reaching. A fundamental change is an emphasis on children's right to knowledge and information. A second emphasis is on children participating in arenas, such as decision-making, that have always been defined as the province of adult authority (Whyness 2000: 128–9).

The move towards children's rights, even though it dates from the 1990s, is quite developed. Many countries have seen the establishment of a children's commissioner or an ombudsman's office for children as well as special units to further children's rights. Perhaps the recent National Children's Strategy in Ireland is one of the most striking developments (Government of Ireland 2000). Based on what is called an inclusive view of childhood, a threefold strategy is laid out to give children a voice and enable them to be more active in decision-making. So while the strategy has some concern with the functional aspects of childhood (childcare and other needs), it targets children as agents with certain participatory rights. Among other measures, a National Children's Parliament has been set up, intended to be a forum wherein children can raise and debate on a periodic basis issues of concern to them. This is complemented by measures to enhance the representation of children's interests at other levels of decision-making (including an Ombudsman for Children and a National Children's Office). As well as institutionalizing the representation of their interests, the Strategy is also strong on service provision for children. Locality-based services are favoured and the degree of coherence and integration among services spanning a number of policy domains is emphasized. A central part of the Strategy is to protect or improve the quality of children's family life. In policy terms, this is translated into measures such as parenting education and support as well as services targeted on disadvantaged families.

Supporting Working (among) Parents

Apart from measures to redefine family roles and relations, there is an independent move to encourage employment among (both) parents. This is a general shift in policy in many European countries and is expressed, on the one hand, by the growth of leaves from employment for parenting purposes and, on the other, by changes in tax and benefit provisions to encourage paid work. While leaves from employment for parents are not unambiguously interpretable as having the encouragement of parental (and especially maternal) employment as their primary objective, it is possible to interpret them in this way since in most European countries such provisions are fashioned as benefits for workers.[2] There is also an associated set of fiscal changes, realized most widely in the introduction of tax credits, which can be generally interpreted as encouraging the growth of dual-income families (and the reduction in the numbers of workless households).

The moves towards fostering if not compelling employment on the part of lone mothers are also noteworthy in this respect. Among other things, the New Deal for Lone Parents in the UK and the Personal Responsibility and Work Opportunity Reconciliation Act (PRWORA) in the USA significantly reduce the extent to which motherhood is valued and protected by the welfare state (Orloff 2002). In fact, in these and other countries the employment of mothers, especially those on benefits, has been made a specific object of public policy. While the reforms also target other objectives, they are critically oriented to transforming the role of lone mother from carer to worker.[3]

The expansion of subsidies and/or allowances for childcare is another development in the direction of fostering employment among mothers (although it also has other aims such as encouraging 'privately' provided childcare). Eschewing the expansion of general or generic subsidies to families with children, financial support to families nowadays is directed towards specific costs such as those associated with service procurement or the loss of (potential) wages. This is a significant change because traditionally in Europe cash support to families was for the purpose of assisting them with the direct costs involved in rearing children (those associated with food, clothing, and education, for example). The move towards assisting with indirect costs spells a change, especially to the extent that it is underpinned by a view that the two kinds of cost are substitutable.

---

[2] In the process leaves and childcare become constructed as a good for parents' employability rather than as a good for children. Germany is the exception in this regard in that receipt of the child-rearing benefit there has not been tied to active employment status.

[3] The foundation of the reform process that led to the PRWORA was also, as Duerr Berrick (2002) points out, built upon the institution of marriage and a reduction in out-of-wedlock births.

*A Move to a Greater Welfare Mix and Declining Popularity of
State Provision*

In the past, the merits of state provision were self-evident: this was the
best form of provision because it was non-profit seeking and operated
for the good of the entire community. Public provision has experienced a
drop in popularity. State-dominated provision is being represented now
not only as curtailing choice but also as inferior to that provided in or by the
market, which is portrayed as virtuous for its efficiency, competitiveness,
profit maximization, and rationality. Such thinking not only opens the way
to market provision but actually serves to portray family and other forms of
non-statutory provision as a form of 'freedom of choice'. The 1990s was a
time in Europe when family-related services were (capable of) being rewritten. The notion of 'collective' (usually public) provision was being undermined in favour of individualized, personalized services. Associated with
this is some restructuring and redistribution of care (understood as the activities involved in providing for the care-related needs of children and adults).
By way of overview one can say that European welfare states are more willing today to (*a*) pay for or subsidize care (especially when provided
privately) and (*b*) pay for or subsidize a diversity of types of care (because
that is in tune with the welfare-mix ideal).

The move to a greater welfare mix in Europe is taking a number of
forms. In those countries that have traditionally had strong state involvement in provision, the state is being flanked by other actors. As Palme
et al. (2002) describe developments in Swedish welfare services during
the 1990s, this was a period of greater decentralization, user financing,
and market orientation. In France, there is occurring what has been called
an individualization of care whereby care becomes a matter of individual
family taste (Morgan 2001). Letablier and Rieucau (2000) speak of a
general move in France towards privatization of action which is, among
other things, transforming the conception of childcare as a public issue.
Historically, the crèche in France not only represented a conception of the
appropriate way of bringing up children but stood for a certain form of
equal opportunities for children from different backgrounds. Now, class
differentiation proceeds, with the wealthier opting for a different form of
provision—almost always a service that is 'bought' (even at low cost)—
whereas crèches are more and more servicing the children of the working
classes. Palme et al. (2002) also identify growing class inequalities as a
feature of recent Swedish developments around childcare. It is interesting
to compare such developments (which essentially differentiate among
children) with those oriented towards universalizing the child as a bearer
or rights.

A Move towards Gender Neutrality

There is very little explicit engagement with gender issues to be observed in social policy in Europe at the present time. This bald statement requires some clarification. What I am referring to is a virtual absence of action within European countries to utilize social policy to address gender inequalities. This is not to say that social policy is not focused on women and/or men (Rake 2001). The discussion to date has shown that welfare states are differentially targeting women and men. My point is, rather, that gender differences or inequalities are not per se being problematized for the purposes of social policy. This is somewhat at odds with the thrust of policy at European Union (EU) level, which underlines the significance of gender inequalities and enjoins member states to take account of gender when preparing their national action plans on employment and social exclusion and in regard to how they spend the Structural Funds. And yet despite this member states had little to offer the EU on gender in their 2001 national plans to combat social exclusion.[4] So poor was the response that the EU reserved some of its most negative feedback to member states under the heading of gender mainstreaming (Council of the European Union 2001). It seems, then, that, at national level anyway, the assumption is that women and men can now act as economically independent worker citizens.

While it is true that women and men are both being targeted by national-level policy and that there is some difference in what is expected of each sex, an over-arching and striking similarity is also to be observed. Women, mothers especially, are being to some extent 'defamilized', mainly in that less attention is given now than in the past to women's family setting or circumstances. While they are still expected to carry out their maternal role (just as men are expected to be 'good fathers'), as workers or potential workers women are paid a childcare allowance or tax credit and it is up to them to sort out their care arrangements in a way that permits them to be employed. In the context of welfare reform in the USA, Orloff (2001: 134) describes a process of gender sameness whereby the institutionalized expectations for mothers are no longer distinguished from those for fathers. Collier outlines a more or less similar process taking place in the UK wherein women and men are increasingly represented in social policy as gender neutral or ungendered beings (2001: 535). For Lewis (2002: 331), this process could be characterized as the generalization to women of the masculinist model of work and welfare. Concepts like work, citizenship,

---

[4] These were submitted in mid-2001 in the first phase of the new 'social inclusion process' which commits member states and the EU to a series of policy and funding initiatives to reduce poverty and combat social exclusion.

and parenthood are increasingly utilized in a generic rather than gender-specific way. Given this, I think it is true to characterize developments at national level as a move towards gender neutrality.

The main trends having been set out, the next task is to try and identify their significance, especially in terms of their implications for the analysis of the relationship between Third Way, family, and contemporary reform of the welfare state. I begin with a few words on how the family fits into Third Way thinking.

2. Developments in the Light of Third Way Thinking

The family is not a central concept in Third Way theorizing. However, it would be inaccurate to say that the family is marginalized. While the Third Way does accord agency to the family, that agency is filtered through the dominant domains (or concepts) of state, community, and society. In Third Way thinking, for example, the family has a role to play in regard to what is considered one of the most challenging tasks for contemporary politics: to forge a new relationship between individuals and the community. Third Way thinking is, as we all know, normative. So a renewal of the family towards a certain type of family is important. The type of family that Giddens devotes attention to, for example, is 'the democratic family'. He suggests that family relations must be governed by principles of equality, mutual respect, autonomy, decision-making through communication, and freedom from violence (Giddens 1998: 93). Democratic family relations also imply shared responsibility for childcare and obligations on the part of children towards their parents. This type of family is part of Giddens' 'Third Way' programme, along with an active civil society, a new mixed economy, a social investment state, positive welfare, and equality as inclusion. However, when it comes to discussing the family in detail, Giddens subsumes it under the heading of the renewal of civil society. So the role and place of the family is not clearly articulated in Third Way thinking. Moreover, Giddens's work is the only place where a position is elaborated. Against this background, what linkages can we identify between Third Way thinking and the reforms under way in European countries in relation to the family? This is a more inductive exercise.

Changes in (the Meaning of) Family Obligations

Contemporary social policy is opening up the black box of the family. Rather than concentrating on family form and structure, social policy is problematizing how family roles and relations are practised. This is for some countries, such as the UK, relatively new, and developments there especially suggest a concern with the family as a feature of Third Way social policy. In terms of interpreting the meaning of what is happening, one could read the increased interest in family obligations as spelling at its root a concern with family solidarity. There is, as Knijn (2002) points out, a vexed relationship between social solidarity and family solidarity. Looking at contemporary developments, it appears that European welfare states are seeking to redefine and reinvigorate family solidarity. There is something new in this, not just in the fact that family solidarity now has to be engineered (whereas in the past it was considered more as organic) but also in what constitutes family solidarity. One could argue that male solidarity has long been defined in terms of men providing income for their families. Now, though, in addition to this fathers are expected to make themselves available to their children and even to participate in their care. When one looks at the detail of what is happening, it does seem plausible to argue that the underlying concern is not men's errant behaviour as such but rather how they act and behave emotionally as family members. Family solidarity is being redefined for women as well in that the best mothers now combine motherhood and employment.

What are the links to the Third Way in these developments? Both solidarity as a general concept and family solidarity specifically find resonance in Third Way philosophy. In distancing itself from liberalism and espousing communitarian principles, solidarity finds favour with the Third Way for its capacity to locate people in a network of social support and to contextualize social relations. Among other things, solidarity functions to improve social cohesion, protecting people and communities from the effects of individualization and preventing social disorder. Solidarity has an additional appeal to Third Way thinking in that it fosters responsibility. To be solidaristic you have to have a clear sense of what your responsibilities are and be motivated to uphold them. Solidarity could even be viewed as a form of capital: as a feature of societies it is equivalent to an asset or social resource and, in the case of individuals, family solidarity augments their personal social capital.

Yet for all that it might be in vogue among policy-makers, I would question the extent to which current policy is actually generating family solidarity. While parental care has some place as a component of contemporary perceptions of solidarity, the predominant interpretation of family solidarity on the part of the state now is that parents should be prepared to entrust their children to others so that they themselves can be workers. Solidarity expressed in this way requires mothers and fathers to distance themselves from the care of their children. What we are seeing, then, is a process whereby the engineering of family solidarity by the state leads to a certain 'emptying' from the nuclear family of some of its caring and exchange activities.

The Move Towards Children's Rights

This development suggests that there is something substantially novel under way in European social policy: what we are in effect witnessing is the emergence of a social policy for children. The citizenship of children suggests itself, therefore, as an interesting point of departure for the analysis of contemporary social policy. One could say that the move towards children's rights is in line with what Beck (1998) calls 'institutionalised individualism' whereby most of the rights and entitlements of welfare states are designed for individuals (rather than families). While Third Way thinking does not have a worked-out position on children, its predilection for the state as a social investment state, as developed by Giddens in *The Third Way* (1998) and others, does have resonance here.[5] In this view the state engages in positive welfare by investing where possible in human capital rather than the direct provision of economic maintenance (ibid: 117). Hence, in a social investment state social policy is utilitarian, especially having the function of generating resources. Investment in children, therefore, could be seen to be part of a strategy of asset creation and protection. Considering the agency involved lends some support to this interpretation of the origins of the move towards children's social policy. While the potential range of actors is relatively broad—international organizations, the national state and its agencies, parents/guardians, professionals, and institutions—it is mainly state actors who have driven the development. At national level, one could see how the indigenous development of children's policy could be tied up with a changing view of the role of the welfare state. However, this does not explain why this policy should take the form of granting children social rights. Indeed, while it is generally comfortable with a discourse of contract, there are currents within Third Way thinking that would put a brake on the granting of rights per se (emphasizing responsibilities and self-reliance). Etzioni (1995), for example, has called for a moratorium on new rights. To explain why a rights-based approach is preferred, we have to take account of agency at the trans-national level, and in particular the UN Declaration on the Rights of the Child. This, signed in 1989, has acted as a catalyst for the global development of rights for children. The movement towards children's rights is a complex matter, though, and is one which reveals the limits of the Third Way as a complete explanation for how state policy on the family is unfolding in Europe.

---

[5] I am grateful to Jane Lewis for this point.

Supporting Working among Parents

Clearly, parenting is being redefined with financial support and other 'gifts' from the state to families being tied increasingly to parental behaviour. One can read the growth of provisions like tax credits, subsidies, and leaves for childcare as indicating a reorientation of state support for families towards parental employment. The manner in which employment-encouraging measures have come to supersede (although not eclipse) the more unconditional child benefits is further evidence of this trend. However, the growing practice of tying family benefits to employment behaviour leads us to question the motives that underlie contemporary policy. Traditionally, family policy was quite a distinct domain of social policy in Europe, with strong anti-poverty and horizontal equity orientations (as well as to a varying extent a gender-equality thrust). These are now generally less visible as principles of family support in Europe as a closer relationship is forged between family policy and employment policy. The rubric 'reconciling work and family' is now the dominant frame in European and especially EU policy on the family/work relationship.

There are clear links here with the productivist theme of Third Way thinking. As Merkel (2000: 4) points out, in a working society access to education, training, and work is the definitive form of equality of opportunity. Involvement in the labour market also accords with the Third Way conception of social inclusion. In this philosophy the most legitimate role for the state is to encourage people into employment and especially to support the transition from benefit recipient to worker. This suggests that family-related matters are not in themselves priorities but are, rather, manipulated by policy as part of a concern about employment and the tax sustainability of pensions. A utilitarian approach to the family is to be seen here again.

There are other ways to interpret these developments. One could, for example, read the policy developments around the family as expressing a tension, if not clash, between horizontal and vertical equity. We know that the former was an important motivator historically of family benefits, especially in Continental European countries, where equity between families with children and those without rivalled the more conventional notion of equity as requiring redistribution among income groups. These two principles or views of equity came to rival if not conflict with each other in a number of countries during the 1990s. France witnessed the most 'extreme' clash. In the end the Jospin government was forced to overturn its policy to subject family benefits to a means test (in 1998) after only a few months because of the stiff opposition mounted by the family associations (which are in France very strong and well-organized). In this instance horizontal equity won out. There is another equity aspect involved as well.

This concerns which families can afford to accept the increasingly diverse forms of help available. There is evidence from a number of countries of increasing class differences in gaining access to family-related services.

In all of this it is also interesting to consider whether people have their desired family arrangement. The evidence suggests that they do not. Despite the significant reforms and the fact that much effort is focusing on reconciling family and working life, there is a wide divergence between the actual employment/family arrangements that people have and those that they would prefer (OECD 2001). In general, across Europe the model that people have too much of is the traditional male breadwinner one (of employed father and home-making mother). In Germany, for example, this is the actual arrangement of 52 per cent of the population but for only 6 per cent is it their preferred arrangement; similar levels of dissatisfaction with employment/family arrangements are to be found in Italy. The model that is too seldom available across Europe as a whole is the one-and-a-half earner arrangement whereby the man works full-time and the woman part-time. In general, the two-earner family form is more sought after than the traditional model of a male breadwinner/female caregiver. One has to ask how sustainable such a gap between expectations and reality is, especially in countries such as Germany and Italy and, to a lesser extent, France and Ireland, where the opportunity for people to realize their preferred family/employment arrangement is very compromised. At root is a more profound question about the assumptions that state actors make about family and whether they are any more capable now than they were in the past of delivering people's preferences.

A Greater Welfare Mix

As Jane Lewis points out in Chapter 10 of this volume, the idea of a mixed economy is central to Third Way thinking and that of New Labour in particular. On the one hand, diversity is prized and, on the other, there is the view that welfare should be provided by a range of actors which should preferably work in cooperation if not in partnership. The mixed economy has, therefore, a strong ideological component and can be, for example, a convenient way of justifying the partial withdrawal of the state. In addition, the idea of a greater welfare mix destabilizes the conventional opposition between public and private and opens the way for increasing diversification in both the identity of those involved in provision and the role of the state in encouraging or subsidizing service provision by other actors. Clearly, then, an increasing welfare mix raises questions about agency as well as ideas in relation to social policy. Traditionally in Continental Europe, family associations have been strong. Now employers are as involved as directly interested (and sometimes provider) parties as is the market and the third sector (the latter to a much larger extent).

As has been pointed out on a number of occasions, it looks as if the trend towards a greater welfare mix, admittedly multi-dimensional, is leading in the direction of increasing class divisions in terms of which services different sectors of the population can access and the quality of the services available to different socio-economic groups. Given this, class is more than ever a highly significant category of analysis in relation to the welfare state; and the class consequences of reforms need to be the focus of specific attention. The Third Way has few terms to deal with continuing and new divisions based on class and so it is of limited utility as an explanation of the factors that are contributing to widening class divisions.

Greater Gender Neutrality

With equality defined as inclusion and inequality as exclusion (Giddens 1998: 105), a gender-neutral approach fits well with Third Way philosophy. Given that the market is the main agent and locus of social inclusion, women and men are treated as more or less undifferentiated workers. This view of social inclusion is fallow ground for considering either how gender differences might be a barrier to social inclusion or how the family might itself be an agent and locus of social inclusion (Daly and Saraceno 2002). There are different justifications for a gender-neutral approach. It is underpinned by an acceptance of a growing convergence in the lives of women. It is assumed, as Irwin and Williams (2002: 8) point out, that individualization of women and men has already taken place. It could not, however, function without an associated assumption that the family has become more democratic. It is as if policy believes its own rhetoric in assuming, against the evidence, greater sharing of family tasks if not the achievement of egalitarianism in parenting and partnering (Daly and Rake 2003).

It is interesting to point out the extent to which the move towards gender neutrality or sameness is at odds with other policy thrusts. Even a cursory examination suggests a contradiction between the push to redefine and reconstitute family solidarity and the movement towards gender neutrality. For if we look at these developments through the lens of familization, what we see is that men are being familized (and in a particular way) while women are being defamilized. There is another set of issues also about how women's welfare and role are being reconstituted. The move towards children's rights is especially important for women given that welfare states have typically supported women in their role as guardians and carers of children. The question has to be posed of how the future welfare of women is to be secured if children are given access to services and benefits in their own right. This move to focus independently on children has, for example, no terms to treat the poverty of children as a gender issue.

3. Overview

This chapter has identified five main trends in relation to the family in contemporary European welfare states. These are: a heightened interest on the part of the state in family solidarity (especially as it relates to the behaviour of men); a move to treat children independently of their families and to grant them individual rights; a tendency to treat both parents as workers; a move towards a greater welfare mix; and a move towards gender neutrality for the purposes of social policy. It has to be emphasized that the research exercise here is broad-brush across countries. What I have done is to take a general overview. Hence each trend is not necessarily to be found in each country. For this and other reasons (including the fact that there are a number of distinct traditions of family policy and hence departure points of reform in Europe), an interpretation of convergence across Europe is inappropriate. But there are some similarities and it is these that the chapter seeks to identify and explain.

In terms of an explanation, many of the five main developments share some common currency with the Third Way. Viewed together in terms of what they reveal about the core concerns of contemporary policy, the trends could be taken as evidence of a greater focus on family processes than on family form or structure. Reforms almost everywhere involve greater intervention in family life and family practices. That is, the state is, to some extent anyway, seeking to affect the distribution and performance of tasks within the family and the nature of relationships among family members. In addition, social policy does not appear to speak any longer in terms of a single type of family but addresses itself to varied family forms. However, for all the diversity, there is a clear model of family informing policy. This is the working family wherein men fulfil their obligation to be good fathers and women act as good citizens by being employed. It is in this regard that the reforms taking place in states' support for families are closest to the Third Way project. Social inclusion (understood as inclusion in the market society) requires that families are solidaristic units, which actually means not only that family members support each other but that the family itself is prepared to give up some of its activities to other institutions. This idea of the family as partner to a host of other social providers sits extremely well with Third Way thinking.

However, we should guard against the assumption that the developments taking place in family policy detailed in this chapter represent, in some simplistic way anyway, the advance of the Third Way project. There are a number of reasons to be cautious on this count. For one, this chapter has taken a broad European sweep and as we know Third Way philosophy and politics are far from universal in Europe. Moreover, the Third Way is also context-specific and is far from a singular entity. For example, many gaps and differences exist in the Third Way programme as it is being pursued in Germany as against the UK. Second, the Third Way is not always a coherent whole; as Driver and Martell (2002: 50) point out in relation to the UK, it is a combination of agendas. Third, there are clear limitations in the extent to which particular trends in relation to the family are in line with or are being driven by Third Way-related developments. The increasing moves to treat children as individual rights bearers, for example, is not necessarily in line with the Third Way philosophy, which is not generally in favour of the extension of rights and certainly not in favour of the extension of unqualified rights (which is what granting children rights implies). There are, in addition, many contradictions to be seen in the approach taken by states to the family and some policy developments can be seen to be at odds with others. For example, in terms of the nature of the modern family, one should point out that the move towards treating children as individuals also 'distances' them from the family and that, while family solidarity is being promoted, there is a certain 'anti-familism' in this in that the meaning of this solidarity is that parents give up caring personally for their children (at least during 'normal' working hours). To the extent that we can see a clear role for it, the state's task in this process is to assist in the great modernization and monetization of society and social life that Simmel (1990) described in *The Philosophy of Money*. By subjecting families to state policies designed to shape behaviours in the direction of more market participation, more employment, more purchased or extra-familial (or indeed extra-neighbourhood/social network) care for 'dependants', the state subjects more of social life to the logic of the market, of calculation, of rationality (in the Weberian sense), thereby diminishing affect, emotion, and traditional norms.

The developments around the family cast an interesting light on welfare state reform. The decline of the male breadwinner model and other changes in the work–family nexus could be argued to pose a different set of challenges to contemporary welfare states from those emanating from globalization and deindustrialization (Mahon 2002: 1). That is, the changing family constellation challenges states to take on new responsibilities (in regard to assisting families with their caring responsibilities, for example) at a time when other pressures are forcing states to shed responsibilities. Not only are they a vibrant area of policy development, but family support policies are becoming increasingly diverse in terms of both their content and their objectives. Among other things, this suggests some of the limits of a retrenchment perspective in understanding change in contemporary European welfare states.

References

Beck, U. (1998). 'The Cosmopolitan Manifesto', *New Statesman*, 20 March.

Collier, R. (2001). 'A Hard Time to Be a Father?: Reassessing the Relationship Between Law, Policy and Family Practices', *Journal of Law and Society*, 28: 520–45.

Council of the European Union (2001). *Draft Joint Report on Social Inclusion*. Brussels: Council of the European Union (http://europa.eu.int/comm/employment_social/soc-prot/soc-incl/joint_rep_en.htm).

Crow, G. (2002). 'Families, Moralities, Rationalities and Social Change,' in A. Carling, S. Duncan, and R. Edwards (eds.), *Analysing Families: Morality and Rationality in Policy and Practice*. London: Routledge.

Daly, M. and Clavero, S. (2002). *Contemporary Family Policy*. Dublin: Institute of Public Administration.

—— and Rake, K. (2003). *Gender and the Welfare State: Care, Work and Welfare in Europe and the USA*. Cambridge: Polity Press.

—— and Saraceno, C. (2002). 'Social Exclusion and Gender Relations', in B. Hobson, J. Lewis, and B. Siim (eds.), *Contested Concepts in Gender and Social Politics*. Cheltenham: Edward Elgar.

Driver, S. and Martell, L. (2002). 'New Labour, Work and the Family', *Social Policy and Administration*, 36/1: 46–61.

Duerr Berrick, J. (2002). 'Marriage, Motherhood and Other Social Conventions: Welfare Reform and the Politics of Enforced Morality'. Paper presented to ESPRN Conference on Social Values, Social Policy, Tilburg, 29–31 August.

Eekelaar, J. and Maclean, M. (eds.) (2000). *Cross Currents: Family Law and Policy in the United States and England*. Oxford: Oxford University Press.

Etzioni, A. (1995). *The Spirit of Community*. London: Fontana Press.

Gauthier, A. (1999). 'Historical Trends in State Support for Families in Europe (post 1945)', *Children and Youth Services Review*, 21: 937–65.

Giddens, A. (1998). *The Third Way*. Cambridge: Polity Press.

Ginsborg, P. (2000). 'The Politics of the Family in Twentieth Century Europe', *Contemporary European History*, 9: 411–44.

Government of Ireland, (2000). *National Children's Strategy*. Dublin: Stationery Office.

Hobson, B. and Morgan, D. (2002). 'Introduction', in B. Hobson (ed.), *Making Men into Fathers: Men, Masculinities and the Social Politics of Fatherhood*. Cambridge: Cambridge University Press.

Irwin, S. and Williams, F. (2002). 'Understanding Social Values and Social Change: The Case of Care, Family and Intimacy'. Paper presented to ESPRN Conference on Social Values, Social Policy, Tilburg, 29–31 August.

Knijn, T. (2002). 'Family Solidarity—Social Solidarity: Communicating Vessels?' Paper presented to ESPRN Conference on Social Values, Social Policy, Tilburg, 29–31 August.

Lansdown, G. (2001). 'Children's Welfare and Children's Rights', in P. Foley, J. Roche, and S. Tucker (eds.), *Children in Society Contemporary Theory, Policy and Practice*. Basingstoke: Palgrave.

Lavalette, M. and Cunningham, S. (2002). 'The Sociology of Childhood', in B. Goldson, M. Lavalette, and J. McKechnie (eds.), *Children, Welfare and the State*. London: Sage.

Letablier, M. and Rieucau, G. (2000). 'The Policy Logics of Action about Caring for Children'. Paper presented at 4th Seminar of the TSER Network Working and Mothering, 'Social Practices and Social Policies', Paris, 23–5 March.

Lewis, J. (2001). 'Debates and Issues Regarding Marriage and Cohabitation in the British and American Literature', *International Journal of Law, Policy and the Family*, 15: 159–84.

—— (2002). 'Gender and Welfare State Change', *European Societies*, 4: 331–57.

Mahon, R. (2002). 'Gender and Welfare State Restructuring: Through the Lens of Child Care', in S. Michel and R. Mahon (eds.), *Child Care Policy at the Crossroads*. New York: Routledge.

Makrinioti, D. (1994). 'Conceptualization of childhood in a Welfare State: A Critical Reappraisal', in J. Qvortrup, M. Bardy, G. Sgritta, and H. Wintersberger (eds.), *Childhood Matters Social Theory, Practice and Politics*. Aldershot: Avebury.

Merkel, W. (2000). 'The Third Ways of Social Democracy into the 21st Century'. Paper presented at the Third Roundtable for Human Rights and Peace on 'The Third Ways of Social Democracy and the Social Movement', Seoul, June.

Montanari, I. (2000), 'From Family Wage to Marriage Subsidy and Child Benefits: Controversy and Consensus in the Development of Family Policy', *Journal of European Social Policy*, 10: 307–33.

Morgan, K. (2001). 'Does Anyone Have a "libre choix"? Subversive Liberalism and the Politics of French Child Care Policy', in S. Michel and R. Mahon (eds.), *Child Care Policy at the Crossroads: Gender and Welfare State Restructuring*. New York: Routledge.

OECD (Organization for Economic Cooperation and Development) (2001). *Employment Outlook*. Paris: OECD.

Orloff, A. (2001). 'Ending the Entitlements of Poor Single Mothers: Changing Social Policies, Women's Employment and Caregiving in the Contemporary United States', in N. J. Hirschmann and U. Liebert (eds.), *Women and Welfare Theory and Practice in the United States and Europe*. New Brunswick, NJ: Rutgers University Press.

—— (2002). 'Explaining US Welfare Reform: Power, Gender, Race and the US Policy Legacy', *Critical Social Policy*, 22: 96–118.

Palme, J. et al. (2002). 'Welfare Trends in Sweden: Balancing the Books for the 1990s', *Journal of European Social Policy*, 12: 329–46.

Rake, K. (2001). 'Gender and New Labour's Social Policies', *Journal of Social Policy*, 30: 209–31.

Simmel, G. (1990). *The Philosophy of Money*. London: Routledge.

Wennemo, I. (1994). *Sharing the Costs of Children Studies on the Development of Family Support in the OECD Children*. Stockholm: Swedish Institute for Social Research.

Whyness, M. (2000). *Contesting Childhood*. London: Falmer Press.

III

Conflicts and Challenges

8

The Third Way's Social Investment State

RUTH LISTER

'"Third way" policy pragmatism involves both a positive view of the ability of the market to provide certain outcomes and a strong emphasis on the active "social investment state" ' (Green-Pedersen, van Kersbergen, and Hemerijck 2001: 309). The location of the 'social investment state' in Third Way thinking and practice is the subject of this chapter. The social investment state can be understood on a number of levels. First, for a number of Third Way thinkers and politicians, it figures as a *normative ideal* in which children and the community stand as emblems of a future prosperous, cohesive, and inclusive society. The values of responsibility, inclusion, and opportunity (RIO), as articulated by New Labour in particular, are its watchwords (Lister 2000*a*; 2002*a*).

Second, at the same time the social investment state represents a *pragmatic response* to the perceived economic and social challenges facing mature welfare states posed by economic globalization and falling birth rates. Social policy is accorded a central role but it is primarily an instrumental role. Through investment in human and social capital, the state can equip its citizens to respond to global economic change. Investment in young children takes on particular strategic importance. Moreover, in the Third Way 'targeted investment' represents a more politically acceptable language than traditional social democratic 'tax and spend'.

More generally, the Third Way's pragmatism lies in the way in which it draws upon conflicting earlier political traditions. Combining elements of social democracy and neo-liberalism, the emergent social investment state can be described as a hybrid welfare regime. As such, it can be understood at a third level, that of *analytical tool*. Some political scientists have

This chapter is based on Lister (2003*b*). It has benefited from comments from the editors and from Alexandra Dobrowolsky, for which I am grateful.

used the notion of the 'social investment state' as a way of making sense of contemporary developments in liberal welfare states.[1]

This chapter explores all three aspects of the social investment state. It begins with a discussion of both its evolution as a normative ideal and its key elements. This is followed by an examination of the emergence of the 'social investment state' as a hybrid form of welfare regime, most notably in Canada and the UK, and of the pragmatic instrumentalism that informs policy developments in these countries. The 'social investment state' also raises issues of governance and citizenship (Lister 2003*b*). As these are the subjects of Chapters 4 and 9, they are not discussed in any detail here. The one exception is a critical analysis of the way in which the child as citizen-worker of the future has emerged as an icon of the social investment state.

1. The Ideal of the 'Social Investment State'

The Evolution of the Ideal

The term 'social investment state' was coined by Anthony Giddens in his articulation of the Third Way. The guideline, he argues, 'is investment in *human capital* wherever possible, rather than direct provision of economic maintenance. In place of the welfare state we should put the *social investment state*' (1998: 117, emphasis in original). The previous year the OECD commented that 'by shifting from a social expenditure to a social investment perspective, it is expected that considerable progress can be made in transforming the welfare state' (1997: 14, quoted in Jenson and Saint-Martin 2001). An earlier template can be found in the report of the Commission on Social Justice.[2] The central proposition underlying its vision of an 'Investors' Britain' was that 'it is through investment that economic and social policy are inextricably linked'. 'High investment—in skills, research, technology, childcare and community development— is the last and first step' in a 'virtuous circle of sustainable growth' (Commission on Social Justice 1994: 97, 103). The emphasis was on economic opportunity in the name of social justice as well as of economic prosperity and on the achievement of security through investment in and redistribution of 'opportunities rather than just . . . income' (Commission on Social Justice 1994: 95).

---

[1] Notable here is the work of a team of political scientists led by Jane Jenson of Montreal University, which has inspired my own work on the topic.

[2] The Commission on Social Justice was established by the late John Smith, leader of the British Labour Party, to guide the Party's thinking on social and economic reform.

More recently the EU has taken up the theme. The 2000 Lisbon Summit saw investment in people as key to modernization of the European social model (Vandenbroucke 2002). A follow-up communication to the Nice European Council states that:

the European social model, with its developed systems of social protection, must underpin the transformation to the knowledge economy. People are Europe's main asset and should be the focal point of the Union's policies. Investing in people and developing an active and dynamic welfare state will be crucial both to Europe's place in the knowledge economy and for ensuring that the emergence of this new economy does not compound the existing social problems of unemployment, social exclusion and poverty. (Council of the European Union 2000: point 7, quoted in Esping-Andersen, 2002)

The Belgian presidency of the European Union then commissioned Gøsta Esping-Andersen and colleagues in 2001 to draw up 'a scientific report on the evolving architecture of the European welfare states' (Vandenbroucke 2002: ix).[3] The report articulates the general goal of 'a child-centred social investment strategy' as the foundation stone for a 'new European welfare architecture' (Esping-Andersen 2002: 6, 26). More specifically, with regard to child poverty, it argues that 'minimizing child poverty now will yield an individual and social dividend in the future. And in the far-off future, it should diminish the risks of old age poverty' (2002: 55). Although his report adopts a sceptical tone towards New Labour's variant of the Third Way, Esping-Andersen was also commissioned by the Policy Network (chaired by Peter Mandelson, a key protagonist of the Third Way) to produce an expert report for the international Progressive Governance Conference held in London in July 2003 to take forward thinking about the Third Way.

In an abridged, published version of this expert report Esping-Andersen argues that 'the first and most important step towards a positive new welfare equilibrium entails major investments in our children' and that 'a social investment strategy directed at children must be a centrepiece of any policy for social inclusion' (2003: 30, 127). In support, he points to 'evidence concerning the long-term consequences of childhood depriva-tion' for education and adult earnings potential (2003: 141). He points to how

life chances are powerfully over-determined by what happens in children's life prior to their first encounter with the schools system. It is this that explains why a century of educational reform has failed to diminish the impact of social inheritance; why parents' social status continues unabated to dictate children's

---

[3] A revised version of the report has been published as Esping-Andersen (2002).

educational attainment, income or occupational destination. For both welfare and efficiency reasons this impact must be weakened . . . The question, then, is how to combat social inheritance. (2003: 142–3)

His answer is 'a double-barrelled strategy: an effective guarantee against poverty in childhood coupled to measures that equalise the cognitive stimulus that pre-school age children receive' (2003: 148). 'Universal access to high quality day care' is proposed as 'an effective tool in the war against social inheritance' (2003: 151). At the Progressive Governance Conference, Giddens highlighted Esping-Andersen's ideas as key to 'policy innovation' in what he termed the second phase of the Third Way. In his Introduction to the conference volume, he suggests that 'abolish social inheritance!' might even become the new Third Way slogan (Giddens 2003: 30). Although Giddens no longer appears to use the term 'social investment state', having most recently adopted the notion of the 'ensuring state', its key elements are still central to his, and others', exposition of the Third Way.[4]

Unpacking the 'Social Investment State'

The key elements of the 'social investment state' are listed in Fig. 8.1. The central ones are described here and others emerge in the following section.

- A discourse of social investment in place of 'tax and spend'.
- Investment in human and social capital: children and community as emblems.
- Children prioritized as citizen-workers of the future; adult social citizenship defined by work obligations.
- Future-focused.
- Redistribution of opportunity to promote social inclusion rather than of income to promote equality.
- Adaptation of individuals and society to enhance global competitiveness and to prosper in the knowledge economy.
- Integration of social and economic policy, but with the former still the 'handmaiden' of the latter.
- A preference for targeted, often means-tested, programmes.

FIGURE 8.1. *Key features of the social investment state*

[4] The concept of the 'ensuring state' was articulated at the Progressive Governance Conference by Folke Schuppert. He writes that 'the concept develops on, but is significantly different from, the idea of the "enabling state" that has been central to much of the thinking that has guided state reform during the last two decades [see Chapter 4 this volume] . . . The

A discourse of social investment is counterpoised to a more traditional social democratic commitment to social spending. Proponents of the Third Way have attempted to distance themselves from the latter. In their joint statement of the Third Way/Die Neue Mitte, Tony Blair and Gerhard Schröder assert that 'public expenditure as a proportion of national income has more or less reached the limits of acceptability. Constraints on "tax and spend" force radical modernisation of the public sector and reform of public services to achieve better value for money' (1999: 29).

Unlike social spending, social investment is at times portrayed as somehow cost-free. For example, in his speech to the 2003 Labour Party conference, Blair cited the example of:

Holly in Southampton. Teenage mum. Now through Sure Start with childcare. Given help to study so she can become a midwife so she can work in the NHS so another mother can benefit. Why does it take so long for us to realise when we invest in people like her, it's not a cost, it's our future? (Blair 2003: 10)

Social investment is also contrasted with social democracy's traditional belief in the need for redistribution of income and wealth through the tax–benefits system. As Frank Vandenbroucke points out, this 'politically convenient' opposition represents something of a false dichotomy (2001: 167). Social investment can be costly and can itself involve an element of redistribution even if less obviously so than social security expenditure.

Esping-Andersen takes the social investment argument further, drawing an analogy with the distinction made by national accounting systems between current consumption and investment. While he accepts that it is difficult to draw a precise line between 'consumption' and 'investment' in relation to spending on children, he emphasizes the need to acknowledge the future dividends of policies that promote children's welfare. 'Good cognitive abilities to start with', he contends, 'will yield individual returns later on because they are an absolute precondition for educational attainment . . . They also yield a social dividend because we need to offset the limited numbers within coming cohorts with greater productivity' (2002: 9).[5] The costs and benefits of investment in children need to be calculated on a long-term basis.

"ensuring state" emphasises the responsibility of the state in areas where non-state agents play a dominant role in the provision of public services. It argues that there exists a public responsibility "after enabling" and that there are certain guarantees that the state has a moral and political responsibility to provide. Even if public goods or services are provided by private or third sector organisations and bodies, the state still has a major role in ensuring these public goods, whether it is by audit, regulation or funding' (2003: 75).

[5] This argument also illustrates how proponents of the social investment state draw on scientific research, which stresses the importance of early childhood for children's future development (Dobrowolsky and Jenson 2003).

This argument illustrates both the future orientation of the social investment state and, as discussed further below, the pivotal status of children—
particularly young children—within it. Jenson and Saint-Martin sum up
the future oriented nature of the social investment state:

There is also a notion of *time* that underpins the social investment approach about
the role of the state. The results produced by an investment are located in the
future, whereas consumption . . . is something that occurs in the *present*. For state
spending to be effective, and therefore worthwhile, it must not simply be con-
sumed in the present, to meet current needs, but it must be an investment that will
pay off and reap rewards in the future . . . In an 'investment-driven' citizenship
regime . . . any measures of generous and innovative spending must be justified in
future-oriented terms. Thus, spending may legitimately go: to supporting and
educating children, because they clearly hold the promise of the future; to promoting health and healthy populations because they pay off in lower future costs;
to reducing the probability of future costs of school failure and crime, again with
a heavy emphasis on children; and to fostering employability, so as to increase
future labour force participation rates. (2001: 5, emphasis in original)

This future orientation and focus on children are also reflected in a
preoccupation with equality of life-long opportunity rather than the more
traditional social democratic concern with equality as such. 'All of the
notions we associate with equality of opportunity, such as investments in
human capital, social investment, training, and so on are most relevant for
the young' (Jenson 2001: 122). This shift is particularly marked in New
Labour's version of the Third Way and its commitment to social inclusion
rather than equality (Lister 2000*a*, 2001, 2002*a*). According to Giddens,
'the contemporary left needs to develop a dynamic, life-chances approach
to equality, placing the prime stress upon equality of opportunity'. It should,
he argues, accept the consequences: 'that incentives are necessary to
encourage those of talent to progress and that equality of opportunity typically creates higher rather than lower inequalities of outcome' (2000: 86).

Blair and Schröder's statement declares that 'the most important task of
modernisation is to invest in human capital: to make the individual and
businesses fit for the knowledge-based economy of the future' (1999: 29).
This they dub 'a new supply-side agenda for the left' which emphasizes
'lifetime access to education and training' as part of the necessary investment in human capital (1999: 31, 35; Streek 1999). The social investment
state feeds the knowledge economy in a globalized world (Giddens 2000).

This supply-side agenda is complemented by 'an active labour market
policy for the left' in which 'the state must become an active agent for
employment, not merely the passive recipient of the casualties of economic failure' (Blair and Schröder 1999: 31, 35). Both exemplify Bob
Jessop's formulation of the post-fordist 'Schumpetarian workfare state'

in which 'redistributive welfare rights take second place to a productivist re-ordering of social policy' in the name of international competitiveness and the need to equip the population to respond to global change (Jessop 1994: 24; 2000; see also Holden 1999). Although proponents of the social investment state tend to emphasize the need to integrate economic and social policy, it is on terms which do not challenge the traditional subordinate 'handmaiden' relationship of the social to the economic (Titmuss 1974: 31; see also Beck, van der Maesen, and Walker 1997).[6]

As well as investment in human capital, the social investment state is concerned to strengthen *social* capital: 'investors argue that investment in social institutions is as important as investment in economic infrastructure' and that 'the moral and social reconstruction of our society depends on our willingness to invest in social capital', which is both 'a good in itself' and 'also essential for economic renewal' (Commission on Social Justice 1994: 306, 308; Oppenheim 2001). Giddens states that 'the cultivation of social capital is integral to the knowledge economy . . . Like financial capital, social capital can be expanded—invested and reinvested' (2000: 78).[7] According to Blair, a 'central goal' and 'a key task for our second term is to develop greater coherence around our commitment to community, to grasp the opportunity of "civic renewal". That means a commitment to making the state work better. But most of all, it means strengthening communities themselves' (Blair 2002*a*: 9, 11; 2002*b*). The appeal to community has played a key role in the Third Way differentiation of New Labour from the New Right and Old Left, for it posits 'an alternative to both the untrammelled free market (of neo-liberalism) and the strong state (of social democracy)' (Levitas 2000: 191).

2. The 'Social Investment State': A Hybrid Welfare Regime

Two countries that have emerged as prototype 'social investment states' are Canada and the UK, both governed by political parties committed to the Third Way, in reaction to the neo-liberal governments that preceded them.[8]

---

[6] This is typical also of European Union policy-making (see Taylor-Gooby 2003).

[7] Interestingly, Bo Rothstein and colleagues suggest that the most effective way for the state to invest in social capital, understood as trust, may be through strengthening universal social welfare programmes, which instil public trust, rather than through supporting civil society institutions (Kumlin and Rothstein 2003; Rothstein and Stolle 2003).

[8] To my knowledge the label has not yet been applied to other welfare states, although Leisering observes that in Germany 'it remains to be seen . . . if there will be a shift from the "transfer state" to a "social investment state" with more emphasis on education and employment, and less on paying for time off employment' (2001: 178). More generally, the social policy agenda advocated by the European Commission encourages member states to move towards the social investment state model.

These are countries that are typically categorized as 'liberal' in welfare regime analysis. In both cases, though, the increasingly dominant liberal character of their welfare regimes, exemplified by growing reliance on targeted, means-tested forms of welfare, has been tempered by a residual social democratic impulse, most strongly expressed through universal healthcare systems (Esping-Andersen 1990; O' Connor, Orloff, and Shaver 1999; Jenson and Phillips 2001). With their more recent emergence as social investment states, the hybrid nature of these welfare regimes has become more marked (Dobrowolsky and Saint Martin 2002; Jenson and Saint-Martin 2002).[9]

A strong commitment to social investment has always been the hallmark of social democratic regimes (Green-Pedersen, van Kersbergen, and Hemerijck 2001; Esping-Andersen 2002). This does not, however, make them 'social investment states' in the sense used here, for it is the particular configuration of social democratic and liberal/neo-liberal policy approaches outlined above and the dominance of a particular instrumentalist discourse of social investment that marks the Third Way 'social investment state'. As Esping-Andersen has observed, 'the Third Way may be criticized for its unduly selective appropriation of social democratic policy', one example being its 'tendency to believe that activation may substitute for conventional income maintenance guarantees' (2002: 5). This appropriation is typical of the pragmatic 'pick and mix', 'jackdaw politics' of the Third Way (Powell 2000; Bonoli and Powell 2002). The emergence of hybrid welfare regimes of this kind underlines the complex, non-linear nature of welfare state change (Pierson 2001; Clarke 2004). The discussion here focuses mainly on the UK but includes first a brief summary of the position in Canada.[10]

Canada

Jane Jenson (2001) and Sylvia Bashevkin (2002) have both traced the continued impact of late twentieth century neo-liberalism on the Canadian welfare state. The line between state and individual responsibility for welfare has been shifted towards the latter. To the extent that collective responsibility continues to be recognized, it has been through a new focus on children. This is 'expressed in the "children's agenda" now traversing

---

[9] Esping-Andersen himself suggests a bifurcation between 'youth-oriented' liberal regimes and a group that is 'ever more aged-biased and service-lean' (1999: 166). He includes the UK in the latter (with the US) but this was before the emergence of New Labour's social investment state.

[10] Where not stated, the information on Canada is taken from Beauvais and Jenson (2001); Jenson (2001); Jenson and Saint-Martin (2001, 2002).

federal policy communities and in the redesign of federalism and inter-governmental relations via the social union agreement' (Jenson 2001: 112). The children's agenda has formed the central plank of the Liberal government's social policy strategy. Social investment has been its leit-motif. In his preface to the Liberals' 2000 election pamphlet, the then Prime Minister Jean Chrétien declared 'we have invested for the future', claiming that 75 per cent of spending since 1997 represented social investment (Dobrowolsky 2004). Beauvais and Jenson (2001) describe the changes as a shift in emphasis from a 'family responsibility paradigm' to an 'investing in children paradigm'.

A series of policy instruments has been developed at both federal and provincial levels to realize the philosophy of the social investment state. Child poverty and active labour market participation are at the heart of the social policy agenda. Key has been the introduction of the National Child Benefit (NCB), an income-tested tax credit available regardless of parental employment status. One of the goals of the NCB, together with new employability and work activation programmes, is

to foster the labour force participation of *all* parents. Gone is the notion that parental child care can supplant employment in the case of lone parent families. Instead, all parents, at least when their children are school-aged, are required to seek employment and, in many cases, even when their children are much younger. (Jenson and Saint-Martin 2001: 14, emphasis in original; see also Bashevkin 2002*b*.)

Dobrowolsky (2004) observes that labour market participation is seen as a means of combating social exclusion and fostering social cohesion. She also draws attention to the selective, typically means-tested nature of new social programmes in the social investment state of Canada (see also Bashevkin 2002*b*). Universal family allowances, abolished under the previous Conservative government, are not to be reinstated (McKeen 2001). Dobrowolsky and other Canadian scholars emphasize the significance of the wider context in which responsibility for welfare has increasingly been shifted from the federal government to provincial governments, but without adequate funding (Dobrowolsky 2004; Bashevkin 2002*b*).

A document published by one of the provincial governments, titled *Our Children . . . Today's Investment, Tomorrow's Promise*, sums up the new social investment philosophy. It promotes the idea of investment

in the early years as an economic strategy . . . The fiscal argument for investing in early childhood programs has gained momentum. Recent shifts in economic policy emphasize open economies and require a well-educated and flexible labour force in order to compete globally. Therefore, it is vital that we support and value children in order to ensure their futures. (Province of Nova Scotia 2001: 8, cited in Jenson and Saint-Martin 2001).

On the service side a raft of early childhood initiatives has been developed to support children's early health and educational development at both federal and provincial levels. These include a Community Action Program for Children, which invests in programmes for high-risk young children in selected areas. The main areas of intervention are family resource centres, child development centres, parenting education, and infant stimulation. The rationale of the programme is that 'early investment in children' enables them to get a better start in life and equips them for school (cited in Jenson and Saint-Martin 2001: 15). In this ' "social investment state" . . . investments—in services and also in income transfers in the name of equity—are justified by their supposed long-term pay offs in terms of school success and future well-being. Rather than focusing on equity now, they seek to provide equality of opportunity for future success' (Beauvais and Jenson 2001: 5). Hopes that the Liberal government might instigate a national childcare programme, based on earlier promises, were, however, dashed by a combination of the priority given to reducing the federal deficit and the attendant decentralization of welfare responsibilities to the provinces (Bashevkin 2002*b*; Dobrowolsky and Jenson 2003).

The United Kingdom

In a key Strategic Audit, drawn up by the government's Strategy Unit, the first 'strategic priority' is described as 'ready for the future'. Key to its achievement is 'ensuring people have the skills and qualities for future jobs, lives and citizenship', with 'the importance of human capital to future growth' highlighted (Strategy Unit 2003: 37). Later the Audit emphasizes the 'high returns' to be gained from early years programmes in light of 'the very strong evidence on the cost-effectiveness of targeted investment in children' (Strategy Unit 2003: 78–9). This is the strategic context in which the priority given by New Labour to children has to be understood.

The Commission on Social Justice declared that 'children are 100 per cent of the nation's future' and 'the best indicator of the capacity of our economy tomorrow is the quality of our children today' (CSJ 1994: 311). Children emerged as key figures in New Labour's nascent social investment state early in 1999. In his Beveridge Lecture, the Prime Minister pledged the government to eradicate child poverty in two decades, explaining that 'we have made children our top priority because, as the Chancellor memorably said in his Budget, "they are 20% of the population but they are [echoing the CSJ] 100% of the future" ' (Blair 1999: 16). Around the same time, the Treasury published a document titled

Tackling Poverty and Extending Opportunity, which emphasized the impact of poverty on children's life chances and opportunities (HM Treasury 1999).

Although the pledge to end child poverty was made by Blair, much of the policy impetus on children has come from the Treasury, which under Brown has become a key actor in the development of social policy (Deakin and Parry 2000). Brown has described child poverty as 'a scar on Britain's soul', arguing that 'we must give all our children the opportunity to achieve their hopes and fulfil their potential. By investing in them, we are investing in our future' (Brown 1999a: 8). He has developed these themes in a series of speeches, together with the argument that 'tackling child poverty is the best anti-drugs, anti-crime, anti-deprivation policy for our country' (Brown 2000). In his foreword to the pre-2002 Budget report, he states that 'our children are our future and the most important invest-ment that we can make as a nation is in developing the potential of all our country's children' (Brown 2001: iv). While this report does acknowledge that 'action to abolish child poverty must *improve the current quality of children's lives* as well as investing to enable children to reach their full potential as adults' (HM Treasury 2001: 5; emphasis added), the point is not developed.[11] The futurist and economistic rationale for the priority given to child poverty was taken to an extreme in the 2003 Budget Report. Having pointed to how poverty affects both childhood and children's 'experience as adults and the life chances of their own children', it explains that 'support for today's disadvantaged children will therefore help to ensure a more flexible economy tomorrow' (HM Treasury 2003: para. 5.4).

Brown presented his 2002 Budget as 'building a Britain of greater enter-prise and greater fairness, and nothing is more important to an enterpris-ing, fairer Britain than that, through education and through support for the family, we invest in the potential of every single child in our country' (Brown 2002: col. 586). He also announced 'one of the biggest single investments in children and families since the welfare state was formed in the 1940s' (Brown 2002: col. 587). He was referring primarily to additional investment in an evolving tax credits system that reflects the influence of the Canadian (as well as the Australian and US) models. According to Myles and Quadagno, this 'model of welfare state redistribution . . . is particularly compatible with Third Way principles in liberal welfare states' and with 'the new politics of austerity' (2000: 159, 161). It promotes the

---

[11] The November 2002 Pre-Budget Report does acknowledge that poverty 'excludes children from the everyday activities of their peers' (HM Treasury 2002b).

recommodification of labour and represents what Sylvia Bashevkin has described as an increasingly 'fiscalized social policy' (2002*a*: 114; 2002*b*).

Means-tested benefits for children are being replaced by a child tax credit (CTC), which provides 'a single, seamless system of income-related support for families with children' paid direct to the caring parent with the universal child benefit (HM Treasury 2002: para. 5.17).[12] In addition, a new working tax credit incorporates a childcare element (payable to the caring parent). These tax credits represent a further shift in the balance of financial support towards the means-testing typical of liberal regimes. It is justified by reference to the principle of 'progressive universalism', that is, 'giving everyone a stake in the system while offering more help to those who need it most' (HM Treasury 2002: para. 5.5).[13]

Prior to the introduction of the CTC, the amount of money available for the children of both employed and non-employed parents had already been increased significantly. This includes a phased improvement in the social assistance rates for children so that by October 2002 the real value of assistance for under-eleven-year-old children had virtually doubled. This improvement deviates from the Third Way in welfare as initially articulated by New Labour: improvements in out-of-work benefits were dismissed as 'dependency'-inducing 'cash handouts' to be rejected in favour of 'a modern form of welfare that believes in empowerment not dependency' (DSS 1998: 19). It has therefore not been trumpeted as loudly as other policy developments, so much so that many people are still unaware of it. It is an example of a wider phenomenon: 'redistribution by stealth'.

Redistribution of resources, as opposed to redistribution of opportunities, does not fit the New Labour template. When pressed on the issue, Brown has therefore described it as redistribution based on 'people exercising responsibilities' to work and bring up children in contrast to old forms of redistribution based on 'something for nothing' (Brown 1999*b*). The exercise of responsibility to undertake paid work, in return for the opportunities provided by government, lies at the heart of New Labour's Third Way citizenship and social inclusion philosophy, which, as suggested in the Introduction, can be summed up as 'RIO' (Lister 2000*a*, 2002*a*). The main policy instruments are a series of New Deal programmes and the JobCentre Plus agency (described in Chapter 9). These

---

[12] A higher children's tax credit is paid during the year of a child's birth as part of a package to improve support in the early years of a child's life (see HM Treasury 2002).

[13] The government did implement a significant increase in the universal child benefit in its first term, but all the indications are that this will not be repeated. There is considerable criticism of the heavy reliance on means-testing, not least from the former social security minister, Frank Field, who has described tax credits as 'a form of permanent serfdom' (Field 2002).

too are promoted by using a discourse of investment. For example, commenting on research which suggests that welfare-to-work policies boost output as well as employment, the Work and Pensions Secretary, Andrew Smith, declared that 'the evidence is increasingly clear that government investment to help people back to work gives a good return to society as a whole' (DWP 2003).

Two further examples of New Labour's strategy of investing in children and young people are the piloting and introduction of means-tested educational maintenance allowances to encourage young people from low-income families to stay on at school and the planned introduction of a universal 'child trust fund', a form of 'asset-based welfare' under which every newborn child will be given a modest capital sum, accessible only when they reach eighteen years of age (Kelly and Le Grand 2001; Inland Revenue/HM Treasury 2003). Indeed, asset-based welfare has itself been characterized as representing a transition to a social investment state (Sherraden 2002).

Important also to the development of the 'social investment state' is a series of service-based initiatives. Of particular significance is Sure Start, which was inspired by the US Head Start programme (see HM Treasury 2001). Although its initial focus was more on health and child development, one of its architects, Norman Glass, a former Treasury official, has warned that it is in danger of 'becoming a New Deal for toddlers', dominated by the ' "what parents need is work" policy line' (*Society Guardian* 2003). Sure Start is to be combined with early years education and childcare within a single interdepartmental unit with an integrated budget. A further injection of funds into New Labour's national childcare strategy is promised, in the face of evidence that the policy is flagging. This will involve the creation of children's centres and of an additional 250,000 childcare places by 2005–6 (Strategy Unit 2002). Newspaper reports suggest that major investment in a comprehensive network of children's centres could form the 'big idea' for New Labour's next election manifesto (*Observer* 2003a; *Independent* 2003).

For all its weaknesses, the national childcare strategy represents a breakthrough in British social policy. It represents the first time that government has accepted that childcare is a public as well as a private responsibility. Birte Siim has argued that 'from the point of view of social policies towards women and children, Britain . . . represents an exception to the rule of European social policies', particularly in the area of childcare services (Siim 2000: 92). This, she suggests, reflects the dominant liberal philosophy of the separation of public and private spheres and (partial) non-intervention in the latter (see also Lewis 1998; O'Connor, Orloff, and Shaver 1999).

Hitherto this philosophy has framed general policy towards children other than those deemed at risk of abuse or neglect. Despite the introduction of family allowances and their extension and replacement by child benefit, children have been the subject of public neglect. The UK has been described as 'a serious contender for the title of worst place in Europe to be a child' (Micklewright and Stewart 2000*b*: 23; 2000*a*). Arguably this reflects not only the liberal strand in the dominant social welfare philosophy but also an ambivalence in British attitudes towards children (Lister 2000*b*). A tendency to sentimentalize and idealize children has existed alongside a reluctance to accommodate their presence in the adult world and an element of hostility and fear, as reflected in the recent demonization of 'feral children'.[14] In addition, during the Thatcher years there was an increasingly strongly expressed view that having children is 'essentially a private matter', akin to other expensive consumer goods (Beenstock 1984, cited in Brown 1988). This ambivalence is reflected in the ways in which children figure in policy both as our future hope, deserving of investment, and as anti-social terrors, needing regulation and punishment (Reeves 2003).

3. The New Citizens

In both Canada and the UK, the Third Way governments that came to power in the 1990s, in the wake of neo-liberal restructuring of the welfare state, were committed to fiscal responsibility, continued limits on social spending, and reducing welfare 'dependency'. At the same time, in contrast to their neo-liberal predecessors, once in power they developed a social investment strategy that represents a real increase in expenditure on children. The reality has not always matched the rhetoric, particularly in the area of childcare provision (Bashevkin 2002*a*, 2002*b*; Jenson and Saint-Martin 2002; Children's Rights Alliance 2003; Dobrowolsky 2002, 2004). Nevertheless, it would appear that we are witnessing a genuine, unprecedented attempt to shift the social priorities of the state and nation to investing in children. Arguably, the motivation behind this shift is a mixture of pragmatic instrumentalism and a vision of what Esping-Andersen calls the 'Good Society' (2002: 1). In this final section, I explore the implications of the child-centred 'social investment state' for the citizenship of both children and adults, with reference in particular to the UK.

---

[14] The 'feral child' figured prominently in a number of newspapers reports of the acquittal of the young people charged with the murder of the Black teenager Damilola Taylor. See, for instance, the *Daily Mail* (2002) and Anderson (2002) and, for a critical account of its wider use, Hari (2002).

Children as Citizen-Workers of the Future

Jenson, writing in the Canadian context, has suggested that, in the social investment state, children have become the 'model citizens' but they are so symbolically because, as minors, they cannot be full citizens able 'to employ the force of democratic politics to insist on social reform in the name of equality' (2001: 122, 125). In a more recent paper with Denis Saint-Martin, she traces a shift in the 'ideal-typical representation of citizen' from 'citizen-worker' in the 'social rights' citizenship regime to 'the child as citizen-in-becoming' in the 'social investment' regime (Jenson and Saint-Martin 2001: table 2).

In the UK, the 'citizen-worker' is still centre stage (see Chapter 9). In so far as he or she is being joined there by the child, it is the child as 'citizen-*worker*-in-becoming' or 'citizen-*worker* of the future'. It is the future *worker*-citizen more than *democratic*-citizen who is the prime asset of the social investment state. Moreover, the future orientation and discourses of the social investment state encourage not just the elision of demands for equality in the here-and-now[15] but also, paradoxically, the partial disappearance of childhood and of the child qua child, including the child as a rights-bearer (under the UN Convention on the Rights of the Child). The child as cipher for future economic prosperity and forward-looking modernization overshadows the child as child-citizen.[16]

This reflects the Third Way's instrumentalist orientation to children, as summed up by Myles and Quadagno:

if Third Wayism has a soft spot, it is for children. The soft spot comes less from benign spirits than from hard-headed economic considerations about the longer-term implications for economic performance of a large number of children growing up poorly educated or in poor health. Children matter because 'human capital' formation matters. (2000: 166)

In many ways, the discourse of social investment in children reflects that deployed by organizations and individuals, in the UK and elsewhere, making the case for better state financial support and services for children.[17] As such it has arguably proved its utility in persuading politicians. In turn, it may also represent a politically astute discourse for politicians

---

[15] See Jenson (2001); Jenson and Saint-Martin (2001); Dobrowolsky and Saint-Martin (2002).

[16] According to one participant, when ministers were asked at a seminar in 1998 why they were focusing on children, the response was that 'children are the future; we are not interested in the past' (Seminar for Hilary Land, 25 March 2002, London).

[17] See for instance Brown (1988); England and Folbre (1999); European Forum for Child Welfare (2002). Indeed, I have used the argument myself, particularly in my former role as Director of the Child Poverty Action Group.

to use in a culture unsympathetic to children and alongside a rhetoric hostile to cash benefits. However, there are also dangers: Sanford F. Schram has cautioned in the US context that the deployment of the economistic discourse of investment represents 'a slippery politics' (1995: 24). As Valerie Polakow warns, if children are seen to 'matter instrumentally, not existentially', expenditure on them will be justifiable only where there is a demonstrable pay-off, so that there is no room for 'expenditure which merely contributes to the well-being or enjoyment of children as children' (1993: 101).

In the UK, while there is strong support for the commitment to eradicate child poverty, there is also an emergent critique of the social investment paradigm from a child-centred perspective as well as ongoing criticism of the government's patchy record on children's rights. According to Alan Prout, the central focus of policy 'is on the better adult lives that will, it is predicted, emerge from reducing child poverty. It is not on the better lives that children will lead as children' (2000: 305). Prout does not reject the discourse of investment in children but warns that 'on its own a focus on futurity is unbalanced and needs to be accompanied by a concern for the present well-being of children, for their participation in social life and for their opportunities for human self-realisation' (2000: 306; see also Roche 1999; Ridge 2002). Such a concern reflects a 'new paradigm' of childhood in which children are seen as 'beings' rather than 'becomings' (Fawcett, Featherstone, and Goddard 2004). As the Children's Forum declared in its official statement to the UN General Assembly, 'you call us the future, but we are also the present' (cited in Stasiulis 2002: 508). This stance was reflected in the UN's 2002 resolution on *A World Fit for Children*. While it too affirms the importance of investment in children, it also offers a vision of

a world in which all girls and boys can enjoy childhood—a time of play and learning, in which they are loved, respected and cherished, their rights are promoted and protected, without discrimination of any kind, where their safety and well-being are paramount, and where they can develop in health, peace and dignity. (UN 2002: para. 9)

Although the UK is a signatory to this document, it is telling that no mention is made of it in the recent Green Paper *Every Child Matters* (Willow 2003). In New Labour's 'social investment state', goals and targets tend to be future-oriented rather than focused 'on the quality of children's lives—goals of achieving childhoods that are, as far as possible, happy, healthy and fulfilled' (Piachaud 2001: 453; see also Thomas and Hocking 2003). Education is reduced to a utilitarian achievement-oriented measurement culture of tests and exams, with little attention paid to the actual educational experience. As the children's author Philip Pullman has warned, in what amounts to a critique of the social investment state's construction of children, the government wants 'to turn children into bright little units of production and consumption'. That, he responds, is 'not what education is about; education is about developing the whole. It's not like investing in a company where you expect a regular dividend . . . It ought not to be regarded in costs and benefits, price and profit terms' (quoted in the *Observer* 2003*b*).

The target-oriented construction of children as citizen-workers of the future provides only limited space for the 'imaginary of the child citizen as an active participant in governance', personified in and promoted by an emergent international children's movement (Stasiulis 2002: 509; see also Roche 1999).[18] Although, in the UK, this imaginary has been promoted by the official Children and Young Person's Unit, it does not have very deep roots in wider government thinking about children and children's rights, as codified in the UN Convention on the Rights of the Child.[19]

Under Article 12 of the Convention, children have the right to express their views and have them taken seriously in all matters affecting them. Gerison Lansdown (2002) has argued that this article 'is far from adequately implemented in respect of children in the UK'. The second UK report of the UN Committee on the Rights of the Child highlighted the extent to which the government's approach to children's rights has been piecemeal and partial (CRC 2002; Featherstone, Fawcett, and Goddard 2002). A particular focus of criticism in the report is the 'unequal enjoyment of economic, social, cultural, civil and political rights' by vulnerable groups of children including asylum and refugee children (CRC 2002: para. 22). There has, for instance, been a reluctance to extend to the children of asylum-seekers the welfare and educational rights enjoyed by other children (Maternity Alliance 2002; Sale 2002; see also Stasiulis 2002; Children's Rights Alliance 2003). In a review of government action on the UN report a year on, the Children's Rights Alliance for England, while acknowledging where progress has been made, expresses 'huge disappointment that not more was done to make a reality of children's human rights' (2003: 6). In particular, it criticizes *Every Child Matters* for its failure to make reference to the Convention on the Rights of the Child.

---

[18] The movement was made visible as children took to the streets in March 2003 to protest against war with Iraq.

[19] The Children and Young Person's Unit was, however, abolished as a free-standing unit in 2003 and subsumed within a new Children and Families Directorate within the Department for Education and Skills.

Adult Citizens of Today

Canadian analysts of the 'social investment state' have drawn attention to how the priority given to children has meant neglect of the needs of adults, both non-parents and parents. Jenson writes: 'adults are left to fend for themselves "responsibly" in the neo-liberal world of individualization and market relations' (2001: 112). The model adult citizen of both genders is expected to support himself or herself in the labour market rather than rely on the state. This is an expression of an individualized 'citizen-worker' or 'adult worker' model that is being promoted by governments more widely (Fraser 1997; Lewis 2000; Lister 2002*b*, 2003*a*).

The implications of the social investment state for women's citizenship and gender equality are of particular concern. Jenson and Saint-Martin (2001) warn that neglect of gender equality issues may be one consequence of the future-oriented social investment state. There is a danger that children's poverty is divorced from that of their mothers and more generally that 'questions of gender power . . . are more and more difficult to raise, as adults are left to take responsibility for their own lives' (Jenson 2001: 125; Dobrowolsky 2004). The discourse of child poverty has dominated policy-making on poverty for longer in Canada than in the UK. A Status of Canada Women report argues that the discourse has served to make the structural causes of poverty less visible; to encourage a response motivated by pity for the helpless child; and to displace women's issues generally and women's poverty specifically (McKeen 2001; Wiegers 2002; Stasiulis 2002). Dobrowolsky (2004) also traces how the women's movement has been marginalized in policy-making in Canada's social investment state (see also Jenson and Phillips 2001).

A focus on children and social investment does not, however, necessarily have to mean the displacement of gender issues, even if it still distorts the construction of women's citizenship. Esping-Andersen, for instance, makes the case—albeit an instrumentalist case typical of the 'social investment state'—for treating the development of 'women-friendly' policies as themselves 'a social investment'. He justifies this position on the grounds that 'in many countries women constitute a massive untapped labour reserve that can help narrow future age dependency rates and reduce associated financial pressures' and that 'female employment is one of the most effective means of combating social exclusion and poverty' (2002: 94). He does, nevertheless, concede that increased female participation in paid work has implications for male participation in the unpaid work of care, which many would argue is critical to a gender-inclusive, woman-friendly model of citizenship (Lister 2003*a*). Hitherto, this has not been treated as a serious policy issue in the social investment states of Canada and the UK.

It would be wrong to say that New Labour has ignored the general issue of gender equality. But the consensus is that it has accorded it relatively low priority, despite the establishment of a Women and Equality Unit and a number of specific policies that will improve women's lives. New Labour's avoidance of a systematic gendered analysis and strategy is not, however, simply a function of its child-oriented priorities. It also reflects a reluctance, symptomatic of the Third Way, to acknowledge structural inequalities and conflicts of interest in a concern to promote consensus and cohesion (Franklin 2000*a*, *b*; McRobbie 2000; Coote 2001). That said, a focus on the child is one way of side-stepping social divisions, even though these frame and shape children's opportunities and adult outcomes: 'because the figure of the child is unified, homogeneous, undifferentiated, there is little talk about race, ethnicity, gender, class and disability. Children become a single, essentialized category' (Dobrowolsky 2002: 67).

The more general question of the construction of responsible adult citizenship in the UK is discussed in Chapter 9. In summary, in return for the promise of investment in economic opportunity by the state, increased emphasis is being placed on the responsibilities of citizens, most notably: to equip themselves to respond to the challenges of economic globalization through improved employability; to support themselves through paid work; to invest in their own pensions; and to ensure the responsible behaviour of their children.

4. Conclusion

The notion of 'the social investment state' has emerged as both a normative ideal of the Third Way and a pragmatic response to the challenges to the welfare state identified by Third Way thinkers and politicians. At the same time, it can also be used as an analytical tool for understanding emergent tendencies in Third Way states. This chapter has discussed each of these aspects, using the case studies of Canada and the UK as the most advanced examples of social investment states in action.

The normative ideal and pragmatic response are intertwined. The child and the community are idealized as emblems of the social investment state. The child in particular takes on iconic status. However, it is the child as 'citizen-worker' of the future rather than the 'citizen-child' of the present who is invoked by the new discourse of social investment. This investment in human and social capital represents a primary function of the social investment state in order to equip its members to cope with the challenges of the global economy. As future citizen-workers, children, and especially children in poverty, take priority but the quality of their *childhood* risks being overshadowed. At the same time, the issue of the poverty of today's citizens of working age is marginalized. More generally, while the importance of social policy is emphasized, its role is essentially instrumental to economic ends.

From an analytical perspective, the idea of the social investment state provides a helpful analytic framework for understanding the emergent new welfare architecture. In the language of welfare regime analysis, it represents a new hybrid model of liberal regime which combines liberal/ neo-liberal and social democratic tendencies. This does not, however, mean that all policy shifts in emergent social investment states are necessarily *reducible* to the 'social investment state' template, even if they are consistent with it. Thus, for instance, New Labour's preoccupation with citizenship responsibility and the obligations associated with the paid work ethic needs to be analysed in its own right as well as simply as an expression of the social investment state. Indeed, it helps us to understand better the true complexion of the model citizen in that state.

Second, neither the state nor welfare state change is monolithic and it is dangerous to assume 'unity or integration' or to flatten out complexity (Pringle and Watson 1992: 63; Clarke 2004). While the philosophical and policy contours of the Third Way may be becoming clearer (as argued elsewhere in this volume), its underlying pragmatism continues to give rise to ambiguities (Lister 2001; Bonoli and Powell 2002). Such ambiguities mean that there are spaces, such as around childhood and poverty, that civil society actors can exploit to argue for a more genuinely child-focused and also more egalitarian approach. Thus, even if the 'social investment state' represents something of a paradigm shift, analysts and activists need to remain alert to complexities and possible inconsistencies within the specific policy configurations to be found in particular emergent social investment states.

References

Anderson, B. (2002). 'The Time for Sentimentalism is Over: Let Us Tame These Feral Children', *Independent*, 29 April.

Bashevkin, S. (2002*a*). 'Road-testing the Third Way: Single Mothers and Welfare Reform During the Clinton, Chrétien and Blair Years', in S. Bashevkin (ed.), *Women's Work is Never Done: Comparative Studies in Care-Giving, Employment and Social Policy Reform*. New York and London: Routledge.

——(2002*b*). *Welfare Hot Buttons: Women, Work and Social Policy Reform*. Toronto and London: University of Toronto Press.

Beauvais, C. and Jenson, J. (2001). *Two Policy Paradigms: Family Responsibility and Investing in Children*. Ottawa: Canadian Policy Research Networks, www.cprn.org.

Beck, W., van der Maesen, L, and Walker, A. (eds.) (1997). *The Social Quality of Europe*. The Hague/London/Boston: Kluwer Law International.

Beenstock, M. (1984). 'Rationalising Child Benefit'. Paper given at Policy Studies Institute Seminar, London, June.

Blair, T. (1999). Beveridge Lecture, Toynbee Hall, London, 18 March. Reproduced in R. Walker (ed.), *Ending Child Poverty*. Bristol: Policy Press.

—— (2002*a*). 'New Labour and Community', *Renewal*, 10/2: 9–14.

—— (2002*b*). 'My Vision for Britain', *Observer*, 10 November.

—— (2003). 'I Want Us to Go Further and Faster'. Speech to Labour Party conference, Bournemouth, 30 September. www.labour.org.uk/tbbournemouth.

—— and Schröder, G. (1999). 'Europe: The Third Way/Die Neue Mitte'. Reproduced in *The Spokesman* 66: 27–37.

Bonoli, G. and Powell, M. (2002). 'Third Ways in Europe?', *Social Policy and Society*, 1/1: 59–66.

Brown, G. (1999*a*). 'A Scar on the Nation's Soul', *Poverty*, 104.

—— (1999*b*). *Today Programme*, BBC Radio 4, 29 March.

—— (2000). Speech to the Children and Young Person's Unit conference, Islington, London, 15 November.

—— (2001). 'Foreword' to HM Treasury, *Tackling Child Poverty: Giving Every Child the Best Possible Start in Life*. London: HM Treasury.

—— (2002). 'Budget Statement', Hansard (HC), 17 April.

Brown, J. (1988). *Child Benefit: Investing in the Future*. London: Child Poverty Action Group.

Children's Rights Alliance for England (2003). *Convention on the Rights of the Child: Review of UK Government Action on 2002. Concluding Observations of the UN Committee on the Rights of the Child*. London: CRAE. www.crights.org.uk.

Clarke, J. (2004). *Changing Welfare, Changing States*. London: Sage.

Coote, A. (2001). 'Feminism and the Third Way: A Call For Dialogue', in S. White (ed.), *New Labour. The Progressive Future?* Basingstoke/New York: Palgrave.

CRC (Committee on the Rights of the Child) (2002). *Concluding Observations of the Committee on the Rights of the Child: United Kingdom of Great Britain and Northern Ireland*. Geneva: Office of the High Commissioner for Human Rights. www.unhchr.ch.

CSJ (Commission on Social Justice) (1994). *Social Justice: Strategies for National Renewal*. London: Vintage.

Deakin, N. and Parry, R. (2000). *The Treasury and Social Policy*. Basingstoke: Macmillan.

Dobrowolsky, A. (2002). 'Rhetoric Versus Reality: The Figure of the Child and New Labour's Strategic "Social Investment State" ', *Studies in Political Economy*, Autumn: 43–73.

—— (2004). 'The Chrétien Liberal Legacy and Women: Changing Policy Priorities with Little Cause for Celebration', *Review of Constitutional Studies*.

Dobrowolsky, A. and Jenson, J. (2003). 'Shifting Patterns of Representation: The Politics of "Children", "Families", "Women" '. Unpublished draft.

—— and Saint-Martin, D. (2002). 'Agency, Actors and Change in a Child-Focused Future: Problematizing Path Dependency's Past and Statist Parameters'. Paper prepared for Canadian Political Science Association Annual Meeting, University of Toronto, 29 May–1 June.

DSS (Department of Social Security) (1998). *New Ambitions for Our Country: A New Contract for Welfare*. London: Stationery Office.

DWP (Department for Work and Pensions) (2003). Press release, 17 October.

Dwyer, P. (1998). 'Conditional Citizens? Welfare Rights and Responsibilities in the Late 1990s', *Critical Social Policy*, 18: 493–517.

England, P. and Folbre, N. (1999). 'Who Should Pay for the Kids?', *Annals of the American Association of Political and Social Science*, 563: 194–207.

Esping-Andersen, G. (1990). *The Three Worlds of Welfare Capitalism*. Cambridge: Polity Press.

—— (1999). *Social Foundations of Postindustrial Economics*. Oxford: Oxford University Press.

—— with Gallie, D., Hemerijck, A., Myles, J. (2002). *Why We Need a New Welfare State*. Oxford and New York: Oxford University Press.

—— (2003). 'Against Social Inheritance', in M. Browne, P. Thompson, and F. Sainsbury (eds.), *Progressive Futures: New Ideas for the Centre-Left*. London: Policy Network.

European Forum for Child Welfare (2002). *Eradicating Child Poverty: Fact or Fiction*. www.efcw.org.

Fawcett, B., Featherstone, B., and Goddard, J. (2004). *Contemporary Child Care Policy and Practice*. London/New York: Palgrave.

Featherstone, B., Fawcett, B., and Goddard, J. (2002). 'New Labour, Children's Rights and the United Nations: "Could Do Better" ', *Journal of Social Welfare and Family Law*, 24: 475–84.

Field, F. (2002). 'Gordon Brown's Invention: A Form of Permanent Serfdom', *Daily Telegraph*, 11 June.

Franklin, J. (2000a). 'After Modernisation: Gender, the Third Way and the New Politics', in A. Coote (ed.), *New Gender Agenda*. London: IPPR.

—— (2000b). 'What's Wrong with New Labour Politics?', *Feminist Review*, 66: 138–42.

Fraser, N. (1997). *Justice Interruptus*. New York and London: Routledge.

Giddens, A. (1998). *The Third Way: The Renewal of Social Democracy*. Cambridge: Polity Press.

—— (2000). *The Third Way and its Critics*. Cambridge: Polity Press.

—— (2003). 'Introduction: The Progressive Agenda', in M. Browne, P. Thompson, and F. Sainsbury (eds.), *Progressive Futures: New Ideas for the Centre-Left*. London: Policy Network.

Green-Pederson, C., van Kersbergen, K., and Hemerijck, A. (2001). 'Neo-Liberalism, the 'Third Way' or What? Recent Social Democratic Welfare Policies in Denmark and the Netherlands', *Journal of European Public Policy*, 8: 307–25.

Hari, J. (2002). 'Yah Boo to a Daily Mail Myth', *New Statesman*, 23 September: 24–5.

HM Treasury (1999). *Tackling Poverty and Extending Opportunity*. London: HM Treasury.

—— (2001). *Tackling Child Poverty: Giving Every Child the Best Possible Start in Life*. London: HM Treasury.

—— (2002). *Budget Report*. London: HM Treasury.

—— (2003). *Budget Report 2003*. London: HM Treasury.

Holden, C. (1999). 'Globalization, Social Exclusion and Labour's New Work Ethic', *Critical Social Policy*, 19: 529–38.

Inland Revenue/HM Treasury (2003). *Detailed Proposals for the Child Trust Fund*. London: HMSO. www.inlandrevenue.gov.uk/ctf.

Jenson, J. (2001). 'Rethinking Equality and Equity: Canadian Children and the Social Union', in E. Broadbent (ed.), *Democratic Equality: What Went Wrong?* Toronto/Buffalo/London: University of Toronto Press.

—— and Phillips, S. (2001). 'Redesigning the Canadian Citizenship Regime: Remaking the Institutions of Representation', in C. Crouch, K. Eder, and D. Tambini (eds.), *Citizenship, Markets, and the State*. Oxford: Oxford University Press.

—— and Saint-Martin, D. (2001). 'Changing Citizenship Regimes: Social Policy Strategies In The Investment State'. Paper prepared for workshop on 'Fostering Social Cohesion: A Comparison of New Political Strategies', University of Montreal, 21–2 June.

—— (2002). 'Building Blocks for a New Welfare Architecture: From Ford to LEGO'. Paper prepared for American Political Science Association Annual Conference, Boston, 29 August–1 September.

Jessop, B. (1994). 'The Transition to Post-Fordism and the Schumpeterian Workfare State', in R. Burrows and B. Loader (eds.), *Towards a Post-Fordist Welfare State?* London and New York: Routledge.

—— (2000). 'From the KWNS to the SWPR', in G. Lewis, S. Gewirtz, and J. Clarke (eds.), *Rethinking Social Policy*. London: Sage.

Kelly, G. and Le Grand, J. (2001). 'Assets for the People', *Prospect*, December, pp. 50–3.

Kumlin, S. and Rothstein, B. (2003). 'Investing in Social Capital: The Impact of Welfare State Institutions'. Paper prepared for delivery at the 2003 Annual Meeting of the Political Science Association, Philadelphia, 28–31 August.

Lansdown, G. (2002). 'Children's Rights Commissioners for the UK', in B. Franklin (ed.), *The New Handbook of Children's Rights*. London and New York: Routledge.

Leisering, L. (2001). 'Germany: Reform from Within', in P. Alcock and G. Craig (eds.), *International Social Policy*. Basingstoke: Palgrave.

Levitas, R. (2000). 'Community, Utopia and New Labour', *Local Economy*, 15/3: 188–97.

Lewis, J. (ed.) (1998). *Gender, Social Care and Welfare State Restructuring in Europe*. Aldershot: Ashgate.

—— (2000). 'Work and Care', in H. Dean, R. Sykes, and R. Woods (eds.), *Social Policy Review 12*. Newcastle: Social Policy Association.

Lister, R. (2000a). 'To RIO via the Third Way: Labour's "Welfare" Reform Agenda', *Renewal*, 8/4: 9–20.

Lister, R. (2000*b*). 'The Politics of Child Poverty in Britain from 1965 to 1990', *Revue Française de Civilisation Britannique*, 11/1: 67–80.

—— (2001). 'New Labour: A Study in Ambiguity From a Position of Ambivalence', *Critical Social Policy*, 21: 425–47.

—— (2002*a*). 'Towards a New Welfare Settlement?', in C. Hay (ed.), *British Politics Today*. Cambridge: Polity Press.

—— (2002*b*). 'The Dilemmas of Pendulum Politics: Balancing Paid Work, Care and Citizenship', *Economy and Society*, 31: 520–32.

—— (2003*a*). *Citizenship: Feminist Perspectives* (2nd edn.). Basingstoke: Palgrave.

—— (2003*b*). 'Investing in the Citizen-Workers of the Future: Transformations in Citizenship and the State under New Labour', *Social Policy and Administration*, 37: 427–43.

McKeen, W. (2001). 'Shifting Policy and Politics of Federal Child Benefits in Canada', *Social Politics*, 8/2: 186–90.

McRobbie, A. (2000). 'Feminism and the Third Way', *Feminist Review*, 64: 97–112.

Maternity Alliance (2002). *A Crying Shame: Pregnant Asylum Seekers and their Babies in Detention* (Briefing paper). London: Maternity Alliance.

Micklewright, J. and Stewart, K. (2000*a*). *The Welfare of Europe's Children*. Bristol: Policy Press.

—— —— (2000*b*). 'Child Well-Being and Social Cohesion', *New Economy*, 7/1: 18–23.

Myles, J. and Quadagno, J. (2000). 'Envisioning a Third Way: The Welfare State in the Twenty-First Century', *Contemporary Sociology*, 29/1: 156–67.

O'Connor, J., Orloff, A., and Shaver, S. (1999). *States, Markets, Families: Gender, Liberalism and Social Policy in Australia, Canada, Great Britain and the United States*. Cambridge: Cambridge University Press.

Oppenheim, C. (2001). 'Enabling Participation? New Labour's Welfare-to-Work Policies', in S. White (ed.), *New Labour: The Progressive Future?* Basingstoke: Palgrave.

Piachaud, D. (2001). 'Child Poverty, Opportunities and Quality of Life', *Political Quarterly*, 72: 446–53.

Pierson, P. (ed.) (2001). *The New Politics of the Welfare State*. Oxford: Oxford University Press.

Polakow, V. (1993). *Lives on the Edge: Single Mothers and their Children in the Other America*. Chicago and London: University of Chicago Press.

Powell, M. (2000). 'Something Old, Something New, Something Borrowed, Something Blue: The Jackdaw Politics of New Labour', *Renewal*, 8/4: 21–31.

Pringle, R. and Watson, S. (1992). ' "Women's Interests" and the Post-Structuralist State', in M. Barrett and A. Phillips (eds.), *Destabilizing Theory: Contemporary Feminist Debates*. Cambridge: Polity Press.

Prout, A. (2000). 'Children's Participation: Control and Self-Realisation in British Late Modernity', *Children and Society*, 14: 304–15.

Reeves, R. (2003). 'The Battle for Childhood', *New Statesman*, 20 October: 18–20.

Ridge, T. (2002). *Childhood Poverty and Social Exclusion: From a Child's Perspective*. Bristol: Policy Press.

Roche, J. (1999). 'Children: Rights, Participation and Citizenship', *Childhood*, 6: 475–93.

Rothstein, B. and Stolle, D. (2003). 'Social Capital, Impartiality and the Welfare State: An Institutional Approach', in M. Hooghe and D. Stolle (eds.), *Generating Social Capital: The Role of Voluntary Associations, Institutions and Government Policy*. New York: Palgrave.

Sale, A. (2002). 'News Analysis', *Community Care*, 20–6 June: 20.

Schram, S. (1995). *Words of Welfare: The Poverty of Social Science and the Social Science of Poverty*. Minneapolis and London: University of Minnesota Press.

Schuppert, F. (2003). 'The Ensuring State', in M. Browne, P. Thompson, and F. Sainsbury (eds.), *Progressive Futures: New Ideas for the Centre-Left*. London: Policy Network.

Sherraden, M. (2002). 'From a Social Welfare State to a Social Investment State', in C. Kober and W. Paxton (eds.), *Asset-based Welfare and Poverty*. London: National Children's Bureau.

Siim, B. (2000). *Gender and Citizenship: Politics and Agency in France, Britain and Denmark*. Cambridge: Cambridge University Press.

Society Guardian, 8 October 2003.

Stasiulis, D. (2002). 'The Active Child Citizen: Lessons from Canadian Policy and the Children's Movement', *Citizenship Studies*, 6: 507–38.

Strategy Unit (2002). *Delivering for Children and Families*. London: Cabinet Office.

—— (2003). *Strategic Audit* (discussion document). London: Cabinet Office.

Streeck, W. (1999). *Competitive Solidarity: Rethinking the "European Social Model"* (MPIfG Working Paper 99/8). www.mpi-fg-koeln.mpg.de/pu/workpap/wp99–8/wp99–8.html.

Taylor-Gooby, P. (2003). 'Introduction: Open Markets versus Welfare Citizenship: Conflicting Approaches to Policy Convergence in Europe', *Social Policy and Administration*, 37: 539–54.

Thomas, G. and Hocking, G. (2003). *Other People's Children*. London: Demos.

Titmuss, R. (1974). *Social Policy*. London: Allen and Unwin.

UN (United Nations) (2002). *A World Fit for Children*. Resolution adopted by the General Assembly, 27th Special Session, United Nations.

Vandenbroucke, F. (2001). 'European Social Democracy and the Third Way: Convergence, Divisions, and Shared Questions', in S. White (ed.), *New Labour: The Progressive Future?* Basingstoke: Palgrave.

—— (2002). 'Foreword: Sustainable Social Justice and "Open Co-ordination" in Europe', in G. Esping-Andersen, with D. Gallie, A. Hemerijck, and J. Myles, *Why We Need a New Welfare State*. Oxford and New York: Oxford University Press.

Wiegers, W. (2002). *The Framing of Poverty as 'Child Poverty' and its Implications for Women*. Ottawa: Status of Women Canada.

Willow, C. (2003). 'Whatever Happened to Happiness?', *Zero2nineteen*, November: 8–9.

9

The Implications of Third Way Social Policy for Inequality, Social Cohesion, and Citizenship

HARTLEY DEAN

In so far as there is an orthodoxy to Third Way approaches, they tend to assimilate issues of inequality, social cohesion, and citizenship under the rubric of social exclusion and inclusion. Giddens claims that 'The new politics [of the Third Way] defines equality as *inclusion* and inequality as *exclusion* . . . Inclusion refers in its broadest sense to citizenship, to the civil and political rights and obligations that all citizens should have . . . to opportunities and to involvement in public space' (1998: 102–3). Social exclusion and inclusion remain contested concepts, but they have been colonized by the Third Way in a manner that subordinates concerns with structural inequality to a concern for social cohesion, albeit a notion of cohesion premised on a predominantly liberal–individualist conception of citizenship. Of particular significance is that, unlike those who define social exclusion and inclusion in terms of whether people have access to enforceable social rights—to healthcare, education, and material well-being (for example, Gore and Figuieredo 1997)—Third Way social policy would seem to prioritize formal civil and political rights, and to accord greater importance to opportunities—and in particular labour market opportunities—than to substantive social protection. Rhetorical calls, such as those once espoused for example by the British Labour Party, for 'the right to work' have been reinterpreted within the nostrums of the Third Way in terms of equal employment opportunities, not guaranteed jobs; of promoting an obligation to engage with the labour market before the freedom to choose one's employment.

It is generally accepted that the term 'social exclusion' was adopted as a euphemism for 'poverty' in discussions about European Union social policy in the 1980s (Atkinson 1998; Burchardt, Le Grand, and Piachaud 2002). At the time, a Conservative (or, more accurately, 'New Right') government in the UK denied the very existence of poverty. Since 1997, however, a so-called 'New' Labour (that is to say, quintessentially Third

Way) government in the UK has been prepared to discuss poverty *and* social exclusion as if the terms were virtually interchangeable and, to a degree, this tendency has become the commonplace in Third Way political discourse across Europe. However, as Room points out

The notion of poverty is primarily focused on distributional issues: the lack of resources at the disposal of an individual or household. In contrast, notions such as social exclusion focus primarily on relational issues, in other words, inadequate social participation, lack of social integration and lack of power . . . It is the liberal vision of society that inspires the Anglo-Saxon concern with poverty, it is the conservative vision of society . . . that inspires the continental concern with social exclusion. (1995: 5–6)

The manner in which the Third Way has embraced the concepts of social exclusion and inclusion would appear to conflate what Room calls the 'relational' paradigm with the 'distributional' paradigm. In previous work (Dean 1999) I have suggested an ideal-typology of welfare regimes in which the relational dimension is understood in terms of a continuum running from a liberal-competitive or contractarian conception of citizenship on the one hand to a republican-solidaristic or collectivist conception on the other. The former, I would argue (contrary to Giddens), is axiomatically *exclusive* since those who fail to take up the opportunities available to them or to observe their obligations are excluded from the benefits of citizenship. The latter is axiomatically *inclusive*: certainly it may have exclusionary consequences for those who are not recognized as citizens, but its organizing principle is the inclusion of those whom it does recognize. The distributional dimension in the typology is understood in terms of a continuum running from an *egalitarian* preoccupation with justice or 'fairness' on the one hand to a preoccupation with social *order* on the other. The former may call upon either formal or substantive notions of equality; upon either economic or social accounts of justice. The latter is by implication inegalitarian or hierarchical, since its concern is with the maintenance of social cohesion within the existing social order, whether this be achieved coercively or by corporate brokerage.

The resulting typology is incorporated into Fig. 9.1, which presents for the purposes of this chapter a more developed taxonomy of competing approaches to inequality, social cohesion, and citizenship. In the rest of this chapter I shall be using this figure, first, to locate or define Third Way approaches; second, to address the policy implications; and third, to discuss the possible consequences. As this is done within the compass of a single chapter, it should be noted that several highly relevant topics—relating, for example, to gender inequality and the exclusion of refugees—must, unfortunately, be left to one side.

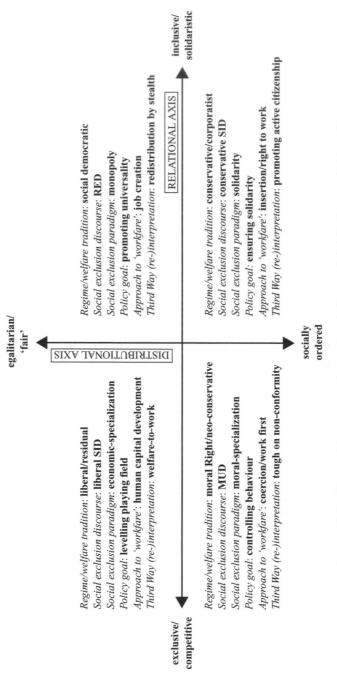

FIGURE 9.1. *Categorizing approaches to inequality, social cohesion, and citizenship*

Note: The taxonomy adapts/draws, *inter alia,* upon Dean (1999), Levitas (1998), Silver (1994), EC (2001), Lodemel and Trickey (2000).

Before moving on I should emphasize that Fig. 9.1 is a heuristic not a descriptive device. The original focus of the typology had been to define four rather than the three welfare regimes that feature in Esping-Andersen's (1990) classic typology. I have characterized Esping-Andersen's liberal/ residual regime in terms of a commitment to formal equality of opportunity alongside a notion of conditional rights and duties premised on a strictly contractarian calculus. His social democratic regime is characterized in terms of a commitment to substantive equality of outcome alongside a solidaristic, and therefore universalistic, notion of rights and responsibilities. His conservative/corporatist regime is characterized in terms of a commitment to a corporately brokered social order alongside a solidaristic republican traditionalism. Additionally, however, I posit a moral Right/neo-conservative regime in which a commitment to a coercively maintained social order goes hand in hand with Hobbesian assumptions about the nature of the human condition and the individual/state contract. I would not for my part contend that any particular country exemplifies any one of these ideal types. There is a sense in which the classic post-Second World War Western European welfare states were all hybrids, combining to various degrees elements of the social democratic and conservative/corporatist regimes; whereas the aspirations of the New Right during the Thatcher/Reagan era combined elements of the liberal/residual and the moral right/neo-conservative welfare regimes. The question now is: how to characterize the Third Way?

1. Locating the Third Way

As should be clear from preceding chapters, to define the Third Way as a middle path between the New Right and the Old Left is somewhat facile. Certainly, the substantive foundations of the path had been laid principally by the New Right. To borrow a different metaphor from the title of a conference organized by Nexus (a 'virtual' think-tank) and the *Guardian* newspaper in the month preceding New Labour's 1997 general election victory, the Third Way project entailed 'Passing the Torch': a torch lit by the now discredited New Right but which now belonged to a reinvigorated centre-left (Levitas 1998: 31–2). The Third Way is an avowedly pragmatic project with what is sometimes characterized as a 'pick and mix' approach to policy (Powell 2000). It is rapidly adapting itself to a variety of contexts and so, potentially, may exhibit different characteristics depending on the circumstances prevailing in different countries (see Chapter 3 in this volume). To switch metaphors one more time, though the centre of gravity of the Third Way project would seem to be located in the top left quadrant of

Fig. 9.1, it is buttressed to a significant degree by each of the other three quadrants. In fact, as we shall later see, it has its own interpretation of each quadrant. The Third Way entails not a wholly unprincipled, still less an entirely random, strategy of 'pick and mix'. It is perhaps more of a fifth than a third way, though this too would be a misnomer: in welfare regime terms, it is, I shall argue, a complex hybrid.

Let us illustrate this. My focus here will be on social policy, though the argument could be extended to take account of other policy arenas and reform agendas. Ruth Levitas (1998) claims that Britain's New Labour government articulates three intersecting social exclusion 'discourses', which she calls by the acronyms RED, MUD, and SID. At times the Third Way approach will resort to an economic redistributionist discourse (RED), consistent with social democratic and/or Old Left traditions, as is evinced in what the British Chancellor of the Exchequer, Gordon Brown, characterizes as the 'fairness agenda'. At times it resorts to a moral underclass discourse (MUD), consistent with moral authoritarian/neo-conservative traditions, as has been evinced in the British context by 'zero-tolerance' approaches, for example, to street crime, anti-social behaviour, teenage pregnancy, and social security benefit fraud. Central to the project, however, is a social integrationist discourse (SID), premised, according to Levitas, upon inclusion through labour force participation. Levitas makes the point (see also Levitas 1996) that, in so far as there is a Third Way consensus, it is not about inclusion so much as integration. The emphasis on supply-side-driven active labour market policies—or 'workfare' (see Lødemel and Trickey 2000)—privileges paid employment. This, according to Levitas and many other commentators (for example, Lister 1998), devalues the care work that is performed predominantly by women, and marginalizes the citizen status of those who cannot participate in the labour market. While in no way demurring from this analysis, I would suggest that there are in fact two kinds of SID. There is a *liberal* social integrationist discourse, which, as Levitas describes, is at the heart of the Third Way project, but there is also a *conservative* social integrationist discourse that may be less evident in the British context, but is strongly redolent of republican and conservative/corporatist traditions and, for example, the French notion of 'insertion' (see, for example, Silver 1994).

Hilary Silver (1994) offers a different analysis in which she identifies three 'paradigms' of social exclusion. One, which she identifies explicitly with social democracy, she calls the *monopoly* paradigm. It interprets exclusion as the outcome of hierarchical and/or exploitative relations of power in which the powerful monopolize resources to the exclusion of the weak. Another, which she identifies with republicanism and would seem to be consistent with the conservative/corporatist tradition, she calls the *solidarity* paradigm. It interprets exclusion as a failure of social cohesion or integration. Her final paradigm, which she identifies with liberalism and the Anglo-American tradition, she calls the *specialization* paradigm. It interprets exclusion as the outcome of processes of specialization within a market economy by which the least successful individuals or groups may become marginalized as a result of the success of the majority. I would suggest, however, that there are two kinds of specialization paradigm and Silver herself acknowledges that the liberal individualism on which the specialization paradigm is premised 'encompasses two streams of thought: libertarian or neo-liberalism and social or communitarian liberalism' (1994: 543). Silver's terminology is perhaps a little confusing and my preference would be to distinguish between *economic* specialization and *moral* specialization. The latter is consistent with the neo-conservatism of the moral Right in so far as it interprets exclusion in terms of moral and behavioural defects.

My extended versions of Levitas's and Silver's taxonomies are mapped into the typology in Fig. 9.1 and what begins to emerge is four competing views of inequality, social cohesion, and citizenship. In the top left quadrant lies a view that inequality of economic outcome is entirely acceptable provided individuals have equality of opportunity; that social cohesion depends on economic participation (which, for most people, entails labour market participation); that citizenship rests on equality before the law and political enfranchisement. In the top right quadrant lies a view that there are limits to the acceptability of substantive social and economic inequality; that social cohesion depends on social justice; that citizenship requires social rights and universal welfare entitlements (cf. Marshall 1950). In the bottom right quadrant lies a view that certain economic inequalities and social differences may be a natural feature of the social order; that social cohesion depends on solidarity and mutual loyalty; that citizenship requires an equality of belonging. In the bottom left quadrant lies a view that inequality is an inevitable consequence of the competition between self-serving individual subjects and the inadequacy of the weak; that social cohesion depends on the enforcement of a moral consensus; that citizenship requires subjection to state authority. My argument would be that it is the overarching hegemonic influence of the top left quadrant, in conjunction with inherently contradictory influences from some or all of the other quadrants, which characterize the Third Way.

2. Policies for Social Inclusion

Although the 'Third Way' stands for the hegemonic influence of a peculiarly Anglo-American policy agenda, there have been discussions across

Europe of 'the new middle' and of 'purple coalitions' (Bonoli and Powell 2002). In this section I consider how the social inclusion agenda has taken hold as the means by which policy-makers now address issues of inequality, social cohesion, and citizenship. I start by looking at the European Union's social inclusion initiative before focusing in particular on workfare policies as the central plank of Third Way hegemony, and then return to discuss other aspects of the Third Way approach as they apply in the British case.

The European Social Inclusion Strategy

Under the Amsterdam Treaty of 1997, the European Union (EU) committed itself to fight against social exclusion and in 2000 the Lisbon European Council declared its aim to eradicate poverty in Europe by 2010. The context of this commitment was a wider strategic goal: 'to become the most competitive and dynamic knowledge-based economy in the world, capable of sustained economic growth and more and better jobs and greater social cohesion' (cited in EC 2001: 9). The language is unmistakably Third Way in tone and substance: the primary challenge lies in the changing nature of the global economy; the required response lies in enhancing economic competitiveness; improved social cohesion is a potential outcome rather than a primary objective. Later in 2000 the Nice Council formulated the European Social Agenda, requiring member states to produce two-year National Action Plans demonstrating their progress towards the following common objectives (cited in EC 2001: 10):

1. To facilitate participation in employment and access by all to resources, rights, goods, and services.
2. To prevent the risks of exclusion.
3. To help the most vulnerable.
4. To mobilize all relevant bodies.

It is significant not only that labour market participation features as the first objective of the social inclusion strategy, but that it is being advanced in parallel with a European Employment Strategy (EC 1997). The primary emphasis stems from the prescriptions of economic liberalism, and yet the reference within the first objective to facilitating access to rights and resources calls upon different traditions.

The remaining objectives are, potentially, equally ambiguous, not least in the manner in which they have been interpreted in the first round of National Action Plans submitted by member states in 2001 (EC 2001). The second objective, which focuses on the risks of social exclusion, is sometimes interpreted in terms of the propensities of individuals: for example, the problems faced or caused by people with erratic labour market records, inadequate educational achievements, poor health status, minority ethnicity, or illegal immigration status. At other times, however, it is interpreted in terms of structural factors: the failure of local labour markets and the limitations of policy frameworks or social institutions. Similarly, the third objective, which focuses on the needs of the most vulnerable, is sometimes interpreted in terms of policies that 'target' particular hard-to-help groups (such as ex-offenders and people with drug dependency problems) with a view to incorporating them wherever possible into labour markets. At other times it is interpreted more broadly in terms of policies that will guarantee financial and social support for children and disabled people. The fourth objective, which focuses on the mobilization of relevant groups in society, is sometimes interpreted— in the language of the 'new managerialism' (for example, Clarke and Newman 1997)—in terms of the implementation of a 'partnership' approach and an emphasis on the direct engagement of community groups and private businesses in local service provision and in the processes of local government. At other times it is interpreted—in the language of corporatism—in terms of involving the 'social partners' (including, and particularly, the trades unions) and non-governmental organizations in the wider priority setting and policy-making process. The agenda can be inflected towards any one or towards different combinations of the competing objectives defined within Fig. 9.1.

The *Joint Report on Social Inclusion* prepared by the European Commission on the basis of the first round of National Action Plans singled out a variety of instances of 'good practice' amongst member states and additionally, without expressing any kind of preference, identified three different kinds of goals currently being adopted by the member states (EC 2001: 25):

- **Universality**: this means ensuring increased levels of adequacy, access and affordability of mainline policies and provisions with a view to improving their coverage, uptake and effectiveness.
- **A level playing field**: this means addressing specific disadvantages that can be overcome by the use of policy (e.g. lack of skills).
- **Solidarity for human dignity**: this means compensating for disadvantages that can only be partially (or not at all) overcome (e.g. disabilities).

These goals articulate with the social democratic, liberal/residual, and conservative/corporatist ideal-type welfare regimes respectively. From a theoretical perspective we might also posit the existence of an unspoken fourth goal which would be consistent with a neo-conservative/moral authoritarian ideal-type regime and which might be concerned with *controlling the behaviour* of the excluded. It may be that the Commission was reluctant to identify the coercive elements of the social policies pursued by member states as 'good practice' and so did not articulate this fourth goal. Nevertheless, all four policy goals have been incorporated into Fig. 9.1, providing yet another layer of interpretation.

At this early stage of the European Social Inclusion Strategy it is clear that not all member states may be said to subscribe to a Third Way compromise, but, significantly, the Commission has concluded that the National Action Plans of 'most' member states (EC 2001: 24):

- recognise the need for policies that **invest in new starts** . . . [for example, for those experiencing] exclusion from the labour market, long-term unemployment, delinquency or addiction, skills redundancy, homelessness, family breakdown, poor or inadequate school behaviour and intergenerational poverty . . . [but which] reflect a framework of rights and duties underpinning the goods, services and other provisions made available to support new starts.
- develop strategic responses that **turn risk and disadvantage unto opportunity** . . . [for example, by seeking increasingly] to bring out and develop the untapped potential of immigrants, people with disabilities, lone parents and older people as well as lagging regions and neighbourhoods.

The emphasis on extending and stimulating labour market participation, on promoting opportunity, on reciprocal duties as well as rights, all clearly bear the stamp of Third Way thinking.

Workfare

The pivotal element of Third Way thinking is the idea that work is the best form of welfare : which is to say that human well-being is best achieved when people support themselves and their families through paid employment. The concept of 'workfare' has always been controversial. Though often presented as a new idea that originated in the late twentieth century in the United States, its fundamental tenets date back to an era when the relief of poverty across much of Western Europe was conditional upon the performance of forced labour (Piven and Cloward 1974). At the beginning of the twenty-first century most developed nations are pursuing active labour market or 'welfare-to-work' policies in which social assistance for some social groups, at least to some degree, is conditional upon the performance of compulsory activities relating to work (whether subsidized or unsubsidized) or training.

It is possible, however, by drawing on comparative studies of workfare regimes (for example, Lodemel and Trickey 2000), to distinguish four conceptually different approaches to, or justifications for, workfare-type policies:

1. The Nordic welfare states, shaken by the global economic upheavals that characterized the last decades of the twentieth century (Kautto et al. 1999), have lately been adopting active labour market policies with elements that are recognizably Third Way in nature, if not provenance. Nonetheless, these traditionally social democratic welfare states were once regarded as 'employers of last resort' (Leibried 1993: 140–1). To an extent, even now, the function of 'activation' in the Nordic states is to incorporate the citizen as a productive member of society. The system is intended to promote universal participation. The emphasis of late is towards retraining for unemployed people and subsidized work-experience programmes rather than the direct provision of public sector jobs for those in need of them. In the not so distant past, however, the unequivocal objective would have been *job creation*.

2. The western continental European conservative/corporatist regimes have correspondingly been characterized as 'compensators of first resort' (Leibried 1993: 140–1). Compensation, however, had always been conditional on prior labour market participation. The tendency has been less marked in strongly Bismarckian welfare regimes, such as Germany, but in France—as guardian of the republican tradition—the function of recent 'insertion' programmes has been to plug the gaps that had been left by social protection systems based on employment-based social insurance. Workfare, in this context, is all about social integration. The system is intended to help the unprotected citizen. Such an objective is compromised, if not actually contradicted, by a simultaneous desire to protect the rights enjoyed by existing workers, but the primary objective is to create labour market opportunities; to assert, but not necessarily guarantee, a *right to work*.

3. Forced labour under the poor laws was an explicit deterrent to idleness and, to a degree, the poor law tradition lives on in the USA where, under the Personal Responsibility and Work Opportunity Reconciliation Act 1996 (especially as it is interpreted in more conservative states), the enforcement of the civic obligation to work overrides the liberty of the subject; the function of workfare is to prevent dependency; the primary objective is labour market attachment; and the system is intended to 'hassle' as much as help the citizen. The approach is essentially coercive. The object is '*work first*'.

4. According to Lødemel and Trickey (2000), there is an emergent 'European centralised' workfare model—epitomized by the Dutch Job-seekers' Employment scheme, Danish activation, and the UK's New Deal policies. The model represents something quite close to a Third Way consensus, strongly influenced by neo-liberal economic assumptions. The function is to foster economic independence. The system is intended—through individualized case-work support on the one hand and sanctions for non-compliance based on the withdrawal of social assistance benefits, on the other—to combine hassling and help; to engender a kind of 'Tough Love' (Jordan 2000). The ostensible objective is *human capital development*.

These four different approaches to 'workfare' have also been added to the model in Fig. 9.1. Elements of all approaches can find expression in the workfare policies of developed countries. In the British case, as we shall see shortly, workfare policies contain elements of a 'work first' as well as a human capital approach. The notion of workfare as a policy objective beyond the English-speaking world, however, is in itself a reflection of the ascendancy of the Third Way.

Most significant is the gradual emergence of the essentially 'managerial' (see Chapter 4 in the volume) human capital approach. The metaphor 'human *capital*' accords recognition to the productive potential of every citizen and to the ideals of self-development and individual empowerment. In so doing the concept calls attention to the role of the citizen as an economic rather than a social actor and as a competitive individual rather than as a cooperative social being.

The British Case

The Third Way is most closely associated with Britain's New Labour government, whose approach towards issues of inequality, social cohesion, and citizenship can be analysed under four headings, corresponding to each of the quadrants in Fig. 9.1.

Central to New Labour's approach has been *welfare-to-work* and the idea that the primary means by which to achieve social inclusion is through labour market participation. This initially entailed a number of 'New Deal' programmes focused on the young and the long-term unemployed; on lone parents and the partners of the unemployed; on disabled people and the over-fiftys. However, since New Labour's re-election in 2001, in a symbolically significant move the Department of Social Security was reconstituted as the Department for Work and Pensions (DWP). The New Deals were incorporated into a new social security benefits regime for *all* those of working age. The regime, administered by a new national governmental agency within the DWP, called JobCentre Plus, requires all but a few exempted claimants to attend job-focused interviews as a condition of receiving benefits. The interviews are used to present claimants with appropriate employment or training opportunities. Certain client groups—at present, the young and long-term unemployed—may be subject to specific benefits sanctions if they do not take up such opportunities. In practice, therefore, while this approach is ostensibly focused on human capital development, there are also elements of a work-first approach (Theodore and Peck 2001; Dean 2003). Welfare-to-work, however, is about more than workfare. It is also about 'making work pay' (DSS 1998), partly through the introduction of a modest National Minimum Wage, but also by way of a new system of Working Tax Credits: means-tested in-work cash benefits that supplement low wages (see Dean 2002*a*). Additionally, the government has expressed the aim of making it easier for people to combine work and family life (Home Office 1998), to which end it has begun somewhat tentatively to develop a 'work-life balance' agenda (Dean 2002*b*). Finally, an important part of the context for New Labour's commitment to welfare-to-work and the promise of 'opportunity for all' (Labour Party 2001) is a legacy of a liberal equal opportunities legislative framework, dating largely from the 1970s, which attempts to outlaw sex and racial discrimination in employment and, in response to EU employment directives, is to be extended to cover age and religious discrimination.

A second and, by its nature, less conspicuous aspect of New Labour's agenda has been *redistribution by stealth*. The key feature that distinguishes 'New' Labour from the Labour Party of old has been a commitment not to 'tax and spend'. Evidence from social attitude surveys (for example, Hills and Lelkes 1999) repeatedly demonstrates that, while the British people feel that something should be done to redress social inequality and improve public services, they are not necessarily in favour of redistribution through the tax and benefits system. Having initially committed itself during its first two years of office to observing the public spending limits imposed by their Conservative predecessors, Britain's New Labour government has continued to refrain from increasing the prevailing rates of income tax. However, by means of changes in pension taxation and to National Insurance contributions and through the effects of 'fiscal drag' (allowing the level of personal tax allowances to lag behind increases in earnings), New Labour has quietly succeeded in making the British personal taxation regime slightly more progressive (Hills 2002). At the same time, there have been significant increases in cash transfers for children, initially through increases in universal child benefit and in the children's allowance element of means-tested social security benefits (Lister 2001) and more recently through the introduction of an 'integrated' Child Tax Credit that has transferred the administration of means-tested assistance directed to children from the DWP to the Inland Revenue (see Dean 2002*a*). Redistribution in favour of children is clearly regarded as more politically acceptable than redistribution to adults and, in a widely publicized speech, the Prime Minister declared the government's intention of abolishing not poverty in general but child poverty by 2019 (Blair 1999). This appears to entail not so much a commitment to social equality as a kind of 'selective universalism' calculated to appeal to the median voter (Hills and Lelkes 1999). Economic redistribution is favoured, perhaps, not so much as a means to redress substantive inequality but as a means of levelling the playing field for the most disadvantaged of tomorrow's citizens (Deacon 2003).

A third element of New Labour's approach is a commitment to be *tough on non-conformity*. One of New Labour's slogans had been its promise to be 'tough on crime, tough on the causes of crime' (Labour Party 1997: 4). The language of moral authority—of 'getting tough' (Fairclough 2000)—has been very much a part of the New Labour project and has played an important part in its approach to social exclusion. Beyond getting people off welfare and into work and achieving some measure of income redistribution in favour of poorer families with children, New Labour had identified a range of interconnected social problems that they wished to address because of

the huge human costs to individuals and society, and the impact on the public finances and the competitiveness of the economy. The human costs were faced by

- **individuals who experience social exclusion**—underachievement in education and the labour market, low income, poor access to services, stress, ill-health and the impact on children; and
- **wider society**—reduced social cohesion, higher crime and fear of crime, and higher levels of stress and reduced mobility. (SEU 2001: 5)

Implicit in this analysis is a chain of association between, on the one hand, social exclusion and the non-conformity of particular individuals or neighbourhoods and, on the other, social exclusion and crime or social disruption. The assumptions were that there are certain kinds of individual behaviour that 'trigger' social exclusion and that there are certain deprived neighbourhoods where basic services are not working or do not reach. The resulting policy approach had two aspects. First, the government set up a central Social Exclusion Unit to coordinate policy-making on specified topics such as school exclusion and truancy, rough sleeping, teenage pregnancy, youth at risk; in each instance, the targets of attention were highly marginalized, non-conforming individuals. Second, the government initiated an array of area-based initiatives. Some entailed the promotion of more coordinated partnership working in specific neighbourhoods through, for example, the Sure Start scheme (focused on services for young children), Health Action Zones, and Education Action Zones. Others were specifically focused on urban regeneration, entailing a National Strategy for Neighbourhood Renewal (SEU 2000) and the creation of a New Deal for Communities initiative (which distributes funds for community-based projects in selected deprived neighbourhoods). The emphasis is on specialized interventions to address individual or neighbourhood pathologics. But, alongside steps intended at the neighbourhood level to empower those who are prepared to become active participating citizens (see below), there have been initiatives that focus on more coercive means of social control, such as the creation of local Crime and Disorder Reduction Partnerships (Cook 1999). These initiatives have coalesced around an anti-social behaviour agenda (Home Office 2003*a*) by which the courts and local authorities have been afforded new powers to control anti-social behaviour, powers that entail measures to be taken against the parents of badly behaved children, a tougher approach to offences in public places, and provision for the withdrawal of housing benefits from anti-social neighbours.

Finally, New Labour has expressed an interest in *promoting active citizenship*. The notion of 'active citizenship' had briefly been promoted by Conservative government ministers in the 1980s as an antidote to the excesses of Thatcherism. Those who flourished in the competitive enterprise culture promoted by the New Right would not to be asked to pay more in taxes, but were encouraged to engage in voluntary activities for the benefit of those who may have fared less well: it was a call for a return to traditional conservative values of philanthropy and *noblesse oblige* (see Dean 2002*a*: 16). Under New Labour the notion of active citizenship has been revived as part of a call for 'civil renewal' (Home Office 2003*b*; see Chapter 6 in this volume). The government has sought on the one hand to introduce citizenship studies into the school National Curriculum (see Crick 1998) in an attempt to promote political literacy and civic virtues. On the other hand it has sought to promote 'a deepening culture of volunteering and giving' (HM Treasury/Home Office 2002: 27) by enhancing the framework of support for the voluntary and community sector and taking measures to boost charitable giving. It has established a target of increasing voluntary and community sector activity, including increasing community participation, by 5 per cent by 2006. In doing so, the Home Secretary, David Blunkett, argues that there is a place for the civic-republican tradition of citizenship alongside more libertarian approaches. He claims that 'the discourse of individual rights finds it difficult to embrace notions of wider social well-being. It cannot tell us much about wider social outcomes, such as social cohesion or justice' (Home Office 2000*b*: 11). He goes on to denounce negative liberty theorists and to celebrate notions of civic virtue, albeit without ever acknowledging that substantive social rights may have a part to play in ensuring social justice. He links active citizenship to notions of social capital (cf. Putnam 2000) or his preferred term 'community capacity'.

These components of the British Third Way may be aligned with the quadrants of Fig. 9.1 and the resulting schema may help to characterize the complex and multi-faceted nature of Third Way approaches in general. Although he categorizes the elements of New Labour's approach somewhat differently, John Hills has suggested that 'In the most optimistic interpretation, embracing both an anti-poverty and anti-exclusion agenda has led to a much richer policy mix, with much greater chance of long-run success' (Hills 2002: 243). In the next section, I shall consider whether such optimism is justified.

3. Assessing the Consequences

Assessing the impact of Third Way policies is difficult: partly because it is impossible in a global context to disentangle the effects of policy from the effects of economic processes, partly because inequality, social cohesion, and citizenship are hard to measure.

Inequality

Inequality is the easiest to measure, although this is not without its problems. Perhaps the most convenient 'rough and ready' statistical measure of inequality is the Gini coefficient, which may be applied to the distribution of incomes or consumption and by which complete equality is represented by 0 and complete inequality by 100. At the global level such indicators have been used to show that, in the course of the twentieth century, while absolute poverty around the world decreased, inequality increased (Bourguignon and Morrisson 2002). According to the latest statistics (see UNDP 2003) the most unequal societies are now to be found in sub-Saharan Africa (Namibia's Gini coefficient is 71; Botswana's and Sierra Leone's are 63), while the most equal are in Scandinavia (Norway's Gini coefficient is 26; Sweden's and Denmark's are 25). Despite being the richest and most powerful nation on earth, the USA continues, with a Gini coefficient of 41, to be a strikingly unequal society, at least in relation to other developed countries. In Table 9.1, using data from the European Union's *Joint Report on Social Inclusion*, I present a variety of inequality and relative poverty indicators relating to four rather different European countries: the UK as the current torch-bearer for the Third Way; Italy as a southern European country; Germany as a classic Bismarckian regime; Denmark as a Scandinavian country. It may be seen that in 1997 the UK was by every measure the most unequal society and Denmark the least.

Have things improved since New Labour came to power? Arguably, it is too soon to say. The latest household incomes data suggest that by 2001/2 overall income inequality had shown little or no change (or may have slightly worsened, depending on the method of calculation); the overall incidence of relative poverty (when calculated *before* housing costs) had slightly worsened; and the incidence of persistent poverty was largely unchanged (DWP 2003). For the time being Britain remains, by European standards, an unequal society.

Other Measures

When we turn to measures relevant to social cohesion and citizenship, one important indicator has been the 'Breadline Britain' relative deprivation measure which establishes the extent to which people are involuntarily deprived of socially perceived necessities—including not just adequate heating, housing, and food but, for example, the ability to buy new (rather than second-hand) clothes and to celebrate special occasions; the sort of things that people require in order properly and without shame to participate in ordinary life (Mack and Lansley 1985; Gordon and Pantazis 1997; Gordon et al. 2000). Surveys using this method in 1983, 1990, and 1999

TABLE 9.1. *Measures of inequality/poverty in four EU countries in 1997*

	UK	Italy	Germany	Denmark
Gini coefficient	34	32	29	21
Ratio of income of richest 20% to that of poorest 20%	7.4	6.0	4.7	2.7
Relative poverty (i.e. proportion of individuals in households with less than 60% median equivalized income—*before* housing costs)	22%	19%	14%	8%
Persistent poverty (i.e. proportion of individuals in relative poverty for three consecutive years)	10%	8%	8%	3%

Source: EC (2001).

indicated that the proportion of people 'in poverty', by reference to a multiple deprivation standard, had risen from 14 per cent to 21 per cent to over 24 per cent. The 1999 survey was extended to include a study of social exclusion as well as poverty. It examined not only income-related deprivation but labour market exclusion, exclusion from services (both public and private), and exclusion from social relations (including social activities, friendships, social support, and civic engagement) (Gordon et al. 2000). It provides important baseline data against which—if the survey can be repeated—it will be possible in the future to assess the longer-term impact of Third Way policies.

A similar attempt to quantify the extent of social exclusion has been made by the Centre for the Analysis of Social Exclusion (CASE) at the London School of Economics (see Burchardt, Le Grand, and Piachaud 2002). The CASE approach draws upon the British Household Panel Study (BHPS) to establish four dimensions of exclusion: consumption (the capacity to purchase goods and services); production (participation in economic or socially valuable activities); political engagement (involvement in local or national decision-making); social interaction (integration with family, friends, and community). The strength of the approach is that, by drawing data from across successive annual waves of the BHPS (from 1991 to 1998), it has explored the dynamics of social exclusion over time. The findings indicate that in the first wave only a very small proportion (1.5 per cent) of the working-age population was excluded on all four dimensions and none remained excluded on all dimensions for more than three years. On the other hand, just over two-thirds were not excluded on any dimension in the first wave, but after four years just over half the population had experienced some degree of exclusion. After eight years nearly two-thirds had at some time experienced exclusion on some dimension. Without a comparative analysis from a different country and without an extension of the study into the period of the New Labour government, this tells us little about how cohesive British society is or about the robustness of citizen participation in relative terms, and it can tell us nothing about the impact of the Third Way. Once again, however, it provides a valuable baseline for future assessments.

Monitoring Social Exclusion

The New Labour government has undertaken to monitor its performance in tackling poverty and social exclusion through a series of annual reports, using a variety of target-related indicators. At the same time, the independent New Policy Institute has, since 1997, been undertaking an annual *Monitoring Poverty and Social Exclusion* exercise, relying for the most part on official data sources, applying an overlapping set of indicators. A small selection of the indicators used and the findings from the latest editions of these reports is compiled in Table 9.2, arranged for the purposes of this chapter under the headings assigned above to the four aspects of New Labour's approach.

In general terms, New Labour's welfare-to-work strategy appears to have been modestly successful, though it is difficult to be sure how much of the overall increase in employment and decline in unemployment in the

TABLE 9.2. *Monitoring social exclusion*

	Opportunity for All (DWP 2002)		New Policy Institute (Palmer, Rahman, and Kenway 2002)	
	Trend Since 1996	Direction of latest data	Trend over medium term	Trend over last year
Welfare-to-work				
employment rate	✓	~		
young people (16–24) unemployed			✓	~
adults (25–retirement) wanting paid work			✓	x
working-age people in workless households	✓	~		
children in workless households	✓	~	✓	x
households without work for two years or more			~	~
working-age without qualifications (England)	✓	~		
adults (25–retirement) without access to training			✓	~
Redistribution by stealth				
children in relative poverty*	✓	✓	✓	✓
working-age in relative poverty*	~	~		
older people in relative poverty*	~	~		
individuals in relative poverty*			~	✓
Tough on non-conformity				
rough sleepers (England)	✓	✓		
teenage conceptions (England)	✓	✓		
births to under-16s			✓	~
school exclusions	✓	x	✓	x
Active citizenship				
non-participation in civic organizations			~	x

*i.e. proportion in households with less than 60% median equivalized income—*after* housing costs

Key: ✓ data moving in right direction/trend improved.
　　x data moving in wrong direction/trend worsened.
　　~ data show broadly constant trend or no significant movement/trend steady.

years following 1997 could be attributed to favourable economic conditions. The evidence indicates that as the economy has slowed the employment/unemployment trends are now flattening out (and in the case of adult unemployment beginning to worsen). Unemployment rates were already relatively favourable compared with some countries. In 1997 the UK's long-term unemployment rate was 2.7 per cent, compared with 8.1 per cent in Italy, 4.9 per cent in Germany, but only 1.5 per cent in Denmark (EC 2001). Evaluations of the New Deal programmes (see Millar 2000) indicated they had assisted certain people into the labour market, though they had not necessarily been effective for multiply disadvantaged groups. What is more, many of the jobs into which people had been assisted were short-term and low-paid: the programmes have done nothing to combat, and may even have exacerbated, the debilitating low-pay/no-pay cycle experienced by those engaging with the periphery of the labour market (McKnight 2002). The introduction of the national minimum wage benefited some 1.5 million low-paid workers (see Exell 2001), but its significance has been compromised by the low level at which it is set. The new Working Tax Credit will play a part in raising incomes for the working poor, but its design quite deliberately extends the gap between in-work and out-of-work benefit regimes—not only in terms of entitlement levels but in terms of the degree of stigma associated with the latter (see, for example, Dean and Shah 2002). Arguably, it exacerbates the social exclusion of those who cannot work. Additionally, there is some evidence that work–life balance initiatives tend to benefit high-paid rather than low-paid workers, exacerbating class inequalities.

It is argued above that New Labour has attempted a certain amount of redistribution by stealth. The explicit focus has been the aim of combating child poverty, which the government had sought to cut—initially by a quarter in five years. The government's target, therefore, had been to reduce the number of children living in households with incomes that are less than 60 per cent of the national median (before housing costs) from a level of 3.1 million (or 24 per cent) in 1998/99 to around 2.3 million (or 18 per cent) by 2003/4. The government calculated this would be the effect of the policy changes it had planned to introduce, a claim that has been broadly endorsed by independent modelling (see Piachaud and Sutherland 2001, 2002). Success, however, would depend on a number of factors. First, a relative poverty measure based on the proportion of households with incomes below the median has provided a moving target as incomes have risen with economic growth. Second, much depends on the pace of policy implementation and, for example, the level of take-up of means-tested benefits and tax credits, especially by low-paid working families with incomes just below the poverty threshold. More to the point, while it may be relatively easy to lift the first half or three-quarters of a million children out of poverty, reaching those who are deeper in poverty will be much harder and more costly (Piachaud and Sutherland 2002). At the 2001 general election the government claimed already to have taken more than a million children out of poverty, but it subsequently emerged this had been achieved for fewer than half a million children (DWP 2003). As a result, the government's ability to meet its targets is currently in doubt. At the time of writing the government is seeking alternative ways of measuring child poverty with a view to redefining its target. Redistributing incomes in favour of families with children, clearly, should have an impact upon income inequality generally, and to an extent this has been happening, albeit so far only to a limited extent.

When it comes to being tough on non-conformity, New Labour claims to have reduced rough sleeping and teenage pregnancies, but has failed to sustain its initial success in reducing school exclusions. While it can claim some success in reducing the incidence of crimes, such as domestic burglary, it is too soon to say what impact it will have on 'anti-social behaviour'. There is no doubt that phenomena like street homelessness result from intense and complex individual problems (Burrows, Pleace, and Quilgars 1997); that teenage pregnancy, truancy, and school exclusion are all strong precursors of adverse outcomes in later life (Hills, Le Grand, and Piachaud 2002); and that such issues need to be addressed. However, the complexity of these problems and of the individual lives of those who experience them means they cannot readily be addressed by 'zero-tolerance' solutions (see, for example, Dennis 1997). Coercing rough sleepers into hostels is unlikely to address their underlying problems. Educating young women about sex will not change the social and economic milieu in which they must establish and live out their identities. Pressure placed on schools to retain unruly pupils may conflict with countervailing pressures to enhance the performance of their other pupils. Pressure placed on parents to control their children may fail to address wider and highly intractable family problems. Forcing beggars off the streets and anti-social tenants out of their homes may displace them without fundamentally changing their behaviour.

Finally, such evidence as there is concerning the promotion of active citizenship is not necessarily encouraging. Nevertheless, a Home Office Citizenship Survey in 2001 indicated that some 39 per cent of the population were to some extent involved in formal volunteering and 67 per cent in informal voluntary activity (HM Treasury/Home Office 2002). Ostensibly, therefore, commitment to active citizenship was already high. The question that remains unanswered is whether New Labour's 'civil renewal' agenda can reflect a solidaristic republican ideal or whether it will fuel a transition to self-provisioning and the displacement of the welfare state. It has been argued (Mestrovic 1997; and see Rodger 2000) that we are entering an era of 'postemotionalism', in which people's preoccupation with their own and/or their family's self-interest precludes all but inauthentic or synthetic forms of emotion or compassion. Charitable giving and voluntary activity may represent an insubstantial alternative to traditional forms of collective solidarity. The government's aim for citizenship education was to promote not just community involvement but social and moral responsibility and political literacy (Crick 1998: 13). The questions this poses are, first, whether it is a strictly individualistic ethic of responsibility that will be promoted (see Dean 2004); and second, whether greater political literacy can of itself overcome, rather than exacerbate, political cynicism.

4. Conclusion

The Third Way, in so far as it can be defined, may yet turn out to be little more than a complex front for a neo-liberal agenda. If so, one might predict that the priority given by the Third Way to economic competitiveness and fiscal rectitude must in the present global economic context be achieved at some cost to social equality (cf. Iversen and Wren 1990). Inequality puts pressure on social cohesion and places limits upon citizenship. However, there *are* elements within Third Way approaches that may resist or modify that tendency. Third Way approaches may be premised on market liberalism, but their secondary desire or intention is to ameliorate the tendencies to social exclusion and/or to counteract the social dislocations that may result.

  In the British context it is clear that New Labour's interpretation of the Third Way has elements that were not present in the New Democrats' interpretation in the United States (see King and Wickham-Jones 1999). Its approach to social policy has almost certainly been less coercive and more redistributive than would have been the case even if the Democrats had retained control over US social policy. The neo-conservative tradition is, in some respects, weaker and the social democratic tradition—however residual—is historically stronger in Britain than in the US. In the European context it would seem that, though Third Way discourse has established something of a hold within EU strategies for social inclusion, it is being tempered or reconstituted by influences from social democratic and, particularly, corporatist European traditions. The model illustrated in Fig. 9.1 is intended to demonstrate the elements that go to make up the variety of hybrid discourses and policy regimes that may be described as

'Third Way' approaches. These are not generated in an ideological vacuum. If they involve 'picking' and 'mixing' (cf. Powell 2000) it is on the basis of a reactive engagement or negotiation with existing traditions, not mere opportunism or pure pragmatism. They entail attempts to resolve the tensions between exclusionary and inclusionary impulses; to reconcile demands for fairness with demands for order, albeit in ways that may ultimately be unachievable.

The Third Way should not necessarily be understood as a coherently conceived project, nor as a wholly consciously inspired programme, but in terms of its immanent logic. That logic is often contradictory. The risks are evident. Third Way approaches may not be able to contain inequality. They may not prevent societies becoming more atomistic and less inclusive. Citizenship under Third Way regimes may well become more narrowly contractarian and less solidaristic in nature. But the jury is still out.

References

Atkinson, A. (1998). 'Social Exclusion, Poverty and Unemployment', in A. Atkinson and J. Hills (eds.), *Exclusion, Employment and Opportunity* (CASE Paper 4). London: London School of Economics.

Blair, T. (1999). 'Beveridge Revisited: A Welfare State for the Twenty-First Century', in R. Walker (ed.), *Ending Child Poverty: Popular welfare for the 21st Century*. Bristol: Policy Press.

Bonoli, J. and Powell, M. (2002). 'Third Ways in Europe?', *Social Policy and Society*, 1/1: 59–66.

Bourguignon, F. and Morrisson, C. (2002). 'Inequality Among World Citizens 1820–1992', *American Economic Review*, 92: 727–44.

Burchardt, T., Le Grand, J., and Piachaud, D. (2002). 'Degrees of Exclusion: Developing a Dynamic Multidimensional Measure', in J. Hills, J. Le Grand, and D. Piachaud (eds.), *Understanding Social Exclusion*. Oxford: Oxford University Press.

Burrows, R., Pleace, N., and Quilgars, D. (eds.) (1997). *Homelessness and Social Policy*. London: Routledge.

Clarke, J. and Newman, J. (1997). *The Managerial State*. London: Sage.

Cook, D. (1999). 'Putting Crime in its Place: The Causes of Crime and New Labour's Local Solutions', in H. Dean and R. Woods (eds.), *Social Policy Review 11*. Luton: Social Policy Association.

Crick, B. (Chair) (1998). *Education for Citizenship and the Teaching of Democracy in Schools* (Final Report of the Advisory Group on Citizenship). London: Qualifications and Curriculum Authority.

Deacon, A. (2003). ' "Levelling the Playing Field, Activating the Players": New Labour and the "Cycle of Disadvantage" ', *Policy and Politics*, 31/1: 123–37.

Dean, H. with Melrose, M. (1999). *Poverty, Riches and Social Citizenship*. Basingstoke: Macmillan.

Dean, H. (2002*a*). *Welfare Rights and Social Policy*. Harlow: Prentice Hall.

—— (2002*b*). 'Business versus Families: Whose Side is New Labour On?', *Social Policy and Society*, 1/1: 3–10.

—— (2003). 'Reconceptualising Welfare-to-work for People with Multiple Problems and Needs', *Journal of Social Policy*, 32: 441–59.

—— (ed.) (2004). *The Ethics of Welfare: Human Rights, Dependency and Responsibility*. Bristol: Policy Press.

—— and Shah, A. (2002). 'Insecure Families and Low-Paying Labour Markets: Comments on the British Experience', *Journal of Social Policy*, 31: 61–80.

Dennis, N. (ed.) (1997). *Zero Tolerance: Policing a Free Society*, London: Institute for Economic Affairs.

DSS (Department of Social Security) (1998). *New Ambitions for Our Country: A New Contract for Welfare* (Cm 3805). London: Stationery Office.

DWP (Department for Work and Pensions) (2002). *Opportunity for All: Fourth Annual Report* (Cm 5598). London: Stationery Office.

—— (2003). *Households Below Average Income 2001/02*. Leeds: Corporate Document Services.

Esping-Andersen, G. (1990). *The Three Worlds of Welfare Capitalism*. Cambridge: Polity Press.

EC (European Commission) (1997). *The Way Forward: The European Employment Strategy*. Brussels: EU.

—— (2001). *Joint Report on Social Inclusion*. Brussels: EU.

Exell, R. (2001). 'Employment and Poverty', in G. Fimister (ed.), *Tackling Child Poverty in the UK: An End in Sight?* London: Child Poverty Action Group.

Fairclough, N. (2000). *New Labour, New Language*. London: Routledge.

Giddens, A. (1998). *The Third Way*. Cambridge: Polity Press.

Gordon, D. and Pantazis, C. (eds.) (1997). *Breadline Britain in the 1990s*. Aldershot: Ashgate.

Gordon, D., Townsend, P., Levitas, R., Pantazis, C., Payne, S., Pastios, D., Middleton, S., Ashworth, K., Adelman, L., Bradshaw, J., Williams, J., and Bramley, G. (2000). *Poverty and Social Exclusion in Britain*. York: Joseph Rowntree Foundation.

Gore, C. and Figueiredo, J. (eds.) (1997). *Social Exclusion and Anti-poverty Policy: A Debate*. Geneva: International Labour Organization.

Hills, J. (2002). 'Does a Focus on "Social Exclusion" Change the Policy Response?', in J. Hills, J. Le Grand, and D. Piachaud (eds.), *Understanding Social Exclusion*. Oxford: Oxford University Press.

—— and Lelkes, O. (1999). 'Social Security, Selective Universalism and Patchwork Redistribution', in R. Jowell et al. (eds.), *British Social Attitudes: The 16th report— Who shares New Labour values?* Aldershot: Ashgate.

—— Le Grand, J., and Piachaud, D. (eds.) (2002). *Understanding Social Exclusion*. Oxford: Oxford University Press.

HM Treasury/Home Office (2002). *Next Steps on Volunteering and Giving in the UK: Discussion document*, London: Stationery Office.

Home Office (1998). *Supporting Families* (Cm 3991). London: Stationery Office.

—— (2003*a*). *Respect and Responsibility: Taking a Stand Against Anti-Social behaviour* (Cm 5778). London: Stationery Office.

—— (2003*b*). *Civil Renewal: A New Agenda* (CSV Edith Kahn Memorial Lecture, 11 June, by Rt. Hon. David Blunkett). London: Stationery Office.

Jordan, B. with Jordan, C. (2000). *Social Work and the Third Way: Tough Love as Social Policy*. London: Sage.

Kautto, M., Heikkila, M., Hvinden, B., Marklund, S., and Ploug, N. (eds.) (1999). *Nordic Social Policy: Changing Welfare States*. London: Routledge.

King, D. and Wickham-Jones, M. (1999). 'Bridging the Atlantic: The Democratic (Party) Origins of Welfare to Work', in M. Powell (ed.), *New Labour, New Welfare State: The Third Way in British Social Policy*. Bristol: Policy Press.

Labour Party (1997). *New Labour: Because Britain Deserves Better*. London: Labour Party.

—— (2001). *Ambitions for Britain: Labour's Manifesto*. London: Labour Party.

Leibfried, S. (1993). 'Towards a European Welfare State? On Integrating Poverty Regimes into the European Community', in C. Jones (ed.), *New Perspectives on the Welfare State in Europe*. London: Routledge.

Levitas, R. (1996). 'The Concept of Social Exclusion and the New Durkheimian Hegemony', *Critical Social Policy*, 16/2: 5–20.

—— (1998). *The Inclusive Society? Social Exclusion and New Labour*. Basingstoke: Macmillan.

Lister, R. (1998). 'From Equality to Social Inclusion: New Labour and the Welfare State', *Critical Social Policy*, 18: 215–25.

—— (2001). 'New Labour: A Study in Ambiguity from a Position of Ambivalence', *Critical Social Policy*, 21: 425–47.

Lødemel, I. and Trickey, H. (eds.) (2000). *'An Offer you Can't Refuse': Workfare in International Perspective*. Bristol: Policy Press.

Mack, J. and Lansley, S. (1985). *Poor Britain*. London: Allen and Unwin.

Marshall, T. (1950). 'Citizenship and Social Class', reprinted in T. H. Marshall and T. Bottomore (1992), *Citizenship and Social Class*. London: Pluto Press.

McKnight, A. (2002). 'Low-Paid Work: Drip-Feeding the Poor', in J. Hills, J. Le Grand, and D. Piachaud (eds.), *Understanding Social Exclusion*. Oxford: Oxford University Press.

Mestrovic, S. (1997). *Postemotional Society*. London: Sage.

Millar, J. (2000). *Keeping Track of Welfare Reform: The New Deal Programmes*. York: Joseph Rowntree Foundation.

Palmer, G., Rahman, M., and Kenway, P. (2002). *Monitoring Poverty and Social Exclusion 2002*. York: Joseph Rowntree Foundation.

Piachaud, D. and Sutherland, H. (2001). 'Child Poverty and the New Labour Government', *Journal of Social Policy*, 30/1: 95–118.

——— (2002) 'Child Poverty', in J. Hills, J. Le Grand, and D. Piachaud (eds.), *Understanding Social Exclusion*. Oxford: Oxford University Press.

Piven, F. and Cloward, R. (1974). *Regulating the Poor*. London: Tavistock.

Powell, M. (2000). 'Something Old, Something New, Something Borrowed, Something Blue: The Jackdaw Politics of New Labour', *Renewal*, 8/4: 21–31.

Putnam, R. (2000). *Bowling Alone: The Collapse and Revival of American Community*. New York: Simon and Schuster.

Rodger, J. (2000). *From a Welfare State to a Welfare Society*. Basingstoke: Macmillan.

Room, G. (ed.) (1995). *Beyond the Threshold: The Measurement and Analysis of Social Exclusion*. Bristol: Policy Press.

Silver, H. (1994). 'Social Exclusion and Social Solidarity: Three Paradigms', *International Labour Review*, 133: 531–78.

SEU (Social Exclusion Unit) (2000). *National Strategy for Neighbourhood Renewal: A Framework for Consultation*. London: Cabinet Office.

—— (2001). *Preventing Social Exclusion: Report by the Social Exclusion Unit*. London: Cabinet Office.

Theodore, N. and J. Peck (2001). 'Searching for Best Practice in Welfare-to-work: The Means, the Method and the Message', *Policy and Politics*, 29/1: 81–94.

UNDP (United Nations Development Programme) (2003). *Human Development Report 2003—Millennium Development Goals: A Compact Among Nations to End Human Poverty*. New York: Oxford University Press.

10

What is New Labour? Can it Deliver on Social Policy?

JANE LEWIS

There has been a huge debate about what New Labour is, what it stands for, and whether its policies are more Right than Left. The first point of departure is largely about the extent to which there is something 'new' about New Labour: whether it is more accurate to see it as an extension of the Thatcherite consensus (see, for example, Hay 1999); whether it represents a move beyond both the political Right and the Old Left, as Giddens (1998) argued in his early formulation of Third Way politics; or whether there is at least a 'new mix' that is identifiable (Driver and Martell 2002; Deacon 2002). Of these, the last position is the most persuasive. There is certainly a new policy mix that has taken in traditional Labour concerns alongside policies that would not have characterized the post-war Labour agenda: for example, a commitment to public services together with a welcome for more blurring between public and private finance and provision; a return to Labour's traditional concern with employment but implemented via more contractualist policies;[1] and a commitment to abolish child poverty within a generation alongside an extension of means testing.

In part, New Labour's policy approach has to be explained in terms of its policy inheritance (regardless of whether one takes the view that it has continued along the Thatcherite road or not). For example, Heffernan (2001) has argued that privatization was too costly to reverse; certainly, a commitment to the mixed economy of welfare has persisted. In addition, the dramatic growth of inequality in wealth and income during the 1980s (exceeded only by New Zealand) and of child poverty (Hills 1995; Bradshaw 1990; Piachaud and Sutherland 2000) represented huge challenges. After its 1992 defeat, Labour accepted the political impossibility of reversing what had become under successive Conservative governments a

---

[1] Freedland and King (2003) have deemed these to be illiberal, but White (2003) and Deacon (2002) would disagree.

low-tax, low-wage, low-skill, flexible labour market (Soskice 1999). But the nature of the policy mix since 1997 nevertheless owes much to New Labour's commitment to promoting what may be broadly termed 'social solidarity' alongside markets (Hutton 2003). Labour has had firm ideas about, first, how social provision should look, and second, what the state can and cannot do, although, as the consideration of the childcare policy example in the second part of the chapter will show, the details of the particular policy field and the local context in which key ideas about policies and about governance have been worked through matters enormously.

The nature of the relationship between ideas and instruments in respect of both policies and governance has become a matter of considerable interest in the political science literature. With regard to policies, the relationship looks rather different depending on the level of analysis. Thus, there is a degree of consensus in the comparative literature on Third Way politics and welfare state restructuring in Western European countries that there is more similarity between how the actual policies look than there is between the ideas informing them (Green Pedersen, van Kersbergen, and Hemerijck 2001; Bonoli and Powell, this volume). This suggests the difficulty in drawing firm conclusions about the relationship between ideas and policies across very different national contexts.

Nevertheless, on the basis of evidence from a UK case study, Peter Hall (1993: 290) has insisted on the importance of 'the way in which ideas condition policymaking and how they change, organized around the concept of "policy paradigms"', and there is now a rich literature on the nature of the causal relationships and on the influence of ideas on policy change (for example, Stone 1997; Cox 2001; Ross 2000; Schmidt 2002; Braun and Busch 1999; King 1999). But, in the case of New Labour, it has frequently been suggested that there is in fact a separation between its political ideas, however they might be characterized, and policy formation and implementation, such that the latter becomes entirely pragmatic and a matter of 'what works'. Blair (and Schroeder) have sought to play down the role of ideology, but that does not mean that there is an absence of ideas or strategic vision (Blair and Schroeder 1999). The importance that Blair has attached to the notion of 'what works' should rather be understood as a rhetorical device to signal 'flexible thinking', a commitment to effectiveness, and a distancing from the clear and constant connection made between ideology and policies by the Thatcher administrations. Stuart White (2001) has sidestepped the issue of the precise nature of the causal relationship between ideas and policies, arguing that New Labour's notion of a Third Way is not a concept or an ideology but rather a rhetorically defined space inhabited by values *and* by policy instruments (such as welfare-to-work or asset-based welfare). This analysis is persuasive because it both puts the ideas that lie behind policy goals and programmes in the frame, and invites exploration of ambiguities and tensions. I shall seek to build on White's approach rather than pursuing the issue of the causal relationship between ideas and policies, but shall add consideration of ideas about the role of the state—about governance. I shall argue that there is serious tension between the ideas and principles informing policies on the one hand and ideas about the role of the state on the other.

The literature on the relationship between policy ideas and instruments has tended to proceed separately from that exploring the equally important issue of government: the role of the state and how to govern. There is now a huge literature that has grown up in response to the perceived fragmentation of the modern state. Rhodes's (1997) picture of the 'hollowing out of the state'—upward to the supranational level, outward through privatization, and downwards through the creation of quangos and agencies—is one of the more extreme interpretations of the nature of the changes that have taken place, but one that has captured the imagination. It has become commonplace to read in the literature on 'new governance' that the modern state can 'steer' but not 'row' (for example, Pierre 2000; Prakesh and Hart 1999). In the case of New Labour, Wickham-Jones (2003: 26) has argued that the Labour government has resigned itself to 'utter acceptance of the market economy and the forces of globalization', which has profoundly limited its room for manoeuvre in policy-making. Logically, this would lead to a scaling down of policy ambitions. However, Wickham-Jones also acknowledges New Labour's considerable legislative activity in the social policy arena. Indeed, as Pollitt and Bouckaert (2000) have pointed out, New Labour has tended to make large claims for what it will achieve, for example in respect of 'world class' education. Put simply, New Labour 'wants to do things'. However, it has also shown that it is both aware of and a believer in the 'limits' to action by government (for example, Brown 2000). Crucially, it believes that it can carry forward its commitment to welfare ends using new forms of governance that are also more compatible with market competition. However, there is potential for tension between these. It remains an open question as to whether the commitment to new forms of governance in fact signals the more fundamental tensions perceived by Wickham-Jones: between social policy and economic policy and between welfare ends and market means, tensions that are also increasingly present in other European countries and at EU level.

The first section of the chapter argues that it is possible to see that New Labour has had a strong vision of what constitutes the big picture of welfare. I also suggest that Labour has had a strong sense of the limits to state intervention. It is, I think, important to consider these together, just as it is important to look at the programme instruments alongside the new mechanisms for governing. Thus far, the majority of studies look either at (1) and (3) (below) or at (2) and (4):

(1) core ideas and principles informing policy goals;
(2) core ideas and principles informing the role of the state;
(3) policy instruments;
(4) instruments of governance.

This chapter focuses mainly on (1) and (2), and the aim of second section of the chapter is to explore briefly how the tensions between some of these core ideas work out in practice, using the case of childcare policy as an exemplar. All too often the discussion of core ideas remains at a high level of abstraction, while evidence as to the way in which ideas are deployed in a particular policy field or at the local level is confined to empirical work. It is important to consider these dimensions together not least because, while the Labour government was able to radically reform the tax–benefit system in its first term, since re-election in 2001 it has experienced some difficulty in securing 'delivery' in respect of reform of the public services (particularly health and transport). Services have proved the Achilles heel of many continental European social democratic governments at the turn of the century. The reasons for Labour's problems with policy implementation are many and complicated,[2] but I will suggest that, while core ideas at the heart of policy goals can be seen to translate into a coherent picture of welfare in respect of the nature and sequencing of social policy legislation (what White calls the policy instruments), there is the potential for conflict between the ideas informing policy goals as well as between these and the ideas informing the role of the state. As the second section of the chapter shows, these tensions pose substantial difficulties even in a policy field (childcare) where there has been a long tradition of a profoundly mixed economy. In and of itself, this does not constitute even a partial explanation of the difficulties in 'delivery', but it is suggestive as to the kind of disappointment that results 'on the ground'. In the face of this, together with increasing criticism from some of its earlier enthusiastic supporters (for example, by Compass[3]), Labour has

---

[2] Surprisingly little has been written about this, even at the level of political commentary, but any explanation would have to assess the timing and amount of the new money made available and the viability of the many and various new mechanisms used for delivery, as well as the difficult questions about the extent to which this is the first time in the post-war period that a government has tried to change outcomes (I am indebted to Howard Glennerster for this point), and the gap between the paper logic at the departmental level and the situation on the ground (many of the new agencies that have been created to address particular problems have had to work round what already exists).   [3] www.compassonline.org.uk.

felt increasingly constrained to make more changes to the instruments of governance.

There is in addition a larger underlying issue here. It may in fact be that New Labour provides us with an example of a government that wants to address welfare issues but that may be reaching the limits of what is possible given its acknowledgement of the need to reconcile welfare ends with market means. It is significant that, in the middle of its second term, the debate about policy goals has become centred on choice versus equity. This is all the more important because New Labour is far from alone in facing this conundrum. It is, for example, possible to see a similar accommodation between welfare ends and market means being reached at the EU level, where the subordination of social to economic policy has been rather more explicit. It may be that this effort is reaching its limits.

1. New Labour's Core Ideas and Principles

In the late 1990s, several commentators attempted to identify the core policy ideas of New Labour's so-called Third Way. Julian Le Grand (1998) suggested that the Third Way 'begins with Cora': community, opportunity, responsibility, and accountability. Stuart White (1998, 2001) also identified opportunity, 'civic responsibility', and 'genuine community' as key, while Ruth Lister (1998) suggested responsibility, inclusion, and opportunity ('Rio'). There is thus substantial agreement on the importance of opportunity and responsibility in Third Way thinking. Lister is probably right to see these as part of a new focus on social inclusion (through the obligation to enter the labour market); in other words, opportunity and responsibility are narrowly defined. White is also probably correct in seeing them as the constituent parts of New Labour's hopes for the creation of a 'genuine community': community is to be built on new structures and 'social investment' (see also Lister, this volume) guaranteeing opportunity, and on individual responsibility. The stress on opportunity and on education, training, and access to employment as the means of providing it is intimately linked to the Blair government's focus on social inclusion/exclusion. The twin pillars of opportunity and social inclusion very largely replaced the more traditional concerns with equality (it was a year into the new government before 'poverty' was mentioned). The New Labour government's stress on opportunity as a distinguishing characteristic of its new approach was clearly stated in its early Green Paper on welfare reform:

The welfare state now faces a choice of futures. A privatised future, with the welfare state becoming a residual safety net for the poorest and most marginalised;

the status quo, but with more generous benefits; or the Government's third way—promoting opportunity instead of dependence, with a welfare state providing for the mass of the people, but in new ways to fit the modern world. (DSS 1998: 19)

In their key speeches, Blair and the Chancellor of the Exchequer, Gordon Brown, have continued to refer to 'a new, modern understanding of the duties of citizenship' and the need to reclaim 'both the ethic of personal responsibility as we stress obligations as well as opportunities, and affirm the ethic of fairness as we root out economic injustice' (Brown 2000*b*: 2). Responsibility remains first and foremost as the responsibility to enter the labour market but, as Schmidt (2002) has observed, because this was couched in the new discourse of social inclusion, it was represented as an opportunity as well as a duty (see also Lewis 2003); the high proportion of workless households in the UK was from the first a major concern of the government (Brown 1999).

The concept of responsibility seems to owe rather more to right-wing thinking. Mid-1980s American proponents of New Right ideas were influential in switching attention from rights and entitlements to obligations and responsibilities (especially Mead 1986). However, Raymond Plant (1998), in one of the most cogent examinations of New Labour's thinking, argued that both (1970s, British-style) social democracy, with its stress on entitlements, and neo-liberalism, with its faith in the individual pursuing his or her self-interest, ended up with a 'dutiless individualism'. White (1998) pointed out that responsibility is not the same as 'self reliance'; individuals are not expected to be entirely self-sufficient under all circumstances. The New Labour government has stressed above all the obligation to engage in paid employment:

It is the Government's responsibility to promote work opportunities and to help people take advantage of them. It is the responsibility of those who can take them up to do so. (DSS 1998: 31)

There remains the issue of how far government is prepared to go in *forcing* individuals to be responsible, which as Desmond King (1999) has argued is a hallmark of 'illiberal social policy' in liberal states. The more authoritarian strand in New Right thinking would have no problem in supporting some of New Labour's policies, for example, curfews for schoolchildren, or policy proposals that have been floated, such as removing child benefit from the parents of children who play truant. In the US, Mead (1997) has identified the trend towards enforcing personal responsibility as 'the new paternalism'. In New Labour's thinking, responsibility probably has more resonance with George Orwell's hankering after 'decency', a very 'English' concept which is hard to define but which certainly involves the expectation that people will 'do the right thing' and behave 'properly'. The Labour Party is determined to strive for a balance between rights and obligations. Ruth Levitas (1998) has argued that a 'social integrationist discourse', stressing inclusion via participation, above all in the labour market, has taken priority over a 'redistributive egalitarian' discourse. This is undoubtedly correct, but the former has by no means replaced the latter in practice in so far as there has been considerable redistribution by stealth. Levitas also suggests that as in the US there has been resort to a 'moralist underclass discourse'. This is more difficult. Reference of this kind can be shown to be present, but the approach is not explicitly punitive, although it is certainly paternalistic and individualistic in so far as the aim is to change behaviour (see also Dean, this volume).

Opportunity and responsibility as the means of achieving social inclusion and revitalized communities are perhaps the most central principles of New Labour's approach. However, Giddens's (1998) book on the Third Way ranged rather more widely, addressing additionally the relationship between state and civil society. This takes in the desire for a more democratic, open, and ethical society, but also raises the question of the role of the state in securing its social policy goals. The neo-liberal conservatism of the 1980s and 1990s wanted above all to roll back the state in terms of public expenditure, but at the same time it succeeded in completing Britain's transformation from a relatively decentralized country in the late nineteenth century to the most centralized late twentieth-century Western European state, particularly in respect of fiscal control. In respect of the major social services of the post-war welfare state (education, housing, health, and social care), which arguably have been more at the heart of British social provision than cash benefits, certainly in terms of the public support they command, successive Conservative governments sought both to infuse the public sector with market principles and to pass responsibility for provision to the private sector, the voluntary sector, and the family. Above all, competition between providers was encouraged. Relations between the state and other providers of 'welfare' were often seen in adversarial terms.

When it came to power in 1997, New Labour foreswore both tax increases and major organizational change (although large numbers of additional interdepartmental and cross-cutting bodies have been set up in an effort to ensure delivery), and confirmed its commitment to the 'mixed economy' of welfare. But the nature of the relationship between the state, the market, the voluntary sector, and the family was reformulated in terms of 'partnership'. Indeed, partnership has become a key concept and actually has a double meaning, signalling the idea that actors other than the state will play a major role in policy delivery, as well as comprising a specific instrument of governance. As Newman (this volume) notes, partnership must be understood as part of larger structural processes and in particular as new coordination strategies in the face of state modernization and fragmentation. The role of public–private partnerships in renewing and extending infrastructure—whether in respect of transport, schools, or hospitals—which was begun by the Conservatives, has been taken much further by Labour (IPPR 2001). In other words, the mixed economy of provision has become much more a mixed economy of finance, and the boundaries between market and state have become considerably more blurred (see the observations of Burckhardt, Hills, and Propper 1999). This in turn has brought the other major role of government in relation to service provision into sharp relief: that of the state as regulator. Labour promised to seek to deliver measurable outcomes from services that were increasingly fragmented, albeit at one step remove. The new instruments of governance have thus included the setting of national standards for public services and performance targets, together with the creation of interdepartmental units, such as the Social Exclusion Unit, designed to provide the kind of 'joined-up' government required to push forward the new policy instruments. The imposition of national standards and performance indicators designed to achieve welfare ends by government 'at a distance' were closely related to the further watchword identified by Le Grand and examined by Power (1997): accountability. Securing accountability on the part of professionals in particular—whether teachers, social workers, doctors, or even lawyers—via performance indicators was central to the endeavours of 1980s and 1990s Conservatism too. Given the reluctance (and indeed the impossibility) of reversing the Conservative legislation pertaining to the creation of 'quasi-markets' in social services (Le Grand and Bartlett 1993), together with the taking forward of the mixed economy of finance, accountability was bound to be a continuing principle (and concern).

However, with 'partnership' as the new defining characteristic of the mixed economy of welfare, the hope has been to invigorate rather than to attack the public services. Partnership was defined in the New Labour government's first major White Paper on the National Health Service (NHS):

In paving the way for the new NHS the Government is committed to building on what has worked but discarding what has failed. There will be no return to the old centralised command and control systems of the 1970s. That approach stifled innovation and put the needs of institutions ahead of the needs of patients. But nor will there be a continuation of the divisive internal market system of the 1990s. That approach which was intended to make the NHS more efficient ended up fragmenting decision making and distorting incentives to such an extent that unfairness and bureaucracy became its defining feature. Instead there will be a 'third way' of running the NHS—a system based on partnership and driven by performance. It will go with the grain of recent efforts by NHS staff to overcome the obstacles of the internal market . . . It will be neither the model from the late 1970s nor the model from the early 1990s. It will be a new model for a new century. (Department of Health 1997: paras 2.1 3)

The content of 'partnership', as with opportunity and responsibility, is vexed and has shifted since 1998, but it bears further examination. The idea of partnership between the different elements in the mixed economy of welfare was designed in large measure to change the way in which the introduction of market principles into public services was experienced. Thus, while many accounts of 'partnerships' have stressed above all the possibilities they present for obtaining 'magic money' (that is, money that does not show up in the national accounts as a public sector borrowing requirement) to finance the public services (Redwood 2002), the idea of partnership also entails a new approach to mixed governance. As Pollitt and Bouckaert (2000: 176) have argued, New Labour's insistence on 'modernization', which was intended to encompass more bottom-up change via partnerships than the simple top-down deregulation associated with 'marketization', introduced a 'different spirit' into public management and policy implementation, especially in respect of human services. During Labour's first term, the idea of partnership emphasized collaboration rather than competition, and more recently has stressed the importance of a shared public service ethos between providers from different sectors.

The pattern of social policy-making since 1997, in terms of both the order in which policy areas were tackled and the nature of the policies that were chosen, reflects these core ideas. Many Labour supporters assumed that the new government would begin by pumping money into public services, particularly the NHS. However, most of Labour's first term was dominated by tax–benefit reform. After the introduction of a minimum wage, Labour sought to implement its welfare-to-work strategy via a series of 'New Deals' and its policy to 'make work pay'. The most significant were the New Deals for young people unemployed for six months or more and for adults unemployed for two years or more, in which participation is compulsory. The New Deals for lone parents and disabled people are not compulsory, although benefits have become conditional on a work-focused interview. The Working Families Tax Credit (WFTC), together with the introduction of a minimum wage, was the centrepiece of Labour's policies to 'make work pay'. Indeed, the 2000 budget was redistributive (IFS 2001) and in 2003 the system of tax credits for children and for adults was overhauled and extended, such that the meaning of means-testing has been substantially changed.

The reform of the tax–benefit system was radical and relatively quick, but it may well be that reform of cash benefits is more 'controllable' than attempts to reform the public services. In respect of the latter, the Labour Party's election manifestos and Tony Blair's speeches made most of 'education, education, education', with the health service (always regarded by voters as the centrepiece of the UK welfare state) a close second. The NHS Plan, published in 2000, finally produced a major cash injection for the service, the results of which did not begin to be felt until the end of 2001. A similar cash injection was given to education again more than mid-way through the parliamentary term. The delay was in large part due to Labour's commitment to abide by the Conservatives' spending policies for the first two years. Only after acting to redraw the work–welfare relationship to embody the ideas of opportunity and responsibility via the new instruments of the New Deals and tax credits did New Labour begin to justify vastly increased expenditure on health and education as necessary investments in human capital.[4]

It is also crucial to note that Labour Party leaders expressed caution about how much the state could actually do to achieve these ideas at the heart of its policy goals. In a speech on 'modernising central government' in 1998, Tony Blair said: 'Big government is dead. The days of tax and spend are gone. Much of the deregulation and privatisation that took place in the 1980s was necessary. But everything cannot be left to the market. We believe there is a role for active government' (quoted in Richards and Smith 2002: 240). This neatly encompasses both the desire to act and the perception that there are real limits on government in terms of finance and provision. In a speech to the National Council for Voluntary Organisations, Gordon Brown said: 'We politicians are no longer looking for the opportunity to expand government, but government is looking always to expand opportunity. All this is humbling for government because it forces government to recognise its limitations . . . government must recognise that it does not have the solution to every problem' (Brown 2000*a*: 6). Thus, the role of government in the field of social policy had to be chiefly 'to enable' (Blair 2002) via partnerships, and Brown (2002: 4) referred to the 'sterile war for territory between the public and private sectors'.

The complicated nature of the work done by the term 'partnership' begs crucial questions as to what it is really all about. The next section looks at a rapidly expanding social service, childcare, and at the way in which the idea of partnership has run into a complicated series of unanticipated conflicts with the principles underpinning the policy to increase high-quality

---

[4] This policy logic bodes ill for elderly people. Indeed, social and healthcare services for this group have not attracted major attention; pensions have received more attention mainly because of the crisis in UK occupational schemes.

provision. In the final analysis, it may be that these conflicts are part of a much wider picture of tensions between welfare ends and market means. It may also be the case that the idea of partnership cannot hold the profound tension between markets and state regulation, and between economic and social policies.

2. Childcare: The Tensions between Partnership, Social Inclusion, and Community Building

Labour has moderated its commitment to the mixed economy of welfare in public services via the concept of partnership. The operation of a mixed economy of welfare under the Conservatives in the late 1980s and early 1990s showed the difficulties of reconciling a competitive, adversarial quasi-market with a commitment to equity and quality in human services (see, for example, Lewis and Glennerster 1996). Neither the idea of partnership nor the reality of partnership working has eradicated the problems. The aim here is not to evaluate partnership as a vehicle for delivering policy goals, but rather to explore the tension between Labour's ideas about governance and the principles underpinning its policies.

The promotion of childcare provision has been a significant new initiative of the New Labour government, paralleling similar initiatives in other Western European countries which have historically had low levels of provision (for example, Germany). The ideas driving childcare policy can be seen to reflect the central preoccupations of New Labour with social inclusion (by facilitating the employment of mothers and increasing opportunities among children for 'early learning') and community building (by concentrating new provision on areas of social disadvantage). Childcare in the UK has historically been a very mixed economy of finance and provision, with the private sector playing the largest role. New Labour made an explicit commitment to continue to promote a mixed economy, and local 'partnerships' between private, public, and voluntary providers have been set up at the instigation of central government in order to provide a forum for debate, to disseminate best practice, to coordinate the development of provision, and to make decisions regarding the distribution of supply-side public finance. Improved access to better-quality childcare, defined in terms of early years 'education' rather than 'care', is intended to promote social inclusion, while the concentration of new childcare initiatives on deprived areas, together with local control over policy implementation, is intended to promote community building. However, partnership as an approach to governance that embodies a commitment to a mixed economy of finance and provision, albeit controlled by representatives from different provider interests, finds itself in conflict with both the key policy ideas.

Childcare developed in the UK as a profoundly mixed economy and as the labour market participation rates of mothers, particularly among those with children aged under five years, rose rapidly—from 40 per cent in 1986 to 54 per cent in 1996—so provision of childcare by the 'independent sector' (a mix of private and voluntary providers, but chiefly the former) increased dramatically (Land and Lewis 1998). Until 1998, the UK had never had an explicit 'childcare strategy', and compared with all its northern and western continental European neighbours, access to affordable childcare was poor. In 1998, the Labour government announced the guarantee of a free, part-time early years education place for all four-year-olds (achieved at the end of 2000) and the same for all three-year-olds, to be achieved by 2004 (Cm. 3959, 1998).[5] In 2001, the government announced its aim of creating 1.6m new childcare places by 2004 (DfEE 2001). The shift in policy and the amount of investment on the demand side (through the childcare tax credits that were part of the WFTC and that are now part of the adult tax credit) and on the supply side (through a huge variety of funding streams aimed at encouraging particular kinds of provision) has been very substantial. Furthermore, in line with its intention to avoid major organizational change and a continued commitment to choice—allowing parents 'to decide what sort of childcare they want for their children' (Cm. 3959, 1998: 6)—Labour did not attempt explicitly to change the mixed economy of childcare. Rather, local authorities were required to promote 'partnerships' between the different providers of care (public, private, and voluntary) known as Early Years Development and Childcare Partnerships (EYDCPs). The workings of these partnerships provides a further illustration of how the 'realities' of partnership and core ideas about policy and governance can come into conflict.

In the planning guidance issued by the Department for Education and Employment in 2001, childcare policy was tied firmly into the 'bigger picture' of promoting 'opportunities for all' (a reference to the government document on tackling poverty and social exclusion: DSS 1999) by building secure and responsible communities and by raising productivity and sustainable growth (DfEE 2001: 7). The most important of the new short-term, supply-side funding streams provided by government under the childcare strategy targeted disadvantaged neighbourhoods in order to

---

[5] The part-time place is defined as 2.5 hours per day, five days a week, for thirty-three weeks a year (that is, during school term time).

reach poor children.[6] Demand-side funding targeted low-income parents as part of the wider welfare-to-work strategy. The report on the first year of the 'opportunities for all' strategy stressed the way in which government had sought to focus 'on the most deprived areas where the childcare market faces barriers to development' (DSS 2000: para. 32), while the 2001 planning guidance in respect of childcare stressed the importance of reducing the number of workless households.[7]

In sum, the policy drivers were: tackling social exclusion by getting 'parents' (in practice mainly lone mothers) into work by providing childcare; and making sure that the new childcare places were in early years education governed by a national standard (in the form of a 'foundation curriculum') in order to give children a better start. The area-based form of much of the new funding also signalled the goal of community-building in deprived areas, with local partnership working as a means to encouraging 'bottom-up' policy development and implementation. The number of childcare places has increased enormously, but major tensions have been exposed, the main one being the extent to which the commitment to the idea of partnership and hence to the mixed economy has failed to secure sustainable supply. In addition, there are tensions between the idea of using a particular form of childcare (early years education) to promote social inclusion on the one hand, and community control in the sense of responding to parental preferences on the other, as well as between partnership as a means of promoting a mixed economy of provision and finance 'friendly' to the development of public services, and partnership as a mode of governance which has not favoured all providers equally.

A large number of different types of centrally provided supply-side funding have been filtered through the local partnerships, which have had the job of selecting successful bidders. Application for such a range of funding has proved time-consuming for providers and there is increasing recognition that economic sustainability is a problem when many funding streams are time-limited, the expectation being that after a few years the provider will become self-sufficient, relying on a mix of fees and the childcare tax credits paid to parents. In its planning guidance for 2001–2, the Department for Education and Employment appeared to recognize the issue of sustainability when it set a target of ensuring that 80 per cent of the places created by one of the major new funding streams remained viable five years on (DfEE 2001: 10), although how this was to be achieved was not specified.

---

[6] This policy has been subjected to considerable criticism because only a minority of poor children live in disadvantaged areas (Land 2002).

[7] The UK has a much larger proportion of these than its continental European neighbours (Gregg and Wadsworth 1999).

The emphasis on childcare as a means to promote social inclusion meant that a crucial criterion for receipt of the new public money was the provision of the early years curriculum. However, the most popular form of childcare in the UK since the 1950s has been in the private sector, by 'childminders', but since 1997 their numbers have declined steeply by over a quarter because of the new focus on education rather than care, the tightening of the regulatory structure for childminding, and an increasingly tight labour market which offers more diverse opportunities for women's employment. In respect of children under three years old using childcare, almost one third were enrolled in 'playgroups' prior to the launch of the Labour government's childcare strategy. Indeed, playgroups were one of the most significant community-based, self-help initiatives of the 1960s and 1970s (Tizard, Moss, and Perry 1976), open for only a few hours a day but involving parents in the running of the groups. The number of playgroups has also declined and many are in the process of changing their form. These changes are due to the emphasis placed by government on the need for more early years *education*, by the need of working parents for longer hours of childcare, preferably provided on one site, and by the way in which the new funding streams have worked to promote these changes. One of the new pots of monies is available to playgroups that become (long-hours) day nurseries. However, this is effectively to narrow the choices available to parents and to diminish further a form of provision that has the distinction of being run by parents and controlled by 'the community'. While the main policy goal of the childcare strategy—social inclusion—did not appear to be in any way at odds with provision in partnership with the voluntary and community sector, the new arrangements—which have promoted primarily private sector provision in disadvantaged areas using short-term, pump-priming funds (HC 564-1 2003)—have proved very difficult for one of the main forms of community-based provision.

Indeed, in an early years education and development partnership in a large English town,[8] there was a feeling, particularly on the part of voluntary and community sector representatives, of being 'outsiders' (see also Taylor 2001; Craig et al. 2002). Yet, in this city, elected members of the local authority were committed to a community development focus first, and only then to childcare as a means of enabling women to work and children to escape poverty. However, an active, equal working partnership with voluntary organizations, which may have goals that differ at least in emphasis from those of government, is not really a possibility given the

---

[8] I draw here on EC-funded research on childcare, grant no. HPSE-CT-2001—00067.

extent to which the goal of promoting social inclusion via employment and the nature of the funding streams has determined the nature of the new provision. This in turn is geared to the promotion of education rather than care or play, and to long-hours provision suitable for working parents. Most new places have been created in the private sector rather than the voluntary or public sectors.

This example demonstrates the difficulty of reconciling the core ideas about social inclusion, community-building, and partnership. In this instance, the determination to create the kind of childcare that government believes will address problems of social inclusion among children and their parents living in poor areas, that is, early years education, trumped an equally strong commitment to maximizing parental choice via diversity of supply. Two of the most popular forms of supply—childminders and playgroups—did not offer the kind of childcare that was necessary to attract new public money. Thus, the local partnerships, intended to promote diversity of providers, in practice became bodies that effectively limited these two popular forms of provision. Top-down decisions regarding the nature of childcare thus also trumped bottom-up, community-based decision-making. Perhaps more important still, it proved yet again difficult to secure sustainable supply via a profoundly mixed economy of both finance and provision in which the private sector has played the largest part, something that had already been demonstrated in the UK during the early 1990s in respect of care for elderly people (Lewis and Glennerster 1996).

Labour clearly values partnership as a means of addressing the problem of governance, and opportunity and responsibility as a means of community building and promoting social inclusion. The statement of these principles has been heartfelt and frequent, and has conveyed the wish to promote social cohesion and cooperation. There is no reason to question the government's sincerity in this regard, but there are real problems in promoting these ideas in the context of a mixed economy that remains a quasi-market. David Runciman (2003) has recently characterized government by New Labour as the 'politics of good intentions'. Among the members of the early years partnership in the large English town, this was echoed by voluntary sector childcare providers on the ground, who shook their heads in sorrow at the erosion of a major form of voluntary provision and at the difficulty of creating sustainable childcare places 'despite all the good intentions' of the new national childcare strategy.

The Blair government is well aware of the importance of what Scharpf (1997) has called 'output-oriented legitimacy'. New Labour has not demonstrated its capacity to solve either the quantitative or the qualitative dimensions of the problem of service delivery in respect of childcare.

To understand why, would require a huge amount of work on all four of the dimensions discussed in the introduction to this chapter, as well as the much larger issues outlined in note 2. But in regard to the future of welfare politics, all this raises a much larger question for EU member states: how to square the circle between the demands of a flexible, competitive economy and high quality, universal social services.

3. Conclusion: Welfare Ends versus Market Means ?

The fear is that, while social policy issues are now more firmly on the political agenda than for many years, the extent to which they are dominated by economic policy has also become more explicit: welfare ends are legitimate only if they serve economic goals. Furthermore, this is an issue that has wider geographical purchase than the UK. Just as Wickham-Jones (2003) has suggested that New Labour has prioritized the market economy in the face of globalization, so many commentators on EU-level policy have argued that social policy goals are subordinate to the goals of economic integration policy, that is, to competitiveness and macroeconomic stability (for example, Scharpf 2002; Leibfried and Pierson 2000; Kleinman 2002). The European Commission's Social Policy Agenda, published in 2000, sought to strengthen 'the role of social policy as a productive factor', pointing to the economic benefits of health and education expenditure, of protection against a range of social risks, and of measures to facilitate adaptability in the labour market (EC 2000: 5). As in the UK, the language of responsibility, opportunity, and labour force participation has come to the fore, and employment growth has increasingly been seen as the key to social inclusion (Vandenbroucke 2001).

But in this approach social policies are justified above all in terms of the social investment that is necessary to sustain competition and growth. In addition, changes in ideas about governance that parallel those in the UK are also manifest at the EU level. Top-down, 'hard' instruments like 'Directives' have been abandoned in favour of the 'open method of coordination' (OMC), which leaves national governments free to determine how to make progress towards common objectives. Common values are incorporated in the objectives (for example, in respect of social inclusion: Atkinson et al. 2003), but the OMC is primarily a new method of governance, of government at a distance. The OMC is not only easier to reconcile with national policy objectives but is also much more compatible with European competition policy, which is increasingly being applied to public service provision (Leibfried and Pierson 2000). In the case of childcare policy, as O'Connor (2003) has observed, the implementation of

EU policies had more conspicuous success when governed by Directives. But government by some combination of common standards and performance indicators is one way, perhaps the only way, that states can hope to reconcile welfare ends and market means, which is, I think, a persuasive way of interpreting similar developments in the UK case.

These changes at the EU level raise the possibility that new approaches to governance—via the OMC—are as much the product of an approach to social policy that regards it as legitimate only in so far as it contributes to economic competitiveness, as they are an attempt to take on board the need to accommodate historical and institutional differences between countries in the way they approach policy-making. In which case, new ideas and practices in respect of governance become the means of reconciling the desire to achieve welfare ends with market competition. This has become the fear with regard to New Labour's renewed emphasis on the importance of public–private partnerships in respect of finance as well as provision in its second term. The promotion of Foundation Hospitals, which promises to introduce a new form of local governance for the highest-standard hospitals will, in the view of many, open a window for more patient charges and encourage more competition between hospitals (for example, Mohan 2003). The fear in this instance on the part of some is that new governance is more a Trojan horse for the market (and with it more inequality) than a radical new model of governance that will help to achieve more choice and a more efficient and effective public service (Mayo and Lee 2002; Walsh 2003; Klein 2003). Legal judgements such as that in favour of the BetterCare group, a private company selling nursing and residential care, ruling that contracting out in health and social services trusts is an economic rather than a welfare activity and therefore subject to competition rules, fuels the fears that more user charges and top-up fees for users are on the way (Pollock and Price 2003).

The conclusion of commentators such as Wickham-Jones (2003) would suggest that New Labour's position is similar to that of the EC: it firmly prioritizes the market economy to the extent, in his view, of moving from 'reformism' to 'resignation'. But this hardly characterizes the vigour of New Labour's policies in respect of the tax–benefit system in its first term, and its determined attempts to tackle public service reform in its second term. The issue is more that of the problem of reconciling a desire to pursue pretty clear-cut policy goals with an equally strong belief in the limits of government and the priority it gives to the market. New Labour, like the EC, thus prioritized economic growth and competitiveness and macroeconomic stability. Certainly this has been the essence of the Treasury's message. But whether this has resulted in social policy being treated as a mere handmaiden of economic policy is more difficult to assess. The legislative record would seem to suggest a genuine desire to 'do both'. The worrying underlying issue is whether the limits of such ambitions have now effectively been realized.

The clash between the core principles informing policy and the role of the state is not being claimed as a determining cause of the very real difficulties the Blair government is experiencing in service delivery, but it is a source of confusion and disappointment on the ground. Furthermore, this confusion and disappointment results in a rather frantic search for new principles, particularly in relation to the role of the state. Thus decentralization (Thomson 2003) has recently moved up the political agenda. Government does want to govern, notwithstanding its recognition of the limitations to so doing, and it has demonstrated considerable firmness of purpose in respect of the ideas and principles informing its policy goals and of its chosen policy instruments. But there is, as Newman (this volume) also observes, increasing instability in respect of Labour's ideas about the role of the state (and the instruments of governance), which is in large measure the result of the difficulty it has experienced in reconciling its core principles regarding policy goals and governance.

References

Atkinson, A., Cantillon, B., Marlier, E., and Nolan, B. (2002). *Indicators for Social Inclusion in the European Union*. Oxford: Oxford University Press.

Blair, T. (2002). 'Welfare Reform', www.number-10.gov.uk/output/Page1716.asp 4/4/03.

—— and Schroeder, G. (1999). *Europe: The Third Way/Die Neue Mitte*. London: Labour Party.

Bradshaw, J. (1990). *Child Poverty and Deprivation in the UK*. London: National Children's Bureau.

Braun, D. and Busch, A. (eds.) (1999). *Public Policy and Political Ideas*. Cheltenham: Edward Elgar.

Brown, G. (1999). 'The New Mission for the Treasury', speech given to Institute of Fiscal Studies, www.hm-treasury.gov.uk/newsroom and speeches/speeches/chancellorexchequer 4/4/03.

—— (2000). Speech given to the National Council for Voluntary Organisations Annual Conference, www.hm-treasury.gov.uk/newsroom and speeches/speeches/chancellorexchequer 4/4/03.

—— (2000a). 'Civic Society in Modern Britain'. Arnold Goodman Charity Lecture, July.

—— (2000b). Speech given at the London School of Economics, www.hm-treasury.gov.uk/newsroom and speeches/speeches/chancellorexchequer 4/4/03.

—— (2002). Speech given to the UNISON Conference, www.hm-treasury.gov.uk/newsroom and speeches/speeches/chancellorexchequer 4/4/03.

Burckhardt, T., Hills, J., and Propper, C. (1999). *Private Welfare and Public Policy*. York: Joseph Rowntree Foundation.

Cox, R. (2001). 'The Social Construction of an Imperative: Why Welfare Reform Happened in Denmark and The Netherlands but not in Germany', *World Politics*, 53: 463–98.

Craig, G., Taylor, M., Wilkinson, M., and Bloor, K., with Monro, S. and Syed, A. (2002). *Contract or Trust? The Role of Compacts in Local Governance*. Bristol: Policy Press.

Deacon, A. (2002). *Perspectives on Welfare: Ideas, Ideologies and Policy*. Buckingham: Open University Press.

DfEE (Department for Education and Employment) (2001). *Early Years Development and Childcare Partnerships: Planning Guidance*. London: DfEE.

—— (1998). *Meeting the Childcare Challenge. A Framework and Consultation Document*. (Cm. 3959). London: Stationery Office.

Department of Health (1997). *The New NHS Modern, Dependable* (Cm. 3807). London: Stationery Office.

Driver, S. and Martell, L. (2002). *Blair's Britain*. Cambridge: Polity.

DSS (Department of Social Security) (1998). *New Ambitions for Our Country: A New Contract for Welfare* (Cm. 3805). London: Stationery Office.

—— (1999). *Opportunity for All: Tackling Poverty and Social Exclusion*. London: DSS.

—— (2000). *Opportunity for All—One Year On: Making a Difference*. London: DSS.

EC (European Commission) (2000). *The Commission and Non-Government Organisations: Building a Stronger Partnership*. Brussels: EC.

Freedland, M. and King, D. (2003). 'Contractual Governance and Illiberal Contracts: Some Problems of Contractualism as an Instrument of Behaviour Management by Agencies of Government', *Cambridge Journal of Economics*, 27: 465–77.

Giddens, A. (1998). *The Third Way. The Renewal of Social Democracy*. Cambridge: Polity Press.

Green Pedersen, C., van Kersbergen, K., and Hemerijck, A. (2001). 'Neo-Liberalism, The "Third Way", or What? Recent Social Democratic Welfare Policies in Denmark and the Netherlands', *Journal of European Public Policy*, 8: 307–25.

Gregg, P. and Wadsworth, J. (eds.) (1999). *The State of Working Britain*. Manchester: Manchester University Press.

Hall, P. (1993). 'Policy Paradigms, Social Learning and the State: The Case of Economic Policy-making in Britain', *Comparative Politics*, 25: 275–96.

Hay, C. (1999). *The Political Economy of New Labour: Labouring under False Pretences?* Manchester: Manchester University Press.

Heffernan, R. (2001). *New Labour and Thatcherism: Political Change in Britain*. Basingstoke: Macmillan.

Hills, J. (1995). *Income and Wealth*, Vols. 1 and 2. York: Joseph Rowntree Foundation.

House of Commons (2003). *Work and Pensions Committee. Childcare for Working Parents*. Fifth Report of Session 2002–3 (HC 564–1).

Hutton, W. (2003). *The World We're In*. London: Abacus.

IPPR (Institute for Public Policy Research) (2002). *Building Better Partnerships. The Final Report of A Commission on Public Private Partnerships*. London: IPPR.

King, D. (1999). *In the Name of Liberalism: Illiberal Social Policy in the United States and Britain*. Oxford: Oxford University Press.

Klein, R. (2003). 'Governance for NHS Foundation Trusts', *British Medical Journal*, 326: 174–5.

Kleinman, M. (2000). *A European Welfare State?* London: Palgrave.

Land, H. (2002). *Meeting the Child Poverty Challenge: Why Universal Childcare is Key to Ending Child Poverty* (Facing the Future Policy Papers 3). London: Daycare Trust.

—— and Lewis, J. (1998). 'Gender, Care and the Changing Role of the State in the UK', in J. Lewis (ed.), *Gender, Social Care and Welfare State Restructuring in Europe*. Aldershot: Ashgate.

Leibfried, S. and Pierson, P. (2000). 'Social Policy', in H. Wallace and W. Wallace (eds.), *Policy-making in the European Union*. Oxford: Oxford University Press.

Le Grand, J. (1998). 'The Third Way Begins with Cora', *New Statesman*, 6 March: 26–7.

—— and Bartlett, W. (1993). *Quasi-markets and Social Policy*. London: Macmillan.

Levitas, R. (1998). *The Inclusive Society? Social Exclusion and New Labour*. London: Macmillan.

Lewis, J. (2003). 'Rights and Responsibilities', in N. Ellison and C. Pierson (eds.), *Developments in British Social Policy 2*. Basingstoke: Palgrave.

—— and Glennerster, H. (1996). *Implementing the New Community Care*. Buckingham: Open University Press.

Lister, R. (1998). 'From Equality to Social Inclusion: New Labour and the Welfare State', *Critical Social Policy*, 18: 215–25.

Mayo, E. and Lea, R. (2002). *The NHS and Mutuality*. London: New Economics Foundation.

Mead, L. (1986). *Beyond Entitlement. The Social Obligations of Citizenship*. New York: Free Press.

—— (1997). *The New Paternalism: Supervisory Approaches to Poverty*. Washington, DC: Brookings Institution.

Mohan, J. (2003). *Reconciling Equity and Choice? Foundation Hospitals and the Future of the NHS*. London: Catalyst.

Newman, J. (2001). *Modernising Governance: New Labour, Policy and Society*. London: Sage.

O'Connor, J. (2003). 'Measuring Progress in The European Social Model: Policy Coordination, Social Indicators and the Social Policy Agenda in the European Union'. Paper given to the RC19 meeting, Toronto, August.

Piachaud, D. and Sutherland, H. (2000). *How Effective is the British Government's Attempt to Reduce Child Poverty?* (CASE Paper 38). London: London School of Economics.

Pierre, J. (ed.) (2000). *Debating Governance: Authority, Steering and Democracy*. Buckingham: Open University Press.

Plant, R. (1998). *New Labour—A Third Way?* London: European Policy Forum.

Pollit, C. and Bouckaert, G. (2000). *Public Management Reform: A Comparative Analysis*. Oxford: Oxford University Press.

Pollock, A. and Price, D. (2003). 'The BetterCare Judgment—A Challenge to Health Care', *British Medical Journal*, 326: 236–7.

Power, M. (1997). *The Audit Society*. Oxford: Oxford University Press.

Prakash, A. and Hart, J. (eds.) (1999). *Globalisation and Governance*. London: Routledge.

Redwood, J. (2002). *Third Way—Which Way? How Should We Pay for Public Services?* London: Middlesex University Press.

Richards, D. and Smith, M. (2002). *Governance and Public Policy in the UK*. Oxford: Oxford University Press.

Rhodes, R. A. W. (1997). *Understanding Governance: Policy Networks, Governance, Reflexivity and Accountability*. Buckingham: Open University Press.

Ross, F. (2000). 'Framing Welfare Reform in Affluent Societies: Rendering Restructuring More Palatable?', *Journal of Public Policy*, 20/3: 169–93.

Runciman, D. (2003). 'The Politics of Good Intentions', *London Review of Books*, 8 May: 3–10.

Scharpf, F. (1997). *Governing in Europe: Effective and Democratic?* Oxford: Oxford University Press.

—— (2002). 'The European Social Model: Coping with the Challenges of Diversity', *Journal of Common Market Studies*, 40: 645–70.

Schmidt, V. (2002). 'Does Discourse Matter in the Politics of Welfare State Adjustment?', *Comparative Political Studies*, 35/2: 168–93.

Soskice, D. (1999). 'Divergent Production Regimes: Coordination and Uncoordinated Market Economies in the 1980s and 1990s', in H. Kitschelt, P. Lange, G. Marks, and J. Stephens (eds.), *Continuity and Change in Contemporary Capitalism*. Cambridge: Cambridge University Press.

Stone, D. (1997). *Policy Paradox: The Art of Political Decision Making*. New York: W. W. Norton.

Taylor, M. (2001). 'Partnership: Insiders and Outsiders', in M. Harris and C. Rochester (eds.), *Voluntary Organisations and Social Policy in Britain*. Basingstoke: Palgrave.

Thomson, W. (2003). 'L'Expérience Britannique de Reforme: Un Modèle à Suivre?' Speech given to the Economist Conference, Paris, 29–30 January. www.number-10.gov.uk/output/page254.asp 4/4/03.

Tizard, J., Moss, P., and Perry, J. (1976). *All Our Children*. London: Temple Smith.

Vandenbroucke, F. (2001). 'European Social Democracy and the Third Way: Convergence, Divisions, and Shared Questions', in S. White (ed.), *New Labour: The Progressive Future?* Basingstoke: Palgrave.

Walsh, K. (2003). 'Foundation Hospitals: A New Direction for NHS Reform?', *Journal of the Royal Society of Medicine*, 96: 106–10.

White, S. (1998). 'Interpreting the Third Way: Not One Road but Many', *Renewal*, 6/2: 17–30.

—— (2001). 'The Ambiguities of the Third Way', in S. White (ed.), *New Labour: The Progressive Future?* Basingstoke: Palgrave.

—— (2003). *The Civic Minimum*. Oxford: Oxford University Press.

Wickham-Jones, M. (2003). 'From Reformism to Resignation and Remedialism: Labour's Trajectory through British Politics', *Journal of Policy History*, 15/1: 26–45.

INDEX